LF

MARKETS AND FAMINES

Markets and Famines

MARTIN RAVALLION

CLARENDON PRESS · OXFORD

1987

Oxford University Press, Walton Street, Oxford OX2 6DP

Oxford New York Toronto
Delhi Bombay Calcutta Madras Karachi
Petaling Jaya Singapore Hong Kong Tokyo
Nairobi Dar es Salaam Cape Town
Melbourne Auckland

and associated companies in
Beirut Berlin Ibadan Nicosia

Oxford is a trade mark of Oxford University Press

Published in the United States
by Oxford University Press, New York

British Library Cataloguing in Publication Data

Ravallion, Martin
Markets and famines.
1. Famines—Economic aspects
I. Title 338.1'9   HC79.F3
ISBN 0-19-828514-0

Library of Congress Cataloging in Publication Data

Ravallion, Martin
Markets and famines.
Bibliography: p.   Includes index.
1. Famines.   2. Famines—Bangladesh. I. Title.
HC79.F3R38 1987   381'.456413'0095492   86-23724
ISBN 0-19-828514-0

Set by Katerprint Typesetting Services, Oxford
Printed in Great Britain by
Billings & Sons Ltd
Worcester

PREFACE

This is a study in the economics of famine. The potential reader-ship for any book on famine is likely to be a diverse one. Prospective readers of this book will vary considerably in terms of their initial familiarity with the methods of analysis that I have used. Readers for whom these methods are new will find some help in various appendices, footnotes, and the relatively non-technical summaries at the end of each chapter. But elsewhere it is often assumed that the reader has had a prior introduction to both economics and the elementary concepts from mathematics and statistics that are becoming a familiar part of that subject. I appreciate that some readers would prefer I had not made even this assumption. However, there is a trade-off; the assumption permits a particularly concise presentation of certain sorts of arguments. It also makes the book more accessible to other potential readers, well versed in these subjects. For I nurture hopes that this book will stimulate further research of a similar kind, as well as offer some new knowledge. The problem studied here is certainly no less important than many of those our more analytically and quantitatively orientated economists have dwelled on, and their efforts have been known to pay off.

Many people have helped me at various times and in various ways over the history of this study. The formative time for my interest in these questions was in Oxford during 1982–4. It will be evident that the underlying premises of this book owe much to Amartya Sen's work on famines, and I had some valuable discussions with Amartya as the study progressed. For their help and encouragement in this period, I am also grateful to Tony Atkinson, Christopher Bliss, James Boyce, Keith Griffin, Arthur Hazlewood, David Hendry, John Knight, M. G. Quibria, and Frances Stewart. A special acknowledgement is due to Abhijit (Manik) Sen with whom I had a continual and fruitful discussion on these issues over a number of years in Oxford. My visit to the Bangladesh Institute of Development Studies during the winter of 1983–4 helped in many ways, not least with the field work. I am grateful to a number of people at that institute and elsewhere in Dhaka, including Mahabub Hossain, Wahiduddin Mahmud, M. A. Quasem, Rehman Sobhan and especially to Abu Torab for his invaluable research assistance. The book was written during 1985–6 under excellent conditions at The Australian National University. For their comments and other forms of assistance during this period I am grateful to Max Corden, Richard Cornes, Lorraine Dearden, Meghnad Desai, Rod Falvey, Hilda Heidemanns, Sisira Jayasuriya, Frank Milne, Tony Shorrocks, R. M. Sundrum, Rod Tyers, Etienne van de Walle, Neil Vousden and Peter Warr. Financial support in the early stages of the study, particularly for research assistance and field work, was provided by the Overseas Development Administration (UK) and the Economic and Social Research Council (UK), although neither institution should be held responsible for the results. In writing this book I have drawn quite heavily in places from my articles on these issues published in *The Bangladesh Development Studies, The Economic Journal, Oxford Bulletin of Economics and Statistics, American Journal of Agricultural Economics, Explorations in Economic History,* and *Journal of Public Economics*; the book embodies many of the comments made by the editors and referees of these journals to whom I am grateful.

The final acknowledgement goes to Dominique van de Walle, who has helped me with this study in so many ways since it began that it is fitting the book be dedicated to her.

CONTENTS

1

Introduction and Summary

1.1 Motivation

A great many people are threatened by starvation at one time or another. Still others are susceptible to diseases induced by inadequate food. Much of the time, the survival chances of different people are independent; when low for one person at one instant, survival chance is not also low for many others. But occasionally this is not so; during famines one finds large numbers of people dying as a direct or indirect result of inadequate food.

To understand starvation deaths, one must understand the relationship between individual food consumption and individual survival chances. To understand famine also, one must explain why the risk of starvation is positively correlated amongst a large number of people.

When famine occurs in a poor agricultural economy, the weather is often blamed. Such economies are rarely well protected against bad weather, and this is often positively correlated over large areas. Thus it is not uncommon for many farmers to experience a crop failure simultaneously.

As an explanation for famine, this begs many questions. Even the simplest subsistence economy can use storage to buffer food consumption from output fluctuations. Occasional bad weather need not mean famine. Nor is the subsistence economy a particularly good characterization of the economies in which famines occur. Typically, the relation between output and consumption is more complex. The rural poor are often households with little or no land; this is the case in South Asia and is an emerging characteristic of rural poverty in Africa. The poor rely heavily on exchange for their consumption needs, rarely being able to offer more than their capacity for work in return for food or the money to buy it. Bad weather alone could not produce a famine in this setting since there will generally be possibilities for storage by markets, and also for external trade with other economies which have stored grain or have had better harvests.

For the same reasons, one must be suspicious of all 'explanations' for famine which cite a decline in aggregate food availability. Plainly, such an event is not implied by famine, nor does it imply it. This is not to say that aggregate food statistics are irrelevant. They may well be important parameters. But on their own they are quite uninformative about the causes of famine. Recently Amartya Sen has argued this case forcefully; as Sen (1981*a*, 154) puts it:

A food-centred view tells us rather little about starvation. It does not tell us how starvation can develop even without a decline in food availability. Nor does it tell us—even when starvation is accompanied by a fall in food supply—why some groups had to starve while others could feed themselves.

Instead, Sen advocates study of the food 'exchange entitlements' of famine victims, defined as the food consumption possibilities attainable by all legal means from the individual's available resources. Production using the individual's own means of production is one such means. Trade is another. If the conditions of trade change sufficiently to make it impossible for an individual to attain sufficient food for continued survival then 'trade entitlement failure' is said to occur.[1]

As far as it goes, Sen's argument is persuasive. But, as a number of people have pointed out (and Sen acknowledges),[2] the exchange entitlements theory begs the important question: what caused the shift in the conditions of exchange which gave rise to the entitlement failure?

This book is about the causes of famine in economies in which markets are an important influence on the relation between aggregate food availability and individual survival chances. 'Markets' are defined in the broad sense of all those situations in which voluntary trade takes place. Thus, in Sen's terminology, this book is an investigation of the causes of trade entitlement failure.

A recurrent theme of this study is that market performance influences famine mortality by determining important aspects of the *distribution* of food between people and over time. This immediately prompts two questions:

Why does food distribution matter? The relationship between food consumption and human survival chances is bound to be a 'noisy' relationship, reflecting imprecision in the link between food consumption and nutrition, and also the importance of non-nutritional causes of death. Nonetheless, allowing for these, one can reasonably assume that, on average, diminished food consumption by the poor over an interval of time will lower their survival chances.

But this need not mean that food distribution between points in time also matters for famine mortality. Redistribution raises survival chances for some dates at the expense of others. Long-term survival will also depend on the *shape* of the relationship between food consumption and survival chances as well as the direction of its slope; properties of the shape will determine whether survival chances are also affected by the variability of consumption over time. If, as some people have argued,[3] the marginal effect of consumption on survival chance declines with increases in consumption (in which case survival chance is said to be strictly 'concave' in consumption) then there will generally be long-term survival gains from stabilizing consumption over time. Conversely, de-stabilization of consumption over time can worsen or even produce a famine. This study offers a theory to explain why this may happen, and some empirical evidence suggesting that it does.

A similar argument applies to the interpersonal distribution of consumption. Aggregate mortality will increase if there is an increase in the inequality of food consumption between individuals who would otherwise have the same survival chance. There need not be a fall in aggregate food availability; indeed, aggregate mortality will *increase* if an increase in average food consumption is accompanied by a sufficient increase in the inequality of consumption.

These arguments suggest that a study of the way food institutions determine the distribution of food consumption over time and between people may offer important clues in understanding the causes of famine.

Why do markets matter? There are a number of ways in which political and economic institutions affect the food consumption opportunities of the rural poor. Foodgrain markets do so mainly through the effects of arbitrage on the distribution of prices, and hence consumption, over time and space. Arbitrage is achieved by storage and transport. Its effects on consumption opportunities will depend on a number of factors, including how well traders anticipate future prices and prices at other locations, and also the responsiveness of trade and demands to prices. It is hoped that this study will throw new light on the performance of grain markets in poor countries.

Other markets are involved. The food exchange entitlements of the poor also depend on the markets for the goods they sell. Their capacity for work is generally the most important of these, and so rural labour markets can be important influences on food distribution and survival chances during a famine. Savings also influence the way food consumption opportunities are allocated over time. Survival chances, therefore, also depend on the performance of the various markets for assets and credit. Although foodgrain markets will be the primary concern, some relevant aspects of the way these other markets work will be considered in this study.

A recurrent theme of this book is that the way markets use *information* is crucial to understanding their performance during famines, including their effects on famine mortality. The importance of market information in traditional agricultural settings has often been observed,[4] although the realization has found little concrete form in the traditional quantitative methods of investigation used by researchers studying agricultural market performance in poor countries.[5] As a by-product of the main enquiry, this book will offer some new methods for investigating market performance in such settings.

However, it should be emphasized that markets are not the only institutions involved in determining the distribution of food consumption. In South Asia and elsewhere, patronage is an important risk-sharing institution, often linked with market transactions; for example, a worker may accept lower wages in return for the employer's promise to help out in time of crisis.[6] Patronage is probably well suited to sharing risks which are independent (or better still, negatively correlated) amongst clients. But it can be expected to run into difficulties when risks are positively correlated. This would appear to be why patronage ties often break down during famines and also when previously isolated villages are opened up to external trade.[7] Thus, despite the importance of the 'moral economy' in normal times, there are good reasons for concentrating attention on the performance of markets as the main allocative institutions during famines.

Governmental institutions are also involved. By public storage, food aid, pricing policies, and other forms of intervention, governments can sometimes influence intertemporal and interpersonal distribution. And the way political institutions work can have considerable bearing on market performance. Nonetheless, the decision to concentrate on market performance during famines can be defended on two counts: first, the case for governmental intervention often depends crucially on market performance; the case will be weak if it can be shown that markets work well in the absence of intervention. Second, famine relief policies can often fail owing to their proponents' failure to anticipate the response of markets which can undermine or even wholly defeat the most well intentioned policy initiatives.

1.2 An Introduction to the History of Thought on Markets and Famines

A good deal of this book is devoted to a careful empirical investigation of the main assumptions underlying past debates about the role of markets during famines. The main debates have centred on the issue of whether governments should interfere with the way markets allocate consumption between people and over time.

During much of the nineteenth century, British politicians (both Whigs and Tories) abhorred governmental interference in markets. Exceptions were rarely made for famines. Laissez-faire policies were much influenced by Adam Smith's views and his condemnation of intervention (1961, 32–3) was unequivocal:

Whoever examines, with attention, the history of the dearths and famines which have afflicted any part of Europe during either the course of the present or that of the two preceding centuries . . . will find, I believe, that a dearth never has arisen from any combination among the inland dealers in corn, nor from any other cause but a real scarcity, occasioned sometimes, perhaps, and in some particular places, by the waste of war, but in by far the greatest number of cases, by the fault of the seasons; and that a famine has never arisen from any other cause but the violence of government attempting, by improper means, to remedy the inconvenience of a dearth.

Woodham-Smith's history of the mid-nineteenth century famines in Ireland (1962, 54) describes the pervasive influence of these ideas on government policy:

Almost without exception, the high officials and politicians responsible for Ireland were fervent believers in non-interference by Government, . . . The loss of the potato crop was therefore to be made good . . . by the operations of private enterprise and private firms, using the normal channels of commerce. The Government was not to appear in food markets as a buyer, there was to be 'no disturbance of the ordinary course of trade' and 'no complaints from private traders' on account of Government competition.

The British faith in markets during the nineteenth century has been widely condemned by subsequent historians. Woodham-Smith goes on to argue that there was an important fallacy in the government's position in that, for many people in Ireland, the necessary markets simply did not exist.

In the case of the many famines experienced by the Indian subcontinent over the last century or so, the performance of existing markets has also been strongly criticized. Bhatia (1967, 9) characterizes the new form of 'price famines' which is claimed to have emerged during the nineteenth century:

Thus instead of absolute lack of food in one region, famine under the new conditions assumed the form of a sharp rise in prices. The process was helped by the emergence of 'destructive' form of speculation in foodgrains. The disappearance of domestic stocks, which people were accustomed to keep in the past, and the development of a large export trade in grain, which siphoned off annually a substantial part of cereal production of the country, were factors which contributed to the rise in prices of foodgrains during the period of famine. As a result of these developments, the rise in prices and the consequent suffering of the people were out of all proportion to the nature scarcity. The human and institutional factors were becoming more important than the natural scarcity in causing distress and starvation.

Bhatia's description of famine contains many of the propositions which will be discussed and, when possible, tested empirically in this book. One of the most important of these concerns the role of grain speculation.

'Hoarding' has been a popular explanation for famine when there is no apparent shortage of current aggregate grain availability. References to hoarding go back to at least the Great Famine in India during the 1630s (Raychaudhuri, 1985) and have been heard many times since then.[8] The very existence of private stocks during famines has often raised considerable anxiety, not least amongst those threatened with starvation; writing about the famine in Madras during the 1870s, Arnold (1984, 22) gives the following example:

Visiting villages in the Jammalamadugu taluk of northwest Cuddapah in early September 1876, an Indian Deputy Collector was approached by labourers protesting at the withholding of grain from them by raiyats (farmers) and Komatis (Telugu traders). He arrived at the hamlet of Chinna Venuthurla the day after labourers had tried to loot grain from a Komati, but managed to persuade a raiyat to open his grain store to feed needy villagers. The Deputy Collector remarked that the raiyats were most reluctant to feed the labourers who had also ceased to be able to obtain grain on credit.

One can find numerous other descriptions of the (often) hostile relations between grain merchants and the rural poor; see, for example, Darling (1947, ch. 5), Hartmann and Boyce (1983, ch. 14) and Ram (1986). Some descriptions of grain speculation during famines have been slightly more sympathetic with the traders; for example, Digby (1878, 272) argues that:

Grain dealers naturally wish to make the maximum of profit, and the stores are withheld until competition is roused. A famine or scarcity is the grain-dealer's opportunity, and he cannot, more than any other trader, be blamed for making the most of his opportunity.

Nonetheless, history has by and large condemned the activities of grain merchants during famines.

This assessment fails to appreciate the potentially important role of storage as a means of stabilizing consumption over time. Hoarding can be a highly desirable response of current markets to *future* scarcity. And it may well be desirable from the point of view of the survival chances of the rural poor as well as the profits of speculative traders; those who are close to death now would naturally like stocks reduced considerably but there is every possibility that, in doing so, one would create even greater starvation in the future. As Adam Smith realized, whether one does or not will depend, in part, on how well speculative traders have anticipated future scarcity; referring to the judgements about future prices made by the merchant who holds stocks of grain during a famine, Smith (1961, 41) writes that:

If he judges right, instead of hurting the great body of the people, he renders them a most important service. By making them feel the inconveniences of a dearth somewhat earlier than they otherwise might do, he prevents their feeling them afterwards as severely as they certainly would do, if the cheapness of price encouraged them to consume faster than suited the real scarcity of the season.

Popular opposition to 'hoarding' during famines continues and Smith's case in favour of it has been reiterated. Two centuries later, Kenneth Arrow (1982*a*, 25) remarks in his review of Sen (1981*a*):

If the famine is prolonged, then hoarding at the beginning means greater stores will be available later on. In fact, if the hoarder was correct in his expectations, that is, if the farmer does not need to consume his own grain at a later date or if the speculator makes money by selling at a higher price, then hoarding will have improved the availability of food later on, at, to be sure, the cost of making things worse initially.

For both Smith and Arrow, a crucial assumption underlying the case in favour of letting free markets determine the allocation of consumption over time is that private traders predict future prices accurately. Of course, future prices can never be known with certainty and so forecasting errors must be expected. But if traders predict prices as accurately as can be done with the available information *and* those prices provide the right signals for resource allocation, then the case against 'hoarding' during famines certainly seems weak. The following section will return to this point.

A closely related issue in past thought has been the *spatial* performance of foodgrain markets in eliminating localized scarcities. The above quote from Bhatia also attacks the performance of India's external trade. British India (including Burma) was a substantial net exporter of grain during the numerous severe famines of the late nineteenth and early twentieth centuries (Bhatia, 1967; Ghose, 1982). Ireland also exported food during the mid-nineteenth century famines (Woodham-Smith, 1962) and there have been numerous other instances, including recent famines in South Asia and Africa.[9]

Food export during famine has often been viewed as an indication of the failure of markets as a means of relieving local famine by spatial arbitrage. And a number of explanations for these seemingly de-stabilizing food movements have been offered. Recently, Amartya Sen has interpreted them as 'slump famines', arguing that '. . . market forces would tend to encourage precisely such food movements when failure of purchasing power outweighs availability decline' (Sen, 1981*b*, 461).

It is not obvious that food export during a famine is consumption de-stabilizing. The argument that unrestricted trade will help buffer consumption from output risk only requires that exports should fall during a famine; they need not vanish. However, adverse income effects in famine affected areas could certainly mitigate the stabilizing role of trade, by dampening the response of relative spatial prices to the local scarcity. And there are other reasons for suspecting that trade may be rather sluggish in its short-term response to localized scarcities. For example, traders may be constrained by long-term contracts devised to avoid risk. One need not deny that speculative markets will eventually even out spatial price differentials; but in a famine one is also very much concerned with the speed at which markets perform this function.

The speed of market adjustment to initially localized famines has been an important issue for the design of famine relief policy. There was much debate about this aspect of market performance in British India during the nineteenth century. For example, during the severe famine of the mid 1870s, the local government in Madras rebelled against the central government's firm commitment to non-interference.

The Madras government agreed that if time were given to the market, the necessary grain would eventually come, but time was what could not be given. (Ambirajan, 1978, 95.)

By contrast, public policy towards foodgrain markets in the sub-continent has tended to be highly interventionist in recent times. Governments are actively involved in grain storage and restrictions on the movement of foodgrains from surplus to deficit area are common, and often become tighter during famines. Advocates of such restrictions have often based their case on the assumption that markets cannot be expected to perform well in alleviating local scarcities. Of course, if such restrictions are binding then the markets must be moving grain in the right direction and so the case may seem weak. However, the fact that grain is moving in the right direction does not mean that it will be sold to consumers on its arrival. The markets' critics have thought it more plausible that the grain was bound for the speculative stocks of traders in the deficit district than for current sale.[10] Again the policy debate begs the important question of how well traders anticipate future scarcity when making their storage decisions.

1.3 An Introduction to the Economics of Markets and Famines

Since much of this book is concerned with the performance of markets during famines, it is important to make clear from the outset how that performance is to be assessed.

In discussing the performance of markets under uncertainty it is useful to think of the 'goods' in an economy as including all possible contracts that agents may like to devise as a means of avoiding risk. The risks arise from uncertainty about the environment or 'state' the agent will confront sometime in the future. Thus, the contracts are often called 'state contingent commodities'. It is known that if there is a market for each of these contracts, as well as for all other goods, then a unique competitive equilibrium for such an economy will exist and be economically efficient (in the Paretian sense) under the same conditions for which these properties hold in an economy without uncertainty.[11]

However, as is typically the case, the present setting is one in which there are more goods than markets. Probably most importantly, the necessary markets do not exist to permit agents to trade contracts for *future* grain delivery. Thus, current trading decisions are conditional on expectations about the prices which will prevail in future spot markets, and so expectations will matter for the allocation of consumption over time. Competitive equilibria of such an economy are often called *temporary equilibria*.

An important special case is the *rational expectations equilibrium* (REE). This occurs if the expectations on which a temporary equilibrium is based are stochastically self-fulfilling in that all markets eventually clear at prices which, on average, accord with the prior expectations.[12]

The REE is often viewed as a normative benchmark for discussing the performance of other equilibria, although the sense in which the REE is 'ideal' may be quite restrictive. For example, the REE is generally not Pareto efficient under the same conditions for which this holds when the set of markets is complete (Newbery and Stiglitz, 1981, ch. 15; 1982*b*). Nonetheless the information needed by a government to make a Pareto improvement to the REE may be very difficult to obtain and, by at least one reckoning, the efficiency benefits from doing so appear to be small (Newbery and Stiglitz, 1981). Thus there may well remain a convincing efficiency case for using the REE as the benchmark for discussing market performance during famines.

However, 'efficiency' is an unappealing criterion in this context. The anathemas that it can lead to are plain enough; for example, it is unlikely that many people would be willing to judge a famine as warranted because those who died could not have earnt enough had they lived to pay for aid. For most people (and this surely includes potential famine victims), the overriding concern about famines is not economic efficiency *per se* but human survival. Where does this leave us?

This book assumes that the level of famine mortality attained for given aggregate food availability is the overriding concern when discussing market performance and public policy during famines; in my view, any conflicting assumption runs too great a risk of producing an economic analysis with little relevance to the immediate needs of the people most involved in famines: governments, aid agencies and, of course, victims.[13]

But I shall be giving the REE a special status in the analysis. In particular, I shall attempt to compare the level of mortality one may expect in a REE with that resulting from the way *actual* markets and policies worked during a famine. The REE is generally a feasible equilibrium in the sense that it is consistent with the endowments, preferences, and available information in the economy at each point in time.[14] And it has the informational advantages of only requiring decentralized decision making. If it turns out that the specific ways in which actual markets deviated from the REE resulted in higher mortality then it can be concluded that there was a feasible improvement in the economy's performance in terms of both human survival and (with the aforementioned qualifications) economic efficiency. Thus the REE may remain a useful benchmark for discussing market performance in this setting.

Much of this book is devoted to an empirical assessment of the performance of actual markets during famines, where 'performance' is judged relative to this benchmark. However, such an empirical investigation begs an important prior question of a theoretical nature:

Why might an economy not be in a rational expectations equilibrium? The concept of a REE embodies *joint* hypotheses about market structure on the one hand and expectations formation on the other. Specifically, REE assumes that:

(i) the economy is competitive in that spot prices adjust rapidly to clear markets at the notional demands of all traders, conditional on their expectations of future prices (as well as other prices and endowments), and

(ii) those expectations are 'rational' in the sense that future markets will be found, on average, to clear at the expected prices.

In short, the REE embodies the twin conditions of flexible spot prices and (stochastically) self-fulfilling expectations of future prices. Departure from either of these conditions will result in an economy not being in a REE.

The main sources of departure from REE examined in this book concern expectations formation. Violation of the conditions for rational expectations at the individual level can arise from one or both of two sources:

(i) Individuals use an incorrect model of the economy in forming their forecasts.

(ii) Individuals do not use the mean of the forecasted variable (conditional on whatever model they hold) as their forecast.

The first source of non-rational expectations has received a good deal more attention in the literature than the second. Friedman (1979) and Bray (1983), amongst others, have pointed out the difficulties facing any individual in obtaining a 'true model' for forecasting purposes. Indeed, even if the structure of the model is correctly specified, its calibration is unlikely to be an easy matter. It is known that it is difficult to obtain unbiased estimates of the coefficients on stochastic regressors (including lagged values of the forecasted variable) with small samples; the popular 'least squares' estimates, for example, will be biased in all finite samples. For all practical purposes, the best one can hope for is *asymptotically* unbiased estimates, even if the model is correctly specified from the start. More generally, agents will also be estimating misspecified models. Although convergence to a REE is still possible (Bray, 1983), it may take agents a long time to acquire the information needed to generate rational expectations.

Nor is it obvious that individuals always behave as if they are striving for correct models. As Hey (1984) has argued, the probabilities that people choose to assign to uncertain events may be influenced by the consequences of those events; in particular, an 'optimist' ('pessimist') will prefer to revise up (down) the probabilities of favourable events relative to unfavourable ones.[15]

In such circumstances, expectations will be non-rational because subjective and objective probability beliefs diverge; either because of imperfect information about the true distribution or a personal preference for some other distribution. There is a second class of objections to the rational expectations hypothesis which questions whether the conditional mean of the (subjective or objective) distribution is always the appropriate summary statistic of probability beliefs.

It is known from statistical decision theory that asymmetric loss functions (defined on *ex-post* forecasting errors) invalidate the use of the conditional mean as the optimal forecast (Granger, 1969; DeGroot, 1970). To give an example, suppose that the loss to the individual from making a forecasting error is an asymmetric quadratic function of that error and that the forecast is chosen to minimize the expected value of this, given a set of information on the distribution of the forecasted variable. Then the optimal forecast conditional on that information will be a biased and, hence, non-rational expectation. To give another example, it can be shown that minimization of the expected absolute forecasting error requires use of the median of the distribution of the forecasted variable rather than the mean (DeGroot, 1970).[16] The essential feature of these examples is that the mathematical expectation may not be the appropriate summary statistic of the individual's subjective probability beliefs about the future.

It is not obvious that such 'asymmetric loss functions' have a sensible economic interpretation. However, I have argued elsewhere that asymmetry may provide quite a plausible characterization of the intertemporal consumption decision of an individual who gains present satisfaction (dissatisfaction) from contemplating a favourable (unfavourable) future (Ravallion, 1985c). Formally, this 'contemplation effect' means that expectations can affect *ex-post* life time utility independently of any *ex-ante* actions taken by the individual.[17]

In summary: the concept of a rational expectations equilibrium is better viewed as a normative *benchmark* for evaluating the performance of actual markets than as an inherently plausible characterization of that performance. There are reasonable a priori grounds for doubting that unregulated markets will necessarily find their way rapidly (or at all) to a REE. The empirical question remains as to whether or not market performance is in accord with the REE. As this study will attempt to show, the answer to that question can also throw light on the causes of famines in market economies.

1.4 An Overview of the Study

The questions raised by this study, and at least some of the answers given, appear to have wide relevance to understanding the recurrent famines in Asia and Africa. A number of those questions are empirical. And they can be quite difficult to answer carefully. To do so, this study has examined in detail one recent famine for which we have excellent data: the famine in Bangladesh during 1974.

For this famine, and a number of others, Sen (1981*a*) has demonstrated that the victims suffered a severe contraction in the consumption possibilities—or 'exchange entitlements'—attainable from their endowments. Table 1.1 gives estimates of the percentage changes in the rice exchange rates of the two main tradeable endowments—labour and land—in the four districts of Bangladesh widely agreed to have been worst hit by the famine. The sharp increase in the price of the staple foodgrain coincided with a contraction in rural employment opportunities due to extensive

Table 1.1: *Trade Entitlement Decline During the 1974 Famine in Bangladesh*

| District | Percentage change in price from 1973/4 to 1974/5 | | | | |
	(i) Labour	(ii) Land	(iii) Rice	Labour for Rice	Land for Rice
Rangpur	11	26	71	−60	−54
Mymensingh	25	17	109	−84	−92
Dinajpur	41	17	85	−44	−68
Sylhet	29	13	116	−87	−103

NOTE: (i) and (iii) are simple averages of the monthly figures for agricultural labour and coarse rice (retail) given in Alamgir *et al* (1977). (ii) is the simple average of the figures for irrigated land in Bangladesh Bureau of Statistics (1984, Table 11.48).

flood damage and an increase in 'distress sales' of land.[18] Thus, conditions in the markets for labour and land were not conducive to maintenance of the rice purchasing power of these endowments.

Also, prices for the staple foodgrain have often been highly unstable during famines; the sharp price increases are soon followed by equally impressive falls. For example, Figure 1.1 gives the (de-trended) series of rice prices for Bangladesh during 1974. The figure also gives the prices that one would have expected for the same annual mean but on the basis of the pre-famine seasonal structure (as estimated by 12-month moving averages). Similar price instability has been observed during many other famines.[19] While it need not always be true, I shall argue later that this extreme volatility of rice prices in Bangladesh had a de-stabilizing influence on rice consumption over time amongst potential famine victims.

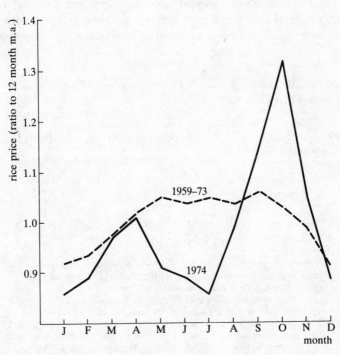

Fig. 1.1

It is also plausible that, at least in the short run, the sharp increase in foodgrain prices added to the inequality of income and consumption. Holding incomes constant, a rice price increase will tend to have a proportionally greater effect on rice consumption by the poor than the rich; this is in keeping with the widely observed tendency (in both low and high income countries) for price elasticities of demand for staple foodgrains to decline with income.[20] Also, in predominately rural economies such as Bangladesh, the rich tend to be net suppliers of agricultural products and the poor to be net demanders. Thus, a rice price increase can also be expected initially to worsen the distribution of income. Adverse effects on the distribution of wealth have also been identified in a number of studies.[21] Longer-term adjustments in factor prices and outputs may well mitigate these adverse distributional effects, but it is the short-run effects that are of most concern during famines.

Combining these considerations, Table 1.2 gives my estimates of the short-run effects on incomes (including agricultural wages) and rice consumption of a rice price increase for some stylized types of rural households. Rice consumption by high income rice supplying

Table 1.2 *Short-run Effects of 10 Per cent Increase in Rice Price on Income and Rice Consumption*

Source of income is from selling:	Demand elasticity		Percentage change in	
	price	income	income	consumption
(i) rice, amount fixed	−0.83	0.94	10	1.1
(ii) rice, amount falls by 10%	−0.83	0.94	0	−8.3
(iii) labour, amount fixed	−1.30	1.19	3.5	−8.8
(iv) labour, employment drops 10%	−1.30	1.19	−6.5	−21

Note: Percentage change in consumption = price elasticity of demand × percentage change in price + income elasticity of demand × percentage change in income. The latter includes a short-run adjustment in the wage rate for (iii) and (iv), using an elasticity of 0.35 as estimated in Chapter 5. Demand elasticities are from Pitt (1983), where (i) and (ii) are assumed to be in the 25th percentile of the expenditure distribution while (iii) and (iv) are in the 90th percentile. Pitt's estimates are higher in absolute value than some others (for example, Ahmed, 1981), but the relative magnitudes between 'poor' and 'rich' are similar and so the distributional effects will also be similar.

households is unlikely to fall much. Indeed, those who do not experience any contemporaneous fall in their rice output are likely to slightly increase their rice consumption during a famine, as illustrated by case (i) in Table 1.2. At the other extreme, agricultural labourers are likely to experience a sharp drop in their consumption of the staple foodgrain, particularly when the price increase coincides with a fall in demand for their labour, as in case (iv).

Thus it can be argued that the Bangladesh famine was associated with a worsening of food distribution, which became both more unstable over time and more unequal between people. Both phenomena appear to be typical of famines in market economies. The twin objectives of this study are to explain how such distributional changes influence famine mortality and how those distributional changes come about.

The theoretical foundation for this study's concern with market performance during famines is laid by Chapter 2. A health-theoretic model is proposed relating famine mortality to food distribution. The model implies that, in addition to the adverse effect on survival chance of a drop in consumption at any one date or for one person, survival chances will be worsened by mean preserving de-stabilizations of foodgrain consumption over time or by unequalizing transfers between people at one point in time. It is also argued that this will remain true in the presence of individual opportunities for storage or savings. Necessary and sufficient conditions are also derived in Chapter 2 for price stabilization to have a beneficial effect on famine mortality. A quantitative assessment is then made of the potential gains in terms of reduced famine mortality from the stabilization of the prices during two famines: the 1877 famine in Madras and the 1974 famine in Bangladesh.

Chapters 3, 4, and 5 are devoted to the 1974 famine in Bangladesh. Chapter 3 attempts to explain the high and unstable rice prices observed during that famine. An econometric model of price formation is proposed and estimated. The model's structure permits an evaluation of the intertemporal allocative performance of a spot market for a storable good when neither private stocks nor price expectations are observed. The method is applied to monthly rice price data for Bangladesh over the period 1972–5. The Bangladesh government's attempts to stabilize prices during the famine are also examined. Chapter 4 looks at the extent of the spatial integration of Bangladesh rice markets during the famine. A model of spatial price differentials for a tradeable good is proposed which avoids the inferential dangers of received methods using static price correlations. While Chapter 3 attempts to explain the sharp fall in the food purchasing power of rural incomes during the 1974 famine in terms of conditions in foodgrain markets, Chapter 5 examines the response of the markets for the main tradeable endowment of the rural poor: their capacity for work. The short-run response of labour markets during a famine is crucial to the famine's effect on interpersonal distribution. An econometric investigation of wage movements before and after the Bangladesh famine is used to test for a structural break in the short-run response of wages to prices at the time of the famine.

In the light of the results of the earlier chapters, it is of interest to take a closer look at some aspects of the workings of a present day Bangladesh rice market. Chapter 6 reports the results of my survey of traders' prices and expectations in one of the country's main wholesale rice markets during the winter of 1983/4. The survey permits assembly of a fairly long time series of *ex-post* forecasting errors at the individual level. These data permit tests of alternative theories of expectations formation in this setting.

Finally, Chapter 7 examines the study's implications for famine relief policies. The main policies that have been used or advocated in the past are critically surveyed from the point of view of their likely effectiveness in reducing famine mortality for given aggregate food availability. A prominent theme of Chapter 7 is that the way markets work has considerable bearing on this issue.

1.5　Summary of the Findings

When potential famine victims rely heavily on current foodgrain markets for their consumption needs, high prices will reduce their survival chances. If those survival chances are also sufficiently concave functions of their incomes, foodgrain price instability will induce famine mortality. A priori considerations and empirical evidence suggest that these conditions are plausible in the South Asian setting. Results for two famines, one hundred years apart, are in close accord and suggest that high and unstable foodgrain prices were major contributing factors to excess mortality.

A study of the causes of the high and unstable rice prices during the 1974 famine in Bangladesh suggests that the markets were de-stabilized by speculation. Rice hoarding prior to anticipated production losses was excessive when compared to the likely outcome under competitive conditions with informationally unbiased expectations. Over-reaction to new information on future scarcity during the famine de-stabilized rice markets. Thus it can be argued that excess mortality in Bangladesh during 1974 was, in no small measure, the effect of a speculative crisis.

The conclusion that rice markets in Bangladesh were informationally inefficient during the 1974 famine is confirmed by a study of recently surveyed expectations in a large wholesale rice market. The traders' forecasts appear to be based on simple 'rules of thumb' which will often be significantly biased. As a consequence, rice markets over-react to new price information; in particular, high current prices will lead to overly optimistic expectations of future prices on the part of stock holders. This has a de-stabilizing influence on the markets.

Nor do the rice markets of Bangladesh appear to have been well integrated spatially during the 1974 famine. Significant impediments to interdistrict trade during the famine are suggested by analysis of the dynamic interaction between prices in Dhaka and its rural hinterland.

At the same time, the flood damage to crops and associated social dislocation during the famine left a sizeable shock to the agricultural labour markets on which Bangladesh's rural poor depend heavily. The results of this study suggest that an increase in the excess supply of labour during the lean season of 1974 resulted in a fall in the long-run real wage rate *and* a sharp drop in the short-run response of nominal wages to rice prices. This added to the unequalizing effect of the high prices on interpersonal distribution and further de-stabilized the real incomes of the rural poor.

The Bangladesh government responded to the volatile conditions in rice markets during the 1974 famine. Price increases appear to have induced government responses aimed at stabilization. The government's attempts at stabilization were evident in the changes in its own stock position and by its policy announcements. But the response lacked credibility: private stockholders' inflated expectations of the effects of crop damage on future prices appear to have been quite correctly premised on a belief that, despite its pronounced aims, the government could not be relied upon to implement a successful stabilizing response to the impending shortage.

Once it is realized that the performance of markets under uncertainty is a crucial factor in determining famine mortality, one can appreciate the possibility that famine may actually occur before any production shortfall. While the 1974 famine in Bangladesh was not associated with a fall in current aggregate foodgrain availability, there is a meaningful sense in which it was caused by a drop in *future* availability. Certain conditions must be met for this to happen. Informational inefficiency in markets is clearly one of them, and this study suggests that this is an important characteristic of rice markets in Bangladesh. However, as I have also emphasised, for private speculation to be de-stabilizing, traders must believe that the domestic government and foreign agencies will be unable to make up for the expected production shortfall. Famine threatens when output *and* political uncertainty are combined.

Notes

1. The importance of trade entitlements in famines has been recognized for some time. For example, in his 'Manual of Political Economy' (1798, 1982 edn., 267), Jeremy Bentham defined 'famine' as 'trade entitlement failure': 'I call it a *famine* when the lowest wages of labour will not produce a family as much bread as it is necessary they should eat, or their healths must suffer by the deficiency.' The Famine Codes of British India also recognized the importance of 'exchange entitlements' (Bhatia, 1967; Currey, 1984; Rangasami, 1985).
2. Both Mitra (1982) and Srinivasan (1983) argue that Sen's theory of famines does not go far enough into the causes of exchange entitlement failure. Sen's (1981a, 164) concluding comments anticipate their criticism.
3. For example, see Preston (1975, 1980), Rodgers (1979), Schultz (1979), Williamson (1984), Goldstein (1985), and Svedberg (1986).
4. This has been noted for a number of countries; on tropical Africa, see Jones (1972); on southern India, see Lele (1971); on Indonesia, see Alexander (1986); and on Bangladesh, see the field work reported in Chapter 6. Also see the survey by Helmberger, Cambell, and Dobson (1981). The special importance of acquiring non-price information in agriculture undoubtedly reflects the fact of output uncertainty, making observed prices a noisy indicator of other traders' private informa-

tion. For an interesting theoretical model illustrating this phenomenon see Grossman and Stiglitz (1980).

5. Traditional methods of analysis in this field have drawn their main theoretical inspiration from the now classic theorems of Paretian welfare economics. It is becoming recognized that these theorems may well be a poor guide for judging market performance under the (typical) conditions of considerable uncertainty and incomplete risk markets found in poor countries, and elsewhere. Section 1.3 will discuss this further.

6. See, for example, Epstein (1967), Bardhan and Rudra (1981), and Greenough (1982).

7. For example, see Epstein (1967), BRAC (1979), Currey (1981), Greenough (1982).

8. See, for example, Arnold (1984) on the severe famine in Madras 1876–8, Das (1949) and Greenough (1982) on the Great Bengal Famine during World War Two, and Meng-Try (1984) on the famine in Kampuchea 1974–5. Nor has the recent famine in Africa been an exception; for example, there have been reports of hoarding by 'grain barons' in Sudan, see Steele (1985).

9. Seaman and Holt (1980) report that food was being exported from famine stricken Wollo province in Ethiopia during 1973–4. There have also been reports of grain export from the Sudan during the 1984–5 famine (Steele, 1985). There were numerous claims of grain smuggling out of Bangladesh during the 1974 famine (see, for example, Alamgir, 1980), although there is conflicting evidence (Reddaway and Rahman, 1975).

10. In India this was argued by, for example, the Foodgrain Enquiry Committee of 1957 and the Agricultural Prices Commission of 1965; see Bhatia (1967) and Chopra (1981).

11. A number of clear and thorough treatments of these topics are available including Debreu (1959), Arrow and Hahn (1971), Allingham (1975), and Varian (1978).

12. There are now a number of useful introductions to the rational expectations hypothesis, starting from elementary principles; see, for example, the first few chapters of Begg (1982). A good introduction to many of the microeconomic applications can be found in Bray (1985).

13. Mortality in poor countries has been viewed as an important welfare economic variable in other contexts; for example, see Kynch and Sen (1983) and Goldstein (1985).

14. Exceptions arise when REE does not exist consistent with initial endowments and preferences. The usual restrictions on the economy's excess demand functions needed to guarantee existence for a complete set of markets (continuity, homogeneity of degree zero and

Walras' law) are sufficient to guarantee existence of temporary equilibria, including REE with shared information (see, for example, Varian, 1978, Chapter 6). However, non-existence problems have arisen under these conditions in rational expectations models with diverse private information. In this case, observed prices will transmit information from informed to uninformed traders. Non-existence problems have arisen when small price changes induce large changes in the deducible information; for discussion and references see Bray (1985), Jordan and Radner (1982).

15. This may also help explain why the revisions of subjective probabilities in the light of new information that experimental psychologists have managed to observe have borne little resemblance to predictions based using Bayes' theorem; see Tversky and Kahneman (1982) and Arrow's (1982*b*) survey. These experiments have generally indicated a tendency to over-react to new information when revising probability beliefs. Recent finance literature also contains a number of tests for such over-reaction to new information on stock markets. Shiller (1981) has argued that US stock prices over the last century have been far too volatile to be rationally attributed to new information on future dividends. Tests based on weaker assumptions by Mankiw, Romer, and Shapiro (1985) have broadly confirmed Shiller's conclusions. Also see DeBondt and Thaler (1985).

16. For other examples, see Granger (1969), Granger and Newbold (1977), and Visco (1984). Mention can also be made of smoothing methods of estimation (see, for example, Silverman, 1985). Here the objective function is also asymmetric; models are chosen to minimize the sum of squared residuals *plus* a 'roughness penalty', such as the integrated squared second derivative. The essential idea is that the appeal of a model depends on its 'smoothness' in describing data (the linear model being a special case) as well as its precision in prediction.

17. The contemplation effect can also be interpreted in terms of the psychological theory of cognitive dissonance (Ravallion, 1985*c*). This has received a good deal of experimental support; see Festinger (1964) and Wicklund and Brehm (1976). For an interesting discussion of the economic implications of cognitive dissonance see Akerlof and Dickens (1982). Hey's (1984) model of optimism and pessimism can also be interpreted as embodying a contemplation effect; contemplation can be manifest in either the probabilities assigned to events or the statistics used to summarize those probabilities. See Ravallion (1985*c*) for further discussion.

18. For evidence on these points and further discussion see Alamgir (1980), Sen (1981*a*), and Muqtada (1981).

19. See, for example, the prices reported for various famines by Alamgir (1980), Sen (1981*a*), Meng-Try (1984), Cutler (1984), Kumar (1986).

20. For Bangladesh see Ahmed (1979, 1981) and Pitt (1983); for India see Radhakrishna (1978) and Swamy and Binswanger (1983). Pinstrup-Anderson (1985) surveys a number of other studies for various countries coming to the same conclusion. More direct evidence of the adverse effect of high prices and/or low real wages in terms of food on rural poverty in India can be found in Saith (1981) and van de Walle (1985).

21. See, for example, Das (1949), Alamgir (1980), Sen (1981*a*), Ghose (1982), Greenough (1982).

2

Markets and Mortality during Famines

2.1 Introduction

This chapter examines how the prices and incomes generated by markets can influence human survival chances. The argument is built on a theoretical model of the relationship between mortality risk, health, and food consumption. This is outlined in Section 2. The model implies that there will be long-term survival gains from mean preserving stabilizations of foodgrain consumption over time and from equalizing redistributions at one point in time. Sections 3 to 5 discuss further aspects of the model: Section 3 offers some caveats concerning optimal stabilization, Section 4 examines the possible stabilizing responses of individuals to exogenous income fluctuations and Section 5 looks at the effects of foodgrain price variability. Section 6 applies the theoretical approach of the previous sections to an analysis of the relationship between mortality and foodgrain prices during two famines: the 1877 famine in Madras and the 1974 famine in Bangladesh. The empirical results are used to make an assessment of the potential gains in terms of famine survival from price stabilization policies. Section 7 presents a simple dynamic model of grain markets which offers some clues to possible causes of price volatility during famines. The clues will be followed up by later chapters.

2.2 Consumption and Survival

It is obvious enough that any person's future survival will depend in some way on the goods which that person is able to consume, including food. But the precise relationship between current food consumption and future survival chances will generally be clouded in uncertainty.[1] One may be confident that a person cannot possibly survive to some future date if food consumption falls below an amount x_0 (say) and that, barring accidents, the same person is very likely to live if at least some larger amount x_1 is consumed. But between x_0 and x_1 the outcome will generally depend on attributes of individual health which are difficult for the individual (or anyone else for that matter) to know with certainty. One can conveniently place these attributes under the rubric 'personal constitution'.

While it is evident that physical health depends on a number of conditions, it is also plausible that there are possibilities for substitution between at least some of these in attaining a given level of physical well-being. For example, a physically strong person can often get by with a lower calorie intake than a weak person. Similarly, a lower metabolic rate permits a lower calorie intake, *ceteris paribus*.

To formalize this, while keeping things reasonably simple, suppose that health is measurable as a non-negative number (h) which depends on current food consumption (x) and personal constitution (y). For concreteness, h can be thought of as the individual's future life span. One can imagine assigning a unique value of h to each possible combination of x and y; let this be represented by the health 'production function' $\phi(x,y)$ which is strictly increasing in x and y. The function ϕ is taken to subsume indirect effects of x and y on health operating through vulnerability to disease.[2]

The importance of personal constitution from the point of view of allocating food depends on the nature of the possibilities for substitution between x and y in attaining a given level of health. To represent these, suppose that the function ϕ traces out strictly convex contours in (x,y), over a suitably restricted domain.[3] This means that, within limits, the food consumption needed to attain a given level of health increases smoothly as personal constitution worsens *and* that the gains in consumption needed to compensate for a poorer constitution also increase. This assumption is intended to capture the (casual) observation that a physically weak person who becomes ill will usually need improved nutrition to remain healthy while a strong person can probably get by with little dietary change.

Food consumption can generally be observed with precision and so it is reasonable to treat this as a non-stochastic variable. But, as I have argued already, this is not so of personal constitution, about which there may be considerable uncertainty. Rather than assign a known value of constitution, I shall assume that probabilities can (at least in principle) be assigned over a range of alternative values. Specifically, I shall assume that personal constitution is a continuous random variable with density function f and distribution function F.

Finally, it is assumed that there is a fixed minimum level of health h_0 which is needed if an individual is to have any (positive) chance of surviving. For example, interpreting h as future life span, $h_0 = 0$. The iso-survival contour at h_0 is the value of $y_0 = g(x)$ such that $\phi(x, y_0) = h_0$ and for which $g'(x) < 0$ and $g''(x) > 0$ under the assumed properties of the health production function. The quantity $g(x)$ will be termed the *survival constitution*; it is the minimum personal constitution needed if a person consuming food in amount x is to have any chance of surviving.

Combining these assumptions, the probability of an individual surviving with consumption x is given by the *survival function*:

$$s(x) = 1 - F(g(x)) \qquad (2.1)$$

with slope

$$s'(x) = -f(g(x))g'(x) > 0. \qquad (2.2)$$

Thus $s(x)$ is the area under the probability density function of personal constitution above the critical value needed for survival, $g(x)$, when consuming food in amount x. Figure 2.1 illustrates this

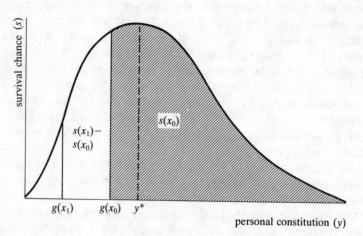

Fig. 2.1

for a unimodal density; an increase in food consumption from x_0 to x_1 reduces the survival constitution from $g(x_0)$ to $g(x_1)$ and so increases survival chance from $s(x_0)$ to $s(x_1)$.

It should be emphasized that the actual relationship between foodgrain consumption and mortality risk in a given individual is likely to be a good deal more complex than this. Elsewhere I have shown how the survival function can be given a much more general interpretation which permits variation in 'needs' such that individuals with the same food consumption can have different survival chances (Ravallion, 1985*d*). I shall use this more general model in Chapter 7 when discussing the interpersonal distribution of food. However, the argument concerning intertemporal distribution can be outlined more simply if it is assumed that needs do not vary within the population at any one date. Section 2.3 discusses the caveats called for when this assumption is relaxed.

The effects on mortality of changes in the spread of consumption over time will also depend on the *shape* of the survival function, as revealed by its second derivative. A concave survival function seems plausible and is in accord with the limited empirical evidence.[4] In this case the increase in survival chance afforded by extra consumption falls as consumption increases until, eventually, extra consumption has negligible benefit.

Under what conditions will this hold? Strict concavity of a (smooth) survival function means that its second derivative is negative. So, from equation 2.2, the necessary and sufficient condition for concavity is that

$$s''(x) = -g'(x)^2 f'(y_0) - g''(x)f(y_0) < 0 \qquad (2.3)$$

This depends on properties of the density function of personal constitution as well as the shape of the iso-health contours. Clearly $s''(x) < 0$ for a uniform distribution (for then $f'(y_0) = 0$). But this seems too restrictive. A more plausible assumption is that the density is unimodal so that $f'(y) \gtrless 0$ as $y \lessgtr y^*$, as in Figure 2.1. Then a sufficient condition for $s''(x) < 0$ is that $y_0 > y^*$. Thus the survival function will be strictly concave if the minimum level of personal constitution needed to survive is less than the mode of its distribution.

Another way of understanding this result is as follows. Consider first the case of a uniform distribution in which all levels of personal constitution are equally probable over some interval.

Suppose that consumption is reduced steadily and by equal amounts. The corresponding increments to the minimum constitution needed for survival will get larger and larger (by the assumed convexity of the iso-health contours). For a uniform distribution, each increase in the survival constitution will yield a proportionate decrease in the area under the probability density function of personal constitution. Thus, since the increments to survival constitution are getting larger and larger as consumption falls, the decrements to survival chance must also be getting larger and larger. But consider instead a non-uniform distribution. Clearly each increment in survival constitution will still reduce the area under the probability density function and, hence, survival chance. But whether the decrements to that area tend to increase or decrease will also depend on the local direction of slope in the density function. If upward sloping (so that the distribution function is convex) then equal increments in survival constitution will yield larger and larger reductions in survival chance. This will reinforce the effect obtained with a uniform distribution and so the survival function will definitely be concave. On the other hand, this need not be so in a downward sloping segment of the density function; the two effects will work in opposite directions and one cannot say whether the survival function is concave or convex. Of course, if the distribution of constitution has only one mode then it must be upward sloping at points to the left of the mode, and so the survival function must then be concave.

This is implausible at low levels of consumption, for then the minimum level of personal constitution needed for survival will be high; if consumption is low enough then y_0 would, in principle, exceed the mode of the distribution of personal constitution. The survival function may well be convex at low levels of consumption. Indeed, with mild restrictions on the limiting properties of the functions f and g, the survival function will be convex at 'low' x and concave at 'high' x (see the appendix to this chapter for details). If one also imposes some restrictions on higher derivatives of f and g then it can be shown that the point of inflexion between the convex and concave segments of the survival function will be unique and so the survival function will look like the top right quadrant of Figure 2.2.[5] Figure 2.2 also demonstrates how the survival function can be constructed geometrically from the underlying health contour (lower right quadrant) and probability distribution of

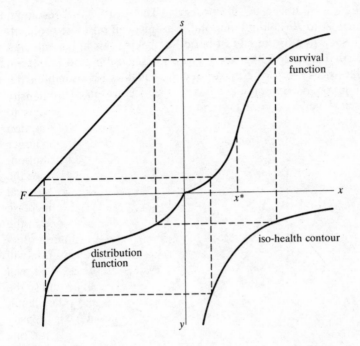

Fig. 2.2

personal constitution (lower left quadrant). The appendix to this chapter gives an example of the mathematical derivation assuming a Cobb–Douglas health production function and log normally distributed personal constitution.

Concavity of the survival function implies that there will be survival gains from stabilizing consumption over time. In particular, *any mean preserving transfer of consumption from a date at which it is high to one at which it is low will raise the chance of surviving to any later date*. To see why, consider the joint probability of surviving to date T when the survival function is concave at each intermediate date. Survival by the terminal date will be the product of the survival probabilities for each intermediate date,

$$s(x_1)s(x_2) \ldots s(x_T) \tag{2.4}$$

The contours of this function are strictly convex to the origin in consumption space whenever the function s is strictly concave.[6]

Figure 2.3 illustrates the property. The transfer of consumption from A to B (holding the total constant) will raise the probability of surviving to the end of period 2. Taking this argument a little further it is clear that for a given total consumption H, terminal date survival will be maximized by equalizing consumption over time; the maximum of equation 2.4 subject to a fixed food stock H is achieved at $x_t = H/T$ for all t.

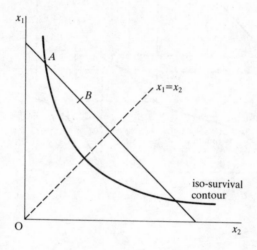

Fig. 2.3

There are two other implications of concavity in the survival function worth noting:

(i) By similar reasoning to that above, it can be readily shown that mean preserving transfers from 'high' grain consumers to 'low' ones will raise both the joint and average probability of survival in a population. In this sense, famines can arise from greater inequality of food consumption. Chapter 7 will explore this aspect further.

(ii) In attempting to uncover the causes of famines, it is natural to look for a sudden shock to the economy, such as war or crop damage. This is typical of past work on famines (as in, for example, Sen, 1981a, 40–1). However, with strict concavity, equal reductions in consumption at each date can be expected to produce ever larger increases in mortality. Thus famines may arise from a steady (even slow) decline in food consumption.

2.3 Caveats

A number of simplifying assumptions have been made in deriving the survival function. Qualifications must be added to the survival case for stabilization when some of these assumptions are relaxed.

1. The case in favour of stabilization can break down at low levels of food availability. Consider the survival function in Figure 2.2. It is clear that the point of stable consumption over time will be found in the concave segment as long as the average availability H/T exceeds x^*. But what if it does not? Then the contours of equation 2.4 will be *concave* to the origin in a neighbourhood of the point of stable consumption, as in Figure 2.4. In this case, some local de-stabilization can be expected to reduce mortality, as in the move from A to B in Figure 2.4. One can, however, be confident that there will be survival gains from eliminating consumption extremes; the iso-survival contours will not be concave over the whole consumption space as long as survival chance falls to zero at zero consumption.[7]

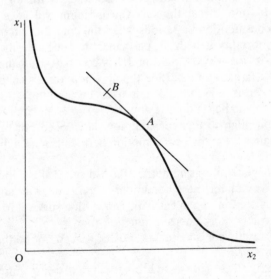

Fig. 2.4

2. It is likely that some deaths during a famine are not (either directly or indirectly) linked to individual food consumption during the famine. This is to be expected during epidemics and if there was malnutrition prior to the famine. The survival function must be modified to incorporate such non-nutritional causes of death. Without loss of generality one can write survival chance during time t in the form

$$s_t = s(x_t) + e_t \tag{2.5}$$

where e_t is the error made in attributing all deaths to inadequate food consumption. The es are independent of current foodgrain consumption. The case for stabilization must be qualified if the survival function has such properties. The optimal intertemporal allocation of consumption now maximizes

$$\prod_{t=1}^{T} (s(x_t) + e_t) \tag{2.6}$$

for a given food stock and so it will equalize

$$s'(x_t)/(s(x_t) + e_t) \tag{2.7}$$

across all t (assuming that the stock is sufficient for an interior solution). It follows that the survival optimum will have higher foodgrain consumption in periods when the contribution of other factors to mortality is high; in particular, it can be easily shown that values x_t for which equation 2.7 is constant are (implicitly) monotonic decreasing in e_t. (See the appendix to this chapter for details.) In terms of Figure 2.3, this arises because the iso-survival contours cease to be symmetric about $x_1 = x_2$. A mean preserving transfer from high to low consumption dates need not raise the survival chance if the high consumption period also has a high risk of death due to other causes.

Although generally asymmetric, the iso-survival contours will remain convex under these conditions. By a similar argument to the previous section, it can easily be shown that survival to date T will be a strictly quasi-concave function of x_t ($t = 1, \ldots, T$) if each s_t is a strictly concave function of x_t; it need not be the same function for all t.

3. The existence of losses due to foodgrain storage also leads one to modify the survival case in favour of stabilization. To see

why, consider again the simplest two period representation in Figure 2.3. If a proportion k of the carryover between periods is lost in storage then $1/(1 - k)$ of period 1's consumption must be sacrificed to increase period 2's consumption by one unit. Then, with symmetric iso-survival contours, the survival optimum will have higher consumption in the first period than the second. Notice that it remains true that mean-preserving transfers from high to low consumption periods will raise the long-term survival rate. The move from A to B in Figure 2.5 will raise the chance of survival to the end of period 2. But for the (given) total foodgrain stock H there may exist feasible consumption plans such as C, dominating A, which yield a higher survival chance than B.

It is clear that the complete stabilization of consumption will not generally be optimal from the point of view of survival. Of course, survival gains can still be expected from eliminating consumption extremes; convexity of the iso-survival contours alone will guarantee this. Also, since famines are typically periods of simultaneously low consumption and high incidence of death due to non-nutritional causes, there will remain a survival case in favour

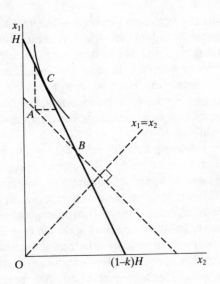

Fig. 2.5

of mean preserving consumption transfers from non-famine periods.

But this does not yet add up to a case for believing that price instability can cause a famine or that government intervention is called for to stabilize foodgrain prices. For one thing, individuals will generally have their own means of stabilizing consumption. For another, even if consumption stabilization is desirable, price stabilization need not be. The following two sections will examine these factors in turn.

2.4 Individual Responses to Uncertain Consumption

If storage or savings can be used with perfect foresight to costlessly re-allocate consumption over time then the survival optimum described in Section 2.2 is fully attainable as an equilibrium of decentralized decision making. Under these conditions, mortality will be invariant to short-run changes in prices or incomes. And so a correlation between mortality and prices during a famine will not be observed (see the appendix to this chapter for details).

How might such a correlation be explained? The invariance property will cease to hold under either of the following conditions:[8]

1. Income changes were unanticipated at the time the consumption plan was made. Random errors in forecasting future income would not be enough; by guaranteeing perfect *stochastic* foresight, rational expectations would still yield the invariance result on average. For a positive correlation between mortality and income, income forecasts would have to be informationally biased such that future income changes are systematically underestimated (see the appendix for details).

2. There are prohibitive costs in using storage or savings to re-allocate consumption over time. To illustrate, suppose that the cost of storage and the rate of interest on savings vary with individual wealth; in particular, a wealthy person can afford good storage facilities which protect well against damp and vermin while a poor person cannot and so incurs a higher average storage cost. Similarly, suppose that only the wealthy can get access to reasonable rates of interest on savings. Furthermore, transaction costs prohibit sufficient co-operation amongst the poor to attain improved storage or credit facilities. Then a poor person might

actually be better off from the point of view of survival chances to rely exclusively on markets to stabilize consumption. In fact this will generally be so; to see why, suppose that the proportionate loss in storage for one period (k) is a decreasing function of initial wealth (w) as $k = g(w)$, $g' < 0$. And let

$$f(k) = s(y_1 - S)s(y_2 + (1 - k)S) - s(y_1)s(y_2) \text{ for } S > 0 \text{ and } y_1 > y_2 \tag{2.8}$$

If $f(k)$ is positive then it is better to store; if negative it is better to let markets determine the intertemporal consumption plan. It is easily verified that $f(0) > 0$ for small S, $f(1) < 0$ and $f'(k) < 0$. Thus (by continuity of f and g) there must exist a value of wealth w^* such that $f(g(w^*)) = 0$; if wealth is above w^* then one stores but otherwise not.

Under these conditions, current food consumption will be constrained by current prices and incomes, in spite of the existence of individual opportunities for saving and storage. The argument that famines can arise from a contraction in current trade entitlements presupposes that capital markets (including markets for storage facilities) have failed or that expectations are non-rational.

2.5 Price Stabilization and Survival

When income changes are unanticipated and cannot be buffered adequately by depleting stocks or savings, consumers will rely on current foodgrain markets for current consumption needs. And such people are typically a high proportion of famine victims.[9] Under these conditions foodgrain markets and government stocking policies may affect survival chances through their effects on foodgrain price variability.

Previous sections have argued the case in favour of consumption stabilization as a famine relief policy. Does this mean that foodgrain price stabilization is also desirable? Past work on the welfare effects of price stabilization has shown that consumers may benefit from unstable prices even when consumption stabilization is desirable.[10] This section will examine the relevance of these arguments to the present problem.

As was the case for consumption stabilization, the survival case for price stabilization depends on the shape of the survival function; if it is strictly concave (convex) in price then long term survival chances will be improved (worsened) by mean preserving price stabilizations.[11] Concavity of the survival function in consumption space does not imply concavity in price space since consumption may well be a convex function of price. Thus the case for price stabilization as a famine relief policy will require further restrictions on the shape of the survival and demand functions.

Continuing to assume (for the moment) that survival chance is determined by consumption of a single good, maximum survival will require that all income at each date will be devoted to consumption of that good. The chance of surviving the tth time interval is then $s(m_t/p_t)$ where m is (exogenous) money income and p is the price of the good. Then, on differentiating twice with respect to p:

$$s_{pp} = x_t s'(x_t)(2 - \gamma)p_t^{-2} \qquad (2.9)$$

where

$$\gamma(x_t) = -x_t s''(x_t)/s'(x_t) \qquad (2.10)$$

is the elasticity of slope of the survival function. This is a measure of the concavity of the survival function (mathematically equivalent to the Arrow–Pratt measure of relative risk-aversion). By interpreting $s'(x)$ as a measure of vulnerability to starvation—the increase in mortality risk associated with a fall in foodgrain consumption—one can interpret γ as the 'elasticity of famine vulnerability'. Equation 2.9 indicates that a necessary and sufficient condition for price stabilization to have a beneficial effect on survival chances, is that the elasticity of famine vulnerability exceeds two. This is best left as an empirical question; the following section will offer some evidence for two famines in South Asia.

However, there is an important caveat on the above analysis. It has been assumed that only one good is consumed which affects survival and that this is the good for which price can be stabilized by storage in markets or by government. Clearly one can readily relax this to permit a Hicksian composite good. But a more interesting question is: what would happen if survival is affected by consumption of a bundle of goods only one of which (or a composite subset) is storable and so amenable to price stabilization? For example, it is common to observe consumption of nutritionally inferior 'famine foods' when rice prices are high in Bangladesh. But, unlike rice, these foods are not generally stored. Assuming that the composition of this bundle of goods is chosen by the individual to maximize survival at each date, the latter will be a function of all prices and money income:

$$s^*(\mathbf{p}_t, m_t) = \text{maximum of } s(\mathbf{x}_t) \text{ subject to } \mathbf{p}_t \mathbf{x}_t \leqslant m_t \quad (2.11)$$

The price vector $\mathbf{p}$ includes the price of the storable good p. The corresponding demands are $\mathbf{x}^* = \mathbf{x}(\mathbf{p}, m)$ at each date. The appendix to this chapter shows that:[12]

$$s^*_{pp} = -sx^*_m(\varepsilon - v(\gamma - \eta)) \quad (2.12)$$

where

$$\varepsilon = -px_p/x \quad (2.13.1)$$
$$v = px/m \quad (2.13.2)$$
$$\eta = mx_m/x \quad (2.13.3)$$

are the own price elasticity of demand (times minus one), income share and income elasticity of demand respectively for the storable good and γ is re-defined as

$$\gamma = -ms^*_{mm}/s^*_m \quad (2.14)$$

Inspecting equation 2.12, we find that the necessary and sufficient condition for price stabilization to improve survival chance is now that the elasticity of famine vulnerability exceeds $\eta + \varepsilon/v$. With both price and income elasticities of demand likely to be high (probably close to unity) for the rural poor, the critical value of γ will now exceed two when at least some income is spent on other (unstored) goods. For example, if both elasticities equal unity and half of income is spent on the 'famine foods' rather than rice, then the elasticity of famine vulnerability must exceed three before price stabilization will be desirable for famine relief.

2.6 Application to Two Famines

The previous sections have identified conditions under which food-grain price stabilization can be expected to reduce famine mortality. This section will test the case for stabilization using monthly data on mortality and foodgrain prices during two famines: the 1877 famine in South India and the 1974 famine in Bangladesh. The Indian data is for Madras Presidency while the Bangladesh data is for Matlab thana in Comilla district.[13] High foodgrain prices have been identified as an important cause of starvation during both famines.[14] A casual inspection of Figures 2.6 and 2.7 suggest that the data are consistent with this view. However, the direction of any curvature in the relationship between mortality

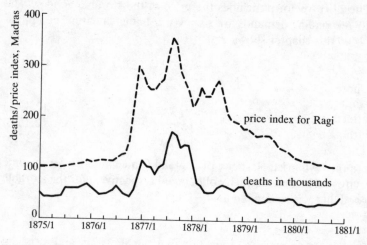

Fig. 2.6

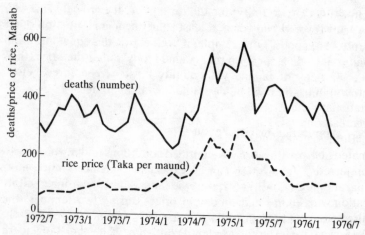

Fig. 2.7

and grain prices is unclear from the figures. An econometric model can throw further light on this question.

For this purpose, the econometric model must not constrain the sign of its second derivative of mortality with respect to price. In view of the likely effects of epidemics, the model should also permit (probably positive) autocorrelation in the mortality series, independently of prices. The following model combines these features with the computational convenience of being linear in parameters:

$$D_t = a_0 + a_1 D_{t-1} + a_2 p_t + a_3 p_t^2 + e_t \qquad (2.15)$$

where e_t is an appropriate error process incorporating non-price effects on mortality; for now it need only be assumed that $E e_t = 0$ although it is plausible that the residuals will be serially correlated. This will be tested and, when necessary, dealt with using an appropriate autoregressive estimator.

In assessing the effects of price stabilization, the sample mean mortality will be compared to a (hypothetical) benchmark in which prices are stabilized at their sample mean ($\bar{p}$) during the study period assuming that the parameters of equation 2.15 remain unchanged. Then the expected value of deaths at stable prices is (in the long run)

$$ED^* = (a_0 + a_2 \bar{p} + a_3 \bar{p}^2)/(1 - a_1) \qquad (2.16)$$

The difference between the sample mean of deaths (ED) and ED^* is a measure of mortality attributable to unstable prices and is given by:[15]

$$ED - ED^* = a_3(Ep^2 - \bar{p}^2)/(1 - a_1) = a_3 \text{var}(p)/(1 - a_1) \qquad (2.17)$$

or simply $a_3 \text{var}(p)$ in the short run. As long as equation 2.15 is stationary ($|a_1| < 1$), the benchmark price stabilization will decrease mortality if (and only if) a_3 is positive.

Both log and linear forms of equation 2.15 were initially estimated, both with an AR1 error process, but the log model was preferred.[16] All residual correlograms passed the Box–Pierce test for randomness at the five per cent level.[17] A more general specification with lagged price effects (one month in both p and p^2) was also tested but the lagged effects were insignificant and so equation 2.15 was preferred. The regressions for Madras included 11 monthly dummy variables to pick up the strong seasonality in mortality (undoubtedly associated with the seasonal incidence of certain diseases). However, no significant seasonality was evident for the Matlab series; probably the series is not long enough to reveal stable seasonality, independently of prices.

Table 2.1 gives the estimates of equation 2.15 for each famine. The main points of interest are:

Table 2.1:   *Parameter Estimates*

Variable	Parameter	Madras 1875–80	Matlab 1972–76
1	a_0	16	12
		(5.3)	(3.5)
D_{-1}	a_1	0.74	0.38
		(15)	(3.1)
p	a_2	−6.1	−3.8
		(5.1)	(2.8)
p^2	a_3	0.61	0.41
		(5.3)	(2.9)
error$_{-1}$		0.52	0.29
		(5.1)	(2.0)
R^2		0.98	0.71
SEE		0.062	0.12
Mean D		4.1	5.9
Box–Pierce Q		14	3.2
		(13)	(8)
n		71	47

Note: Absolute asymptotic *t*-ratios in parentheses, except for the Q statistic which gives the number of degrees of freedom in parentheses.

(i) The quadratic terms are significantly positive for both famines, implying that survival is concave in price. The effect is more pronounced for Madras; indeed, the model's overall fit is a good deal better.

(ii) Positive autocorrelations are evident in both mortality series (independently of prices) and also in the model's residuals; these probably reflect epidemics. Again both effects are stronger for the Madras data.[18]

Table 2.2 summarizes the main findings of interest. The estimated short-run price elasticity of mortality is similar for both famines, although, because of the greater autocorrelation in the Madras series, the long-run elasticities are a good deal higher than for Matlab. It should also be noted that, as can be seen from Table 2.2, the proportionate increase in deaths during the Madras

Table 2.2   *Summary of Results.*

	Madras	Matlab
Famine statistics as percentage increase over mean:*		
(i) mortality	99	36
(ii) prices	64	79
Short-run price elasticity of mortality evaluated at:		
(i) mean	0.12	0.14
(ii) mean + one st. dev.	0.59	0.50
Long-run price elasticity of mortality evaluated at:		
(i) mean	0.45	0.23
(ii) mean + one st. dev.	2.3	0.81
Percentage increase in mortality attributed to price instability		
(i) short-run	9.4	7.7
(ii) long-run	36	12

NOTE: *Famine periods defined as calendar year 1877 for Madras and August 1974–April 1975 for Matlab.

famine was greater than for Bangladesh, while the price change was of a similar magnitude. Thus the excess mortality attributable to high prices during the famine is a good deal larger for the Bangladesh data; in the short run about one in three excess deaths is attributed to high prices for Matlab while for Madras the figure is a little less than one in ten. Of course the long-run values are higher; about one in two for Matlab and one in three for Madras. This difference between the two famines probably reflects greater rural landlessness in Bangladesh and, hence, a greater dependence on the market economy amongst the rural poor.

An increase in mortality of a little under 10 per cent is attributed to short-run price instability for both famines, although as a proportion of the actual increase in mortality, the figure is a good deal higher for the Bangladesh data. When also expressed as a proportion of excess mortality, the long-run figures on the contribution of price instability are in close accord for the two famines. The increase in deaths due to price instability represented about one third of famine mortality.

2.7 Expectations and Price Instability

Having identified price instability as a potentially important cause of the excess mortality observed during famines, the next question is: what causes the volatility in grain markets? The following chapter will test the hypothesis that informational inefficiency was an important cause of price instability during the 1974 famine in Bangladesh. But before embarking on this, it will help to consider the relationship between expectations and price stability in the context of an abstract but simple dynamic model of the market for a storable good. One of the points that will emerge clearly from this is that informational inefficiencies will not necessarily destabilize markets; whether they do or not depends crucially on the precise nature of the inefficiency. And this is an empirical question.

The model assumes that:

1 Markets clear at each date, such that both the consumers' desired consumptions of rice, and any desired increases in rice stocks, are fulfilled with the available output. Consumer demand is a stable decreasing function $f(p)$ of rice price p. The desired stock is denoted S and the available output flow (or 'harvest') is H. Thus the market clearing condition for date t is that:

$$f(p_t) + S_t - S_{t-1} = H_t \qquad (2.19)$$

2. The desired stock at each date is a stable increasing function of the expected change in price.[19] Letting p_{t+1}^e denote the rice price expected for date $t+1$ on the basis of the information at time t and assuming that the latter includes realized price p_t, desired stock is:

$$S_t = g(p_{t+1}^e - p_t) \quad g' > 0 \qquad (2.20)$$

3. Price expectations need not be rational. Since the price is known at each date, the rational expectations hypothesis implies that the *ex-post* forecasting error for future price is independent of current price. A weaker assumption (which permits rational expectations as a special case) is that the *ex-post* forecasting error is:

$$p^e_{t+1} - p_{t+1} = h(p_t) + u_{t+1} \qquad (2.21)$$

where u is a zero mean white noise error process, but no restrictions are placed on the direction of slope (if any) of the function h.

Rational expectations requires that h is invariant to p in the above model. On the other hand, $h' > 0$ means that the effect of current price on future price is overestimated, while it is underestimated when $h' < 0$. For example, suppose that the mean deviations of price move according to a first-order autoregressive (AR1) process,

$$p_t = \alpha p_{t-1} + e_t \qquad (2.22)$$

with unknown autoregression coefficient α and white noise error process e. By repeated observation of the prices generated by equation 2.22, it is possible to obtain an *asymptotically* unbiased estimate of α by minimizing the sum of squared residuals. But, in the mean time, the stockholder's forecasts must be based on biased estimates such as: $p^e_t = \beta p_{t-1}$ for some $\beta \neq \alpha$.[20] In terms of equation 2.21, overly 'static' expectations ($\beta > \alpha$) imply $h' > 0$ while overly 'volatile' ones ($\beta < \alpha$) imply $h' < 0$.

Of course, in practice the price formation process is likely to be a good deal more complex than this, with other variables appearing on the RHS of models such as equation 2.22. If the values of any of these variables are known with certainty at date t, then they may also appear on the RHS of equation 2.21 when expectations are non-rational. For now I shall concentrate on current price as a source of forecasting bias, although other information will play an important role in Chapter 3.

A phase diagram for this model can now be constructed. This depicts the *loci* of price and stock combinations for which both variables are stationary and markets clear at the desired stock levels.

Consider first the rational expectations equilibrium. Then no price change will be expected (on average) when price is in a steady state equilibrium ($p_t = p_{t-1}$). The corresponding desired stock level is $S^* = g(0)$ which is invariant to p. (One may also assume that $S^* = 0$, but this is inessential to the argument.) This is depicted as the vertical line through S^* in Figure 2.8. Similarly,

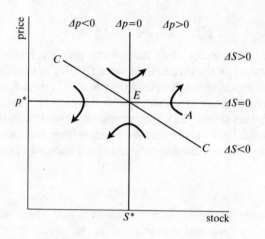

Fig. 2.8

from equation 2.19, the *locus* of (p, S) combinations for which markets clear at constant stock is the horizontal line in Figure 2.8 at price $p^* = f^{-1}(H)$. Considering points off the *loci*, it is plain that price must be increasing when stock exceeds S^* and that stock must be increasing when price exceeds p^*; $p_t \gtreqless p_{t-1}$ as $S_t \gtreqless S^*$ and that $S_t \gtreqless S_{t-1}$ as $p_t \gtreqless p^*$ as indicated by the arrows in Figure 2.8.

Thus the model's equilibrium at E exhibits *saddlepoint instability*; only if the economy starts from points on the convergent path through E (labelled CC) will it reach equilibrium in the long run. The economy will be on explosive paths commencing at points off CC. For example, if the economy starts at point A with stocks falling and prices increasing then, after a while, both stocks and prices will start to increase indefinitely.

Saddlepoint instability is a common property of dynamic models with stock variables (Dixit, 1976, chapter 6; Burmeister, 1980*b*). In models incorporating rational expectations, it is common to assume that those expectations lie on a convergent path; for example, it may be considered implausible that individuals would knowingly participate in an economy which they expected to be explosive.[21]

However, the assumption of dynamic stability begs some interesting questions concerning the possibility of a finitely lived speculative boom (or 'price bubble') in markets.[22] It is not difficult to imagine situations in which high expectations of future prices lead competitive stockholders to bid up present prices to a point where their expectations become (stochastically) self-fulfilling. Rather than assume away such possibilities, it would be nice to know if there is any mechanism which will bring the speculative boom to an end.

In the present setting, foodgrain production is highly seasonal; for example, over half of Bangladesh's annual rice output is the 'aman' crop, harvested in the winter months. Indeed, almost all of the aman crop is harvested between mid-November and mid-January, although the precise dates can vary a good deal. The prime time for speculative activity in rice markets is the relatively lean period of about three months prior to this harvest. While it is theoretically possible for a speculative boom (based on high and self-fulfilling expectations) to survive the aman harvest, in practice even a relatively poor aman crop will bring about a fall in prices and so end the boom. The time when price begins to fall will then depend on stockholders' expectations about the arrival time of the next harvest. Thus, finitely lived speculative booms based on rational expectations may be possible in this setting.

A similar phenomenon is possible in a dynamically stable but informationally inefficient market. To see how, consider a market in which the errors made by stockholders in forecasting future prices are positively correlated with current prices. In other words, high current prices leave stockholders with overly optimistic expectations of the future profitability of their stock position. One need not suppose that this occurs indefinitely; but it is assumed to be a significant feature of the market over the period of time it needs to reach its (saddlepoint) equilibrium from any given point on a convergent arm. An important analytical consequence of this feature is that the *locus* of (p,S) points at which price is stationary will now be positively sloped, as illustrated in Figure 2.9.

As a result, markets in which traders hold biased expectations will have very different dynamic responses to supply shocks as

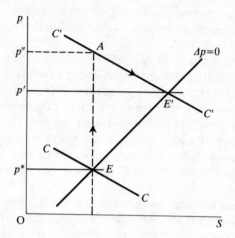

Fig. 2.9

compared to markets in which expectations are rational. Bearing in mind the questions already raised about the assumption, suppose that the market finds its way to a point on its convergent path after a shock. Also assume that this is more easily done by adjusting prices than stocks; in particular suppose that all of the adjustment needed to reach a convergent path is by changes in prices rather than stocks. The market is initially in equilibrium at E in Figure 2.9 with initial output H. There is now a drop in output, leading to an increase in the long-run market clearing price from p^* to p'. However, the initial price response entails a move to point A on the new convergent path $C'C'$, through the new long-run equilibrium at E'. Thus the initial price change due to the supply shock will overshoot the change in the long-run equilibrium price. After the initial shock, price will fall as the economy moves along its new convergent path towards E'.

Although this market is (by assumption) dynamically stable with or without rational expectations, observed price movements in response to output fluctuations will be greater when price expectations are informationally biased than with rational expectations. And, in this specific sense, the informationally inefficient market will exhibit greater price instability.

This conclusion ceases to hold if errors in forecasting future price are negatively correlated with observed current prices. This case is illustrated in Figure 2.10. The *locus* of points with constant prices is now negatively sloped, and so the initial price increase

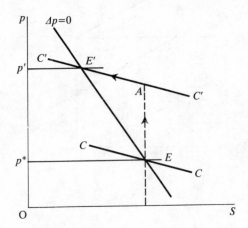

Fig. 2.10

needed to return the market to a convergent path will be less than that needed to reach the new long-run equilibrium.[23]

While the foregoing discussion has concentrated on current price as a correlate of forecasting errors, it is of interest also to consider briefly the effects of other sources of informational inefficiency; for example, the following chapter will look closely at the effects of crop damage information on price forecasting errors in Bangladesh rice markets. Price instability is also possible when price information is used efficiently (so that $h' = 0$ in equation 2.21) but other information is not. To see how, consider an increase in the *ex-post* forecasting error associated with non-price information. This will increase S^* leading to a price jump as illustrated in Figure 2.11, which is drawn assuming that price information is used efficiently, and there is no change in long-run price. Of course, price instability of this sort can also result from unanticipated shocks to an informationally efficient market; in this case stocks would oscillate around S^* inducing price fluctuations around p^*.

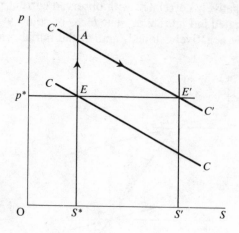

Fig. 2.11

2.8 Summary

The chapter has explored the links between trade entitlements and survival chances. The concept of a *concave survival function* has been used to explain why survival prospects will depend not only on the level of grain consumption but also its variability over time. The theory also suggests that:

(i) Famine mortality will increase if there is an increase in the inequality of food consumption.

(ii) The sharp increase in mortality characteristic of a famine need not mean that there has been any sudden change in food consumption; the phenomenon of a famine could equally well arise from a steady and slow decline in consumption over time.

However, concavity of the survival function need not mean that foodgrain price instability will increase famine mortality. This will be the case if the following conditions hold:

1. *Potential famine victims rely on current foodgrain markets for their consumption needs*. This will be the case if, for example, there are prohibitive costs incurred by the poor in attempting to use storage to reallocate consumption over time *or* if future

income changes tend to be underestimated when forming the expectations relevant to their storage decisions.

2. *The survival chances of potential famine victims are increasing and sufficiently concave functions of income.* If all income is spent on food then the survival function must have an (absolute) elasticity of slope greater than two in order for famine mortality to be reduced by price stabilization. More generally, the critical value of the elasticity of slope will depend on properties of the demand function for foodgrains. In keeping with past work on the welfare effects of price stabilization, high price and income elasticities of demand and low budget shares devoted to the stored good tend to raise the critical level of concavity needed to benefit from stabilization. If the survival function is strictly concave in foodgrain consumption but does not have an elasticity of slope greater than this critical level then grain price stabilization will actually add to famine mortality. And this will be so even though foodgrain consumption stabilization is desirable for potential famine victims.

Econometric investigations of the relationship between mortality and foodgrain prices over periods encompassing two severe famines in South Asia indicate that these conditions are plausible. Both high and unstable prices contributed to the excess mortality.

The revealed concavity of survival chance in price for these famines also implies that the underlying survival function is concave in income; indeed, the elasticity of famine vulnerability must be presumed to be high, undoubtedly exceeding two. This suggests that famine mortality may be quite sensitive to interpersonal inequality.

Comparing these famines, the results on the efficacy of price stabilization are in remarkably close accord and indicate that about one third of excess deaths can be attributable to fluctuations in foodgrain prices alone.

This begs the question: what caused the sudden volatility of foodgrain prices during these famines? This chapter has used a simple model of the dynamics of price adjustment in a stable market to identify conditions under which informational inefficiency in markets can produce greater price variability than would be the case in a rational expectations equilibrium. The plausibility of those conditions remains an empirical question. The following chapter will address this question for the 1974 famine in Bangladesh.

Appendix 2.1

This appendix gives a more formal analysis of the main properties of the survival function used in this chapter.

1. The survival function has the shape depicted in Figure 2.2 if the following assumptions hold:

(a) The density function f approaches (and may or may not reach) zero at extreme values; this will be the case if f is unimodal with finite variance.

(b) The iso-health contour g becomes more linear as one approaches the extremes; for example, g is asymptotic to the axes $x = y = 0$.

(c) $g'''(x) > 2g''(x)^2/g'(x)$; this puts a lower bound on the third derivative of the iso-health contour but does not restrict its sign.

(d) $f''(y_0) < 0$; this restricts the analysis to values of y_0 not 'too far' from the mode. This condition can be weakened somewhat to permit values of $f''(y_0) > 0$ but appropriately bounded above.

From equation 2.3 it can then be seen that:

$$\text{sign } s''(x) = - \text{ sign } h(x)$$

where

$$h(x) = \frac{f'(y_0)}{f(y_0)} + \frac{g''(x)}{g'(x)^2}$$

has the limits:

$$\lim_{x \to 0} h(x) = - \infty \qquad \lim_{x \to \infty} h(x) = \infty$$

under the assumed limiting properties of the density function and iso-health contours (a) and (b). Furthermore:

$$h'(x) = \frac{f''(y_0)g'(x)}{f(y_0)} - \frac{f'(y_0)^2 g'(x)}{f(y_0)^2} + \frac{g'''(x)}{g'(x)^2} - \frac{2g''(x)^2}{g'(x)^3} > 0$$

under the assumed conditions in (c) and (d). Thus, by continuity of h, there exists a unique number x_0 such that $h(x_0) = 0$, with $h(x) \gtreqless 0$ as $x \gtreqless x_0$. And so, $s''(x) \lesseqgtr 0$ as $x \gtreqless x_0$, as illustrated in Figure 2.2.

2. To give an example, suppose that the iso-survival contours are iso-elastic (corresponding to a Cobb–Douglas health produc-

tion function) and that personal constitution is log normally distributed. Then, scaling $\log y$ to have zero mean and unit variance, the survival function is

$$s(x) = \frac{1}{\sqrt{2\pi}} \int_{a_0 - a_1 \log x}^{\infty} \exp\left(-u^2/2\right) du$$

for which

$$s'(x) = a_1 f(\log y_0)/x$$
$$s''(x) = (a_1 \log y_0 - 1) a_1 f(\log y_0)/x^2$$

where a_0 and a_1 are positive constants and f is the normal density function. The point of inflexion is

$$(x^*, y^*) = (\exp((a_0 a_1 - 1)/a_1^2), \exp(1/a_1))$$

This occurs when survival chance is below 0.5. (Noting that the corresponding value of $\log y^* = 1/a_1 > 0$ and so exceeds the mean). For a unitary elasticity of the iso-survival contours, the survival function is concave as long as (the log of) the personal constitution needed to survive does not exceed one standard deviation above the mean. Thus, it is concave as long as survival chance does not fall below 0.16. The point of inflexion falls sharply as the iso-survival contours become less elastic; for example, at an elasticity of 0.5 the point of inflexion is at a survival chance of 0.02 while at an elasticity of 2 inflexion occurs at 0.31.

3. To prove that mean preserving stabilizations reduce mortality, consider two consumption plans $x^0 = (x_1^0, \ldots, x_T^0)$ and $x^1 = (x_1^1, \ldots, x_T^1)$ which differ only in the first two dates and achieve the same time T survival. On taking any convex linear combination of these plans, strict concavity of s means that:

$$s(\lambda x_t^0 + (1 - \lambda)x_t^1) > \lambda s(x_t^0) + (1 - \lambda)s(x_t^1) \text{ for } t = 1, 2 \text{ and } 0 < \lambda < 1$$

Using this fact, the probability of surviving both periods under the combined plan is

$$s(\lambda x_1^0 + (1 - \lambda)x_1^1)s(\lambda x_2^0 + (1-\lambda)x_2^1) >$$

$$s(x_1^0)s(x_2^0) + \lambda(1 - \lambda)(s(x_1^0) - s(x_1^1))(s(x_2^1) - s(x_2^0))$$

Clearly $x_1^0 - x_1^1$ and $x_2^1 - x_2^0$ must have the same sign (otherwise survival must be higher for one of the two plans); so the last term must be positive, in which case the combined plan must have a higher survival chance than the initial consumption plans. Since this is true of all convex linear combinations, it must also hold for mean preserving transfers.

4. Consider next the optimal consumption plan from the point of view of survival. This will maximize $s(x_t)$ for given $H = \sum x_t$. More generally, one can allow non-nutritional causes of death as in Section 2.3. Forming the Lagrangian function, the problem is then to choose $(x_1, \ldots, x_T)$ and the Lagrange multiplier μ to maximize:

$$\prod_{t=1}^{T} (s(x_t) + e_t) - \mu \left(\sum_{t=1}^{T} x_t - H \right)$$

The first-order conditions require that

$$s'(x_t)/(s(x_t) + e_t) = \mu$$

for all t, and that $\sum x_t = H$ (s concave is sufficient for the second order conditions to hold). Consider two dates for which $e_1 > e_2$. To prove that $x_1 < x_2$, as claimed in Section 2.3, suppose that the opposite holds, i.e. $x_1 \geq x_2$. This leads to a contradiction. For then $s'(x_1) \leq s'(x_2)$ by concavity of s and $s(x_1) \geq s(x_2)$ by monotonicity of s. And so

$$\frac{s'(x_1)}{s(x_1) + e_1} < \frac{s'(x_2)}{s(x_2) + e_2}$$

which contradicts the first-order condition for an optimum. Thus $x_1 < x_2$.

5. To see why survival chance at each date will be invariant to anticipated changes in income as claimed in Section 2.4, let income at each date have an exogenous component y_t and an endogenous component z_t. With full information about past, present and future values of y, survival chance to any terminal date will be maximized subject to a fixed $\sum z_t$ and for s concave by choosing z_t to equalize $s'(y_t + z_t)/s(y_t + z_t)$ over all t. Thus $y_t + z_t$ will be invariant to time and hence s_t will be invariant to y_t when z_t is optimal. Relaxing the perfect foresight assumption, let y_t^e denote the expectation held at time $t - 1$ of income at time t. Then by similar reasoning, survival chance at time t will be an increasing

function of the forecasting error $y_t - y_t^e$. Thus, if $y_t - y_t^e$ and, hence, survival chance are positively correlated with y_t then dy_t^e/dy_t < 1 and so income changes must have been underestimated.

6. Consider the dual form (2.11). Applying the envelope theorem:

$$s_p^* = -xs_m^* \tag{2A.1}$$

And so:

$$s_{pp}^* = -x_p s_m^* - xs_{mp}^* \tag{2A.2}$$

Differentiating (2A.1) w.r.t. m and using this to simplify (2A.2) one obtains (2.12) after algebraic rearrangement. This can be used to determine price curvature as in Section 2.5.

Notes

1. Economic theories have had relatively little to say about the relationship between consumption and survival. And the exceptions that I know of have ignored uncertainty in that relationship. This is so in the models of competitive equilibrium which have included sufficient conditions for human survival in equilibrium (see, for example, Arrow and Debreu, 1954, and Malinvaud, 1972, chapter 3) as well as Sen's (1981*a*, appendix A) characterization of exchange entitlement failure as a cause of starvation. In his comments on the Arrow–Debreu model Koopmans (1957, 63) remarks on ' . . . the inadequacies of any model unable to recognize the element of uncertainty in individual survival'.

2. For further discussion of this see Rosenberg (1973), Drasar, Tomkins, and Feachem (1981), and Bang (1981). Also see Chowdhury and Chen (1977) for a general discussion of the linkages between nutrition and mortality risk and Schultz (1979) and Khan (1985) for empirical analyses. The concept of a 'health production function' is also used by Pitt and Rosenzweig (1985).

3. A single valued real function $\phi(x,y)$ is said to have (strictly) convex contours (or, equivalently, to be quasi-concave) if the set of all points (x,y) such that ϕ exceeds any given number is a (strictly) convex set, meaning that all points on a straight line joining any two points in the set are also contained in the set.

4. Results of relevant medical research for Bangladesh are summarized in ICDDR (1979) and are consistent with the concavity property. This property is also found in the international cross-sectional relationship between life expectancy and income (Vallin, 1968; Preston, 1975,

1980; Rodgers, 1979; Goldstein, 1985). Rodgers (1979) also finds evidence of a negative correlation between life expectancy and the Gini coefficient of income within each country. The concavity property has also been found in numerous studies of the effects of low maternal food intake on foetal growth and, hence, infant birthweight, which is considered a major determinant of survival chances; see Stein, Susser, Saenger and Marolla (1975), and Lechtig (1985).

5. The limiting properties guarantee that $s''(x)$ changes sign while the restrictions on higher derivatives guarantee that $s'''(x)$ does not. The intermediate value theorem can then be used to show that there exists a unique point of inflexion. For further details see the appendix to this chapter.

6. Using more advanced methods a simple way to prove that the contours of equation 2.4 are convex is by noting that the survival ranking of consumption plans is preserved by taking the log of the expression in equation 2.4; using Jensen's inequality it can then be shown that $E\log s(x) < \log s(Ex)$ if s is strictly concave.

7. Noting that the iso-survival contours must then be asymptotic to the zero axes.

8. There are other conditions under which the invariance property will not hold. Probably the most obvious is that survival may not be the maximand used in forming individual consumption plans. However, this requires that the correct maximand is not also a concave function of consumption, as seems plausible. Otherwise the optimal consumption plan and, hence, also survival would remain invariant to fully anticipated changes in the exogenous income component.

9. See, for example, the surveys of famine victims reported in Das (1949), Dandekar and Pethe (1972), and Alamgir (1980).

10. See Waugh (1944), Turnovsky, Shalit, and Schmitz (1980), Newbery and Stiglitz (1981), Kanbur (1984).

11. Although, unless aggregate demand functions are linear, mean preserving price stabilizations need not be consistent with maintaining a competitive equilibrium after stabilization. For further discussion see Newbery and Stiglitz (1981). For a convex demand function, stabilization of supply will also lower mean price. Then the following results will underestimate the survival gains from stabilization.

12. Also see Turnovsky *et al.* (1980) and Newbery and Stiglitz (1981 chapter 8) for the analogous result in terms of utility and demand functions.

13. The Madras data is from Lardinois (1985). The mortality series for Matlab was kindly supplied to the author by the International Centre for Diarrhoeal Disease Research, Bangladesh and was obtained by a careful demographic surveillance of Matlab thana. The price data is

from official sources and is for Comilla District; see Alamgir *et al.* (1977).

14. On this aspect of the South Indian famines see Bhatia (1967) and Lardinois (1985). On rice prices and mortality during the Bangladesh famine see Chowdhury and Chen (1977), Alamgir (1980), Ahmed (1981), Sen (1981*a*), and Currey (1981). Note that the prices referred to in the literature and used in this study are nominal rather than real. This is partly imposed by data limitations. But there are good reasons for expecting changes in nominal prices to have (short-run) real effects in this setting, particularly when wealth is held in the form of money and (as I shall argue in Chapter 5), key factor prices are sticky in the short run. This issue has also arisen in studies of poverty; see Sen (1985), and Srinivasan (1985).

15. Note that if price is stabilized at a value p_0 other than the sample mean then the formula in equation 2.17 must be modified to:

$$ED - ED_0 = (a_2(\bar{p} - p_0) + a_3(\text{var}(p) + \bar{p}^2 - p_0^2))/(1 - a_1)$$

For example, one may prefer to use the 'pre-famine' mean as the benchmark.

16. Summary statistics and *t*-ratios were generally better for the log model. Both models are reported and discussed in Ravallion (1985*d*).

17. For discussion of this test see Harvey (1981).

18. One explanation for the poorer performance of the Matlab model is that the quadratic term is not adequately picking up the non-linearity in the relationship. To test this, I re-estimated the model with an unrestricted power term in price rather than a quadratic (using a maximum likelihood method with iterations commencing at the OLS estimates). This gave $a_1 = 0.54(4.9)$, $a_2 = -3.6(5.1)$, $a_3 = 0.48(26)$ and with price raised to the power 1.9(18). Clearly estimator precision is greatly enhanced. The summary statistics (including Table 2.2) are very similar; see Ravallion (1985*d*).

19. This holds for the classic case of a risk neutral profit maximizing stockholder facing a rising marginal cost schedule for storage; then the value of S which maximizes $(p_{+1}^e - p - c(S))S$ is an increasing function of $p_{+1}^e - p$. A more realistic model with the essential properties needed for the following discussion is given in Chapter 3.

20. For example, Marriott and Pope (1954) show that a least squares estimate will have an approximate bias of $2/\sqrt{T}$ (where T is the sample size).

21. For a heuristic argument along these lines see Begg (1982, chapter 3). The transversality conditions for intertemporal consumption efficiency can also be used to justify this assumption; for discussion and references see Burmeister (1980*b*, chapter 3).

22. This has been argued by Samuelson (1957), Blanchard (1979), Bur-meister (1980, chapter 7), Obstfeld and Rogoff (1983), and others. Speculative booms of various sorts have been a popular explanation for financial crises; see, for example, Kindleberger (1978). Flood and Garber (1980) have developed a test for a type of 'price bubble' with rational expectations. Their results do not support this interpretation of Germany's hyperinflation during the early 1920s, although Blan-chard (1979) has shown that there is a broad class of finitely lived price bubbles with rational expectations which the Flood–Garber test is unable to pick up. Nor should one ignore the possibility of finitely lived speculative booms based on (at least temporarily) biased expec-tations. Indeed, this seems a plausible interpretation of many of the financial crises discussed by, for example, Kindleberger, in which case the recent literature on price bubbles with rational expectations may be a misguided approach to understanding speculative crises.

23. To complete the picture one should also mention the possibility that forecasting errors may not be a monotonic function of current prices, being positively correlated over some price intervals and negatively correlated over others. In this case it is also possible to have the sort of dynamic behaviour found in catastrophe theory. This can arise when the $\Delta p = 0$ curve folds back on itself. At the fold point, equilib-rium price will react discontinuously to small changes in the stock level. However, the fold phenomenon seems difficult to rationalize and so catastrophies may be little more than a theoretical curio in this setting. For further discussion of catastrophy theory and attempts to apply it to economic dynamics see Zeeman (1974) and Varian (1979).

3
Rice Markets in Bangladesh during the 1974 Famine

3.1 Introduction

While it is appropriate for the present discussion to concentrate on events over a period of just a few years, it should be appreciated that the 1974 famine had a longer history. There can be little doubt that the food consumption of Bangladesh's rural poor generally declined over a decade or more prior to 1974; nor does the trend appear to have changed since then.[1] This alone would lead one to expect a deterioration in survival chances. And, following the argument of the previous chapter, that deterioration may become dramatic even if the decline in food consumption is not. Superimposing a sudden increase in rice prices onto this period of steady impoverishment, one can readily understand the dreadful mortality experience of 1974–5. But why did prices suddenly increase?

At the time, many people blamed 'hoarders'. For example, the influential Bangladeshi newspaper, *Daily Ittefaq*, claimed on 12 May 1974, that '. . . hoarders, profiteers and black-marketeers were creating the crisis conditions'. When the Prime Minister of Bangladesh, Mujibur Rahman, officially declared famine he was quoted as saying that '. . . a group of sharks, hoarders, smugglers, profiteers and black marketers were trading on human miseries'. (*The Bangladesh Observer*, 23 Sept. 1974)

Recent discussions have emphasized further the role of speculation in foodgrains as a cause of famine.[2] By this reasoning famine is attributed to the expectation on the part of foodgrain stockholders of a substantial future price increase or future rationing.

Heavy flooding during the summer and autumn of 1974 resulted in extensive crop damage over a wide area of Bangladesh. The important 'aman' harvest at the beginning of that year (and prior to the flooding) had been a very good one by past standards. The small 'boro' crop in the spring was partly flooded but, even so, it turned out the highest in official records. Despite heavy localized damage due to flooding, the total 'aus' crop harvested in the summer was higher than in previous years. Indeed, by Alamgir's reckoning (1980), the 1974 aus harvest was 14 per cent higher than for 1973 in the districts worst hit by the famine.

However, the *next* winter's crop, harvested after the worst months of the 1974 famine, was considerably depleted. The aman yield is notoriously vulnerable to damage in the early stages of its growth, particularly around the main time of transplanting the seedlings, namely July and August. Concern over early aman crop damage was very apparent in the newspapers; the following are typical of crop damage reports during the summer and autumn of 1974:

Aman seedlings in the flood affected areas of the country have been totally damaged, making the prospect of the next crop very bleak
(*The Bangladesh Observer*, 5 August 1974)

The Aman seedlings sown after the recession of flood waters have been completely damaged
(*The Bangladesh Observer*, 21 August 1974)

. . . the fresh flood damaged all the paddy seedlings of low-lying areas of the district [of Bogra] planted after the recession of the flood water
(*The Bangladesh Observer*, 21 September 1974)

Thus the exceptionally high rice prices which occurred during the lean months of the latter half of 1974 can be more plausibly attributed to a decline in *future* rice output than to the depletion of recent past harvests.

It is not surprising then, that many people at the time blamed hoarders for the famine. A number of other casual observations add weight to the view that rice stocks were high during the latter part of 1974 and probably well into 1975:

(i) Although the harvests of the summer and spring crops of 1974 turned out to be relatively good, their arrival in markets was widely reported to be unusually slow (see, for example, Appendix 3.2, Table 3A). This suggests that a high proportion of the new rice was being stored.

(ii) Rice prices fell dramatically in November 1974, *prior* to the new (transplanted) aman crop arriving in the markets (Stepanek, 1979, 65–6).[3] This phenomenon is typical of the 'panic' stage after a speculative 'mania'; see, for example, Kindleberger's history of financial crises (1978).

(iii) Rice prices had fallen dramatically within days of the assassination of Mujibur Rahman in August 1975 (Appendix 3.2, Table 3A). While this was at roughly the same time as the aus harvest, it was not an unusually good harvest (in fact it was lower than in 1974). And even exceptionally good aus harvests have only a small effect on August prices (see, for example, the figures reported by Alamgir *et al.*, 1977). As Hartmann and Boyce (1983) argue, a more plausible interpretation of the falling prices in August 1975 is that Mujib's government had fostered confidence on the part of (some) stockholders that future prices would be high and that they were safe from governmental harassment.

However, while a convincing case can be made for believing that rice stocks were high during the 1974 famine, this is not a sound basis for claiming that excessive 'hoarding' was a cause of the famine. If a famine is prolonged, then hoarding at the early stages will improve foodgrain availability later on. Thus hoarding can be a desirable response by markets to discontinuous and uncertain production. Indeed, if there is a complete set of markets, and each one clears at each point in time under Arrow–Debreu assumptions, then one could do no better (at least from a Paretian point of view) than give profit maximizing hoarders a free rein in determining the allocation of consumption over time. Although these are strong assumptions, one can reasonably argue that future scarcity makes at least some storage desirable, even in a famine.

The validity of the 'hoarding' explanation remains in considerable doubt. Nor is it immediately clear how one would go about resolving the issue. This is complicated further by the fact that, as is common, the available information on the level of private stocks during the famine consists of little more than casual observations.

This chapter offers a test for 'excessive hoarding' during the 1974 famine. For this purpose, revealed discrepancies between actual price movements and those implied by rational price expectations formed in competitive markets are taken as an indication of the poor performance of the actual markets. In particular, competitive hoarding is deemed 'excessive' if it can be shown to have been based on price expectations which exceeded the mathematical expectation of future price given all currently available information.

The main problem encountered in applying this criterion to the present setting is that price expectations are not observed. The idea behind the proposed test of market performance based on observed prices can be explained as follows: clearly, it is desirable that storage should respond to future scarcity and, thus, so should the spot price of a storable good. But it is not so clear that such a relationship should exist independently of future prices. I shall argue that if there is convincing evidence that readily available information on likely future scarcity affected current prices independently of realized future prices, then it is reasonable to conclude that either market prices do not adjust to eliminate excess demands, or that the information on future scarcity is leading to biased price forecasts. In either case, markets are not performing well.[4]

The following section outlines the theoretical model to be used in interpreting the movements in rice prices during the period. The model's structure is novel in that, under certain conditions, it permits one to infer deviations of private storage decisions from those implied by rational price expectations, even when neither stocks nor price expectations are observed. The model interprets the monthly rice price series as the outcome primarily of storage decisions in the private and public sectors, and the inherent seasonality of production and transaction costs. Section 3 discusses appropriate estimation methods for the model. Section 4 gives the results and Section 5 examines their implications for market performance. Section 6 tests an alternative explanation for the volatility of Bangladesh rice prices in terms of conditions in world grain markets. Section 7 discusses the causes and effects of the government's activities in rice markets during the period. Finally, Section 8 offers some conclusions.

3.2 A Dynamic Model of the Price of Rice in Bangladesh

I shall assume the following model of the monthly time series of rice prices in Bangladesh (all logarithms are natural):

$$\log P_t = \beta_0 + \beta_1 \log P_{t-1} + \beta_2 \log P_{t+1} + \beta_3 X_t + \beta_4 \Delta L_t + \beta_5 \Delta Z_t + \beta_6 G_t + \mu_t \quad (t = 1, \ldots, n) \tag{3.1}$$

where the βs are parametric and

P = retail price of rice

X = variable(s) determining the flows into storage from the non-storage sectors at given price (production and imports less current consumption)

L = dummy variable for lean months (1 if no rice produced, 0 otherwise)

Z = currently available information on future foodgrain availability

G = net out-flows from the market into public rice stocks

μ = an appropriate error process, to be discussed in Section 3.3

The section offers an economic-theoretic justification for the above econometric model. This will help interpret the empirical results obtained later. Some readers may prefer to skip this section, and go straight to 3.3. However, one result from this section is essential for understanding the later discussion: if price expectations are rational and markets are competitive then $\beta_5 = 0$ in equation 3.1. The main aim of the empirical work is to test that implication.

It is often assumed that competitive storage agents are risk neutral profit maximizers facing a constant marginal cost.[5] Evidence for wheat storage in the United States does not support this assumption. Certainly, marginal storage costs do not seem to vary much with stock level. However, positive stocks are observed even when expected future price falls short of the spot price plus marginal storage cost. Agents perceive a positive marginal benefit from holding stocks, in addition to expected profit.[6]

Although there does not appear to be any comparable evidence for rice storage in Bangladesh, there must be a reasonable presumption that stockholders (farmers, millers, and merchants) were not solely motivated by expected profits during the period. Stockholders are also likely to have viewed their stocks as a desirable precaution in a period of very considerable social instability. Thus I shall assume that storage agents would also have held foodgrain stocks, even if it were not profitable to do so. In particular, stockholders' preferences are defined on the quantity and price of stocks as well as the level of profits from holding stocks. To incorporate this assumption into a manageable econometric model, I shall also assume that:

(i) all stockholders are risk neutral with respect to profits and have identical preferences;

(ii) their preferences can be well represented by a utility function which is strictly concave in stocks at given profitability;

(iii) their utility function is additively separable both intertemporarily and between stocks and profits.

I shall also introduce an additional cost into the storage problem to do with the seasonality in rice availability. Although it is possible to increase private stocks in the lean months (by importing, buying up government stocks or smuggling) it is likely to be considerably less costly to do so at times of harvest. Thus the seasonality of production introduces seasonality in search and transaction costs for buyers. It is assumed that the total transaction cost in lean months is proportional to the value of transactions.

Combining these considerations, the level of private storage in the economy maximizes:

$$U(S_t, P_t) + (P^e_{t+1} - P_t - C_t)S_t - T_tP_t(S_t - S_{t-1}) \quad (3.2)$$

where the function U has the properties: $U_s > 0$, $U_p > 0$, $U_{ss} < 0$, $U_{sp} \geq 0$ and where

S_t = stock level at time t

P^e_{t+1} = price expected for time $t+1$ on the basis of the information available at time t

C_t = unit storage cost at time t

T_t = unit transaction cost at t

The last variable can take two possible values, namely

$$T_t = \phi L_t$$

where $L = 1$ when $S_t > S_{t-1}$ but rice is not produced at time t while $L = 0$ otherwise. In the empirical work it will be assumed that $L = 1$ in all months when, according to a typical crop calendar, little or no rice is produced. Thus, an additional cost of ϕ per unit value of transactions is incurred when a trader attempts to increase stocks in the lean months rather than at the harvests. It also seems a reasonable simplification to suppose that unit storage cost is proportional to current price in the above problem,

$$C_t = cP_t \quad (3.3)$$

where c is a constant. This will be a good approximation when wastage and interest charges are a high proportion of storage cost, as seems plausible in this setting (for further discussion see Moore *et al.* 1973).

The solution to the problem in equation 3.2 will depend on the functional form of U. A convenient assumption with all of the desired properties is that U is linear in P and quadratic in S, in a suitable neighbourhood of the optimum. So U is strictly concave in S but not additively separable between P and S. Then a solution can be obtained of the following form (see Appendix 3.1):

$$S_t = \alpha_0 + \alpha_1(P_{t+1}^e - P_t - C_t - T_t P_t)P_t^{-1} + \varepsilon_{1t} \quad \alpha_1 > 0 \quad (3.4)$$

where the α's are parametric and ε_1 is any appropriate error process. For reasonably static price expectations (P_{+1}^e close to P) the above equation can be well approximated by:[7]

$$S_t = \alpha_0 + \alpha_1(\log P_{t+1}^e - \log P_t - c - T_t) + \varepsilon_{1t} \quad (3.5)$$

Since price expectations are not observed, a theory of their formation is required. Let e_t denote the error made in predicting log price, i.e.

$$e_t = \log P_t^e - \log P_t \quad (3.6)$$

If expectations are rational then they are unbiased predictors conditional on available information, i.e.

$$E(e_t | I_{t-1}) = 0 \quad (3.7)$$

where I_t is the information set available to traders when forming their expectation at time t. By the properties of conditional expectations, e_t will be orthogonal to all elements of I_{t-1}. In short, under these assumptions, storage agents could not have made better use of the available information when forming their price expectations.

One can generalize this model and suppose that expectations need only be partially rational in that only a subset of the available information is used in forming expectations. Then e_t will be correlated with remaining elements of I_{t-1}. Thus the strong form of the rational expectations hypothesis can be nested within a more general model and so tested as a parameter restriction.

Following this approach, suppose that

$$e_t = \gamma_1 Z_{t-1} + \gamma_2 \log P_{t-1} + \varepsilon_{2t} \quad 0 < \gamma_2 < 2 \quad (3.8)$$

for some Z_t in I_t (which may, of course, be a vector). In this setting it is reasonable to assume that I_t includes P_t and this variable is singled out. The restriction that $0 < \gamma_2 < 2$ seems plausible.[8] The 'strong form' of the rational expectations hypothesis is encompassed as the parameter restriction:

$$\gamma_1 = \gamma_2 = 0$$

Following the argument in Chapter 1, this restriction is interpreted as a normative criterion for the informational efficiency of storage decisions.

Combining these assumptions (equations 3.5, 3.6, and 3.8), the change in private stocks during time interval t is given by

$$\Delta S_t = \alpha_1(\Delta \log P_{t+1} + (\gamma_2-1)\Delta \log P_t + \gamma_1 \Delta Z_t - \phi \Delta L_t) \\ + \Delta \varepsilon_{1t} + \alpha_1 \Delta \varepsilon_{2t-1}. \tag{3.9}$$

Given that the rest of the model is log-linear in price it is highly desirable from the point of view of solving the model to assume that this is also the case for flows into storage from non-storage activities (production and imports less current consumption). Denoting the latter by Q it is assumed that:

$$Q_t = a_0 + a_1 \log P_t + a_2 X_t + \varepsilon_{3t} \quad a_1 \geqslant 0 \tag{3.10}$$

This specification can also be given a dynamic structure in prices without altering the main results, for example, by assuming that farmers need not have rational price expectations. To simplify the exposition I have ignored these possibilities.

In testing this model I shall permit a distinction between the recorded prices in the data and the market clearing prices $\log P^*$ which solve

$$\Delta S + G = Q \tag{3.11}$$

at each point in time. Two possible justifications for this distinction can be offered:

(i) While prices may well be recorded accurately by the data collector, the markets may not clear at each point in time at these prices. This will be the case if trading agents perceive a cost of changing their quoted prices independently of the level of any excess demand at the going price.

(ii) While markets may clear continually, the data collector may perceive a cost of reporting price variability. For example, the data collector may find that his or her reports are more readily believed the closer they are to previous reports.

I shall discuss further the possibility of market disequilibrium due to price inflexibility in Section 3.5 when considering alternative interpretations of the empirical results. For now, I shall assume continual market clearing, while permitting extra sluggishness in recorded prices due to imperfect data collection.

Specifically, it is assumed that the data collection agent chooses recorded prices which minimize a loss function which is quadratic in $\log P^*/P$ and $\log P/P_{-1}$. The first quadratic term is interpreted as the expected loss to the data recorder from misreporting the true prices, while the second is interpreted as the perceived cost from reporting price changes. It can readily be shown that recorded prices will then be related to the actual prices according to the familiar partial adjustment model:[9]

$$\log P_t = \delta \log P_{t-1} + (1-\delta)\log P_t^* \qquad 0 \leqslant \delta < 1 \qquad (3.12)$$

Appendix 3.1 outlines the derivation of this result.

Current price in the market can now be expressed in the form of equation 3.1 (substituting (3.9) and (3.10) into (3.11), solving for $\log P^*$ and substituting into (3.12)) where the coefficients have the following interpretation:

$$\beta_0 = -a_0\beta_6 \qquad (3.13.1)$$
$$\beta_1 = \delta + (1-\gamma_2)\alpha_1\beta_6 \qquad (3.13.2)$$
$$\beta_2 = \alpha_1\beta_6 > 0 \qquad (3.13.3)$$
$$\beta_3 = -a_2\beta_6 \qquad (3.13.4)$$
$$\beta_4 = -\alpha_1\phi\beta_6 < 0 \qquad (3.13.5)$$
$$\beta_5 = \alpha_1\gamma_1\beta_6 \qquad (3.13.6)$$
$$\beta_6 = (1-\delta)/(a_1-\alpha_1(\gamma_2-2)) > 0 \qquad (3.13.7)$$

The main task of the empirical work is to test hypotheses concerning γ_1 and γ_2. Provided that β_2 and β_5 are identified, γ_1 is estimatable as a (non-linear) function of the model's parameter estimates:

$$\gamma_1 = \beta_5/\beta_2 \qquad (3.14)$$

However, δ is not identified, and hence estimation of

$$\gamma_2 = 1 + (\delta - \beta_1)/\beta_2 \qquad (3.15)$$

requires a prior assumption about the degree of recorded flexibility. For this purpose it is useful to establish a confidence interval for

$$\delta^* = \beta_1 - \beta_2 \qquad (3.16)$$

since $\gamma_2 \gtreqless 0$ as $\delta \gtreqless \delta^*$ noting that $\beta_2 > 0$.

If one concludes that γ_1 is positive, then price forecasts are biased in that traders systematically over-estimate the effect of crop damage at a given date on future prices. By implication, storage, and hence current price at that date are too high. Similarly, if one believes that $\delta > \delta^*$ and thus that $\gamma_2 > 0$, then price expectations are sluggish in the sense that forecasting errors are correlated positively with past prices.

However, it should be emphasized that all such inferences are conditioned on the validity of the set of prior assumptions outlined above. The most important sources of doubt are probably the treatment of storage decisions, and the assumption that markets clear on the basis of those decisions subject to any short-term costs of adjustment. I shall return to these issues in Section 3.5 and discuss possible alternative interpretations of the empirical results.

3.3 Estimation Methods and Measurement Problems

The theoretical model outlined above has a number of properties which preclude consistent estimation of equation 3.1 by ordinary least squares.

First, autoregressive future prices will be correlated with the error term in equation 3.1. This particular simultaneity problem arises from the model's treatment of price expectations. A number of estimation methods appropriate to models assuming (unobserved) rational expectations have been discussed in the recent literature (for a survey see Wickens, 1982). McCallum (1976) has proposed a convenient and consistent estimator according to which future prices are treated as expectations measured with a white noise error (see also Muth, 1981). The 'errors in variables method' has been adapted to the present problem, the difference being that the present version does not assume the strong form of rational expectations, but contains this as a nested hypothesis.[10] Variables selected from the assumed information set are used as instrumental variables for future price. The main instrumental variables used were lagged prices, seasonal dummy variables, and variables related to crop damage and other damage due to natural causes.

Second, the error term in equation 3.1 is unlikely to be serially independent. The error in equation 3.1 is related to the underlying stochastic terms in equations 3.5, 3.8, and 3.10 as

$$\mu_t = (\Delta\varepsilon_{1t} + \alpha_1\Delta\varepsilon_{2t+1} - \varepsilon_{3t})\,\beta_6 \qquad (3.17)$$

So, even if ε_1, ε_2, and ε_3 are serially and contemporaneously independent, μ will have a negative serial correlation (see Appendix 3.1):

$$\text{cov}(\mu_t\mu_{t-1}) = -\beta_6^2(\text{var}\varepsilon_{1t-1} + \alpha_1^2\text{var}\varepsilon_{2t}) < 0 \qquad (3.18)$$

Of course, serial or contemporaneous correlations amongst the ε's could alter this result. Nonetheless, there is an a priori case for using autoregressive estimation methods.

An important measurement problem is posed by the choice of those variables which are hypothesized to be correlated with price forecasting errors. The selection has been guided by two principles:

(1) It should be highly plausible that the value of the chosen variable was information available to stockholders at the time they formed their price expectations; forecasting errors can obviously be correlated with information which was unknown at the time the forecasts were made (see, for example, Minford and Peel, 1984).

(2) To avoid identification problems, the chosen variable should not also be a determinant of current production or consumption. If it is then it will generally affect current price independently of expected future price, in which case it will be significant in equation 3.1 even when it is uncorrelated with *ex-post* forecasting errors.

In view of the first consideration, it was decided to use only information contained in past newspaper reports. The obvious choices were the main English language newspaper published in Dhaka, *The Bangladesh Observer*, and the main Bengali newspaper, *Daily Ittefaq*. The newspapers are discussed further in Appendix 3.2. Of course, one need not believe that most stockholders read these newspapers (although their circulations are high) to justify the assumption that their contents give a reasonable characterization of the available information on crop damage. (The newspapers are known to have been politically censored at times but this does not appear to have affected crop damage reporting; see Appendix 3.2). A count was made of:

CD_t = the number of reports of crop damage in month t, likely to affect either current output or the time profile of future output. Causes included flood, drought, excessive rainfall, erosion, salinity, crop diseases, and pests.

Counts were also made of other reports of damage to real property and persons, including loss of life, and variables describing government activities. Further details and examples of the newspaper reports and how they were translated, coded, and checked are given in Appendix 3.2.

From the point of view of the second principle above, it was decided to use the information contained in the crop calendar and the reports of crop damage to construct an index of recent damage to future output. 'Recent' is taken to mean within the last four months, and 'future' to mean within the next four months. The index was only constructed for the main (aman) crop. With the exception of a small amount of earlier broadcast rice, this crop is planted between mid-June and mid-August and is harvested between mid-November and mid-January. The aman crop accounts for about 60 per cent of annual production. The index of *aman crop damage* at time $t-i$ is given by:

$$ACD_{t-i} = A_t A_{t-i} CD_{t-i} \qquad (3.19)$$

where

A = 1 for July, August, September, October, and November, i.e. those months for which aman rice is due within the next four months and the crop has been planted.
    = 0 otherwise.

Thus, if ACD_{t-i} is positive, then it is inferred that damage to aman rice occurred i months ago and that this is likely to delay or diminish the future aman crop.

At least some of any crop damage in the months of July and August is likely to affect the relatively small aus crop at the point of its harvesting as well as the future aman crop, thus posing an identification problem in estimating β_5. On a priori grounds, it is implausible that this could account for the high autumn prices of 1974 nationally, since the aus harvest turned out quite well by recent past standards (and, as was noted in the Introduction, it was a good deal higher than in 1973 in the districts worst hit by the famine; see Alamgir, 1980, chapter 6). Nonetheless, an alternative definition for ACD was also considered in which CD was weighted by the proportion of aman rice in total acreage for each month, estimated from the annual acreage data under alternative seemingly plausible assumptions on crop composition for each month. These alternative measures of *ACD* had negligible effect on estimates of β_5 or their standard errors, and so the simpler measure outlined above has been preferred.

In terms of equation 3.1, it is assumed that the price effect of a change in the current information set pertaining to future aman crop damage can be represented by the following polynomial distributed lag:

$$\sum_{i=0}^{4} (\beta_{50} + \beta_{51}i + \beta_{52}i_2)ACD_{t-i} \text{ where } \beta_5 = (\beta_{50}, \beta_{51}, \beta_{52}) \quad (3.20)$$

This specification was tested against an unrestricted distributed lag and a third degree polynomial, and was preferred.

Another measurement problem is posed by the variable L (entering the model in first difference form). Once again, this is a dummy variable, taking the value 1 in months for which no rice is produced but traders want to increase their stocks. Rather than let L vary from year to year (thus posing further measurement and estimation problems) it was decided to fix L on the basis of the crop calendar. Negligible rice is produced from mid-January to mid-April and from mid-August to mid-November. Processing and transportation delays mean that new rice is usually still available late-January and late-August. Furthermore, it is unlikely that traders would want to increase stocks in the week or two prior to harvest. So:

L = 1 for February, March, September, October
   = 0 otherwise.

3.4 Data and Results

The time span of the empirical work is the post-Independence period under Mujibur Rahman, the charismatic leader of the

Bengali nationalist movement prior to 1971. The period was one of considerable internal unrest, as well as bad weather. It would seem that Mujib's early popularity had waned by the famine year and many people had lost faith in their government. (Section 3.6 discusses this further). Mujib was assassinated in August 1975 and there followed a period of many months of political instability.

The model was estimated using monthly data for the period July 1972 to April 1975, giving 30 observations after lags. The starting data was chosen in the attempt to avoid the undoubtedly disruptive effects on markets of the Bangladesh War of Independence in 1971. The terminating date was chosen to avoid the effects of an unprecedented currency demonetization and increase in food aid, mid-1975. However, as will be seen, estimates of the main parameters of interest and their standard errors were found to be quite robust under small changes in the starting and terminating dates, and also for a 43 month version (to mid-1976) estimated on a restricted data set.

With only a few years of monthly data it is difficult to capture convincingly the effects of annual variables such as harvested rice output, or gradually changing ones such as population. Furthermore, one would expect month-to-month price changes to be determined primarily by short-term storage decisions (both in the public and private sectors) and the inherent seasonality in traditional rice production. Also, foodgrain import and distribution policies in Bangladesh during this period are likely to have provided considerable insulation of local rice markets from international prices and trading conditions. The government controlled all foodgrain imports, mainly wheat sold in urban ration shops at controlled prices.[11]

With these points in mind, the following choices were made concerning the specification of the price model reported in Table 3.1.

1. A number of variables likely to influence supplies to the market from the farm sector were tested, including rice output, domestic jute prices, and agricultural wage rates. A number of seemingly plausible monthly allocations of the annual outputs for each crop were considered. All of these performed very well, but generally no better than a simple dummy variable (H) for November and December. The choice made negligible difference to other coefficients in the model. Jute prices and wage rates were

Table 3.1: *Rice Price Equation*

Variable	Parameter	1 Bangladesh Observer	2 Daily Ittefaq
$\log P_{t-1}$	β_1	0.45 (9.3)	0.46 (8.5)
$\log P_{t+1}$	β_2	0.53 (12)	0.54 (10)
H_t	β_3 ($\times 10$)	−0.99 (7.0)	−1.1 (6.6)
$\triangle L_t$	β_4 ($\times 10$)	−0.48 (4.2)	−0.44 (3.5)
$\sum ACD_{t-i}$	β_{50} ($\times 100$)	−0.16 (4.7)	−0.13 (4.6)
$\sum iACD_{t-i}$	β_{51} ($\times 100$)	0.32 (5.6)	0.23 (4.6)
$\sum i^2 ACD_{t-i}$	β_{52} ($\times 100$)	−0.072 (4.3)	−0.047 (3.4)
G_{t-1}	β_6 ($\times 1000$)	0.89 (2.9)	0.63 (2.0)
error_{t-1}		−0.47 (2.1)	−0.35 (1.6)
See		0.027	0.029
Mean $\log P$ (Rho weighted)		10	9.5

Note: Absolute *t*-ratios in parentheses. The TSP programme for IV estimation with a first order serially correlated error has been used; for further details see Hall and Hall (1980).

generally insignificant. On reflection this does not seem too surprising; the poor (and presumably unanticipated) weather conditions during the period suggest that actual outputs were probably less than those chosen by farmers.

2. The results were consistent with the view that the domestic rice markets were reasonably well insulated from foreign foodgrain prices and trading conditions (except in so far as these are reflected in the government's own stock position which does affect domestic prices; see (4) below). The coefficient on foodgrain

imports generally had the expected sign when added to the price model, but had a fairly high variance. Nor were international rice and wheat prices an important determinant of domestic prices. Indeed, world foodgrain prices were, if anything, generally declining during 1974–5. Appendix 3.3 discusses this point further.

3. Excessive money supply growth has been discussed elsewhere as a possible explanation for the famine (for example, see Lifschultz, 1974c). However, the present investigations have not been supportive. Current and lagged values for the log differences of M1 and M2 stocks were tested as additional variables in the price model, but were insignificant. A number of *ad hoc* specifications were also tested with the change in log price regressed against a distributed lag of current and past money supply changes. These models performed poorly. While a reasonable case might be made for the belief that high rates of money supply growth in the first year after Independence did have an inflationary effect, this does not appear to have been a reason for the high rice prices in late 1974.

4. More precise estimates of the effects of changes in the government's rice stockholding (G) were obtained using a one month lag rather than current value. This is presumed to reflect the time required for the transportation and distribution of rice after leaving the government's godowns. Changes in wheat stocks were also tested but did not prove significant. This could reflect the effects of the government's urban wheat rationing system and/or the well-known strength of the Bangladeshi preference for rice.[12]

5. The crop damage counts from *The Bangladesh Observer* were strongly correlated with those from *Daily Ittefaq* ($r = 0.79$) and so it proved difficult to separate their effects in a single regression (see Appendix 3.2). From the point of view of the model, there does not seem to be much difference between the two papers in terms of their crop damage reporting.

6. The log price model (equation 3.1) was also tested against a linear price model. The log model consistently performed better than the linear model; the standard error of estimate was a higher proportion of mean price for the linear model in all specifications tested, and all coefficients except β_1 were estimated with less precision than could be obtained with the log price model. This is consistent with the presumed non-linearity of the storage demand function.

7. The following instrumental variables were used for $\log P_{+1}$: $\log P_{-1,-2}$, H, H_{+1}, G_{-1}, the distributed lags of ACD, foodgrain imports, and newspaper reports of other (non-crop) damage. A number of changes to the set of instrumental variables were considered including the deletion of $\log P_{-1}$, the deletion of G_{-1}, and the addition of agricultural wages, but these changes made negligible difference to estimates of the main parameters of interest, namely β_1, β_2 and β_5. However, estimates of β_6 proved to be quite sensitive and so I have my doubts about how well this parameter has been estimated.

Possibly the most important variable omitted from the model is the level of illegal rice exports into India. The sign of any consequent bias in the estimate of β_5 will equal that of the correlation between smuggling and expected future crop damage (assuming that exports raise the domestic price level). Since crop damage and high prices in Bangladesh are likely to diminish the rewards to smuggling, it seems plausible that any bias due to the missing variable will result in under-estimation of β_5, although the effect on γ_1 is less clear since, by the same reasoning, the omission of smuggling probably results in under-estimation of β_2.

Figure 3.1 gives the first differences of log price and the fitted values using ACD counts from *The Bangladesh Observer*

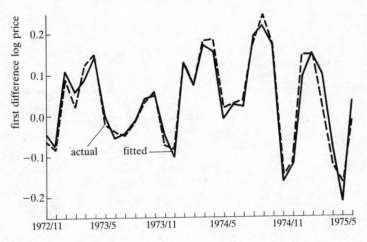

Fig. 3.1

($r = 0.97$). The overall fit of the model is excellent. A check was also made for randomness in the model's residuals. The six month residual correlogram of the first equation in Table 3.1 is given in Table 3.2 and is certainly satisfactory. The residuals very comfortably pass the Box–Pierce test for randomness.[13]

To test the robustness of the model, various changes in specification were tried. Table 3.3 summarizes further estimates obtained for the parameters of the second degree polynomial distributed lag of ACD for various changes to the specifications of the price equation. The model was re-estimated for each of two alternative time periods of approximately 20 and 40 months. For comparison, Column 1 of Table 3.3 reproduces the results for *The Bangladesh Observer* using the 30 month model as reported in Table 3.1. Columns 2 and 3 give results (each for *The Bangladesh Observer*) for the truncated and extended series respectively. In view of the likely measurement error in the CD series, Column 4

Table 3.2 *Residual Correlogram*

Lag	1	2	3	4	5	6
r	-0.098	-0.13	0.036	-0.024	0.063	-0.043
LM	1.2	1.1	0.28	0.18	0.45	0.34

Note: $1/\sqrt{T} = 0.18$, LM = Breusch–Pagan Lagrange multiplier test.

Table 3.3 *Effect of Reported Damage to Future Crop on Current Prices Under Alternative Model Specifications.*

	1 Table 3.1 Col. 1	2 Shorter series ($n = 20$)	3 Longer Series ($n = 43$)	4 IV Estimator (for CD)
$\sum ACD_{t-i}$	-0.16 (4.7)	-0.17 (4.6)	-0.18 (3.3)	-0.19 (3.5)
$\sum iACD_{t-i}$	0.32 (5.6)	0.27 (3.7)	0.31 (3.5)	0.36 (4.0)
$\sum i^2 ACD_{t-i}$	-0.072 (4.3)	-0.053 (2.3)	-0.069 (2.8)	-0.082 (3.1)

of Table 3.3 gives an instrumental variables estimator, in which CD is replaced by a prediction based on predetermined variables.[14]

3.5 Implications for Market Performance

The above results strongly suggest that available information on current and past damage to the future crop affected current prices independently of realized future prices. An *F*-test convincingly rejects the restriction $\beta_5 = 0$ against each of the unrestricted models in Table 3.1 ($F(3,20) = 16$ and 14 respectively). When this empirical result is interpreted in terms of the theoretical model of Section 3.2, it is concluded that price forecasting errors were correlated with available information.

From Table 3.1 the polynomial distributed lag can be seen to give quite a precise representation of the dynamic effect of ACD on current price. In view of equation 3.14, one can use the results of Table 3.1 to estimate the effect of ACD on price forecasting errors. For example, using the first regression in Table 3.1, the following result is obtained for the contribution of ACD to the one month change in log price forecasting errors:

$$\sum_{i=0}^{4} (-0.30 + 0.60i - 0.14i^2)\text{ACD}_{t-i}/100 \qquad (3.21)$$
$$\phantom{\sum_{i=0}^{4}} (4.4) \quad (5.1) \quad (4.0)$$

In terms of stockholders' price forecasting behaviour, the above result suggests that the effect of current damage on the future price is under-estimated, while the effect of recent past damage is over-estimated. On balance, the effect of sustained damage to the future crop such as occurred during 1974 is over-estimated; in particular, if $\text{ACD}_{-i} = \text{ACD}_0$ for all i, then the effect on the change in price forecasting errors is 0.30ACD_0.

Using these results to estimate the price effects of crop damage in the pre-harvest months of 1974, one finds that during September and October ACD added 27 per cent to the price of rice, representing 56 per cent of the actual price increase over those months. These were the months of highest rice price during 1974 and, in terms of starvation, probably the worst months of the famine since they coincide with the low season for agricultural employment (see Chapter 5 for further discussion). ACD also appears to have been an important factor contributing to the instability of prices during the 1974 famine; the variance in ACD (weighted by the parameter estimates from column 1 in Table 3.1) represents 20 per cent of the variance in log price over the last six months of 1974.

Unless one assumes (on a priori grounds) that recorded prices are fully flexible ($\delta = 0$), the results of Table 3.1 also indicate a positive correlation between price forecasting errors and lagged prices. In particular, δ^* is not significantly different from zero; indeed the restriction $\delta^* = 0$ yields a slight reduction in residual variance (a drop of about 0.002 in SEE). This suggests that γ_2 is positive for all positive δ. For example, with seemingly modest sluggishness in recorded prices independently of market conditions $\delta = 0.1$, say, one finds that $\gamma_2 = 0.35$ ($t = 3.0$) using the first equation in Table 3.1. However, it should be emphasized that the data alone cannot be used to choose between this conclusion and the alternative: $\delta = \gamma_2 = 0$.

There is also an alternative to the conclusion that expectations were informationally biased when interpreting the effect on prices of ACD. The model in Section 3.2 assumes that storage is partly motivated by expectations of future scarcity *and* that such scarcity is fully reflected in future prices. Hence, future price expectations are the relevant measure of expectations about future scarcity. However, suppose that prices are generally believed to be inflexible upwards. Then, independently of their beliefs about future prices, traders might store in response to reports of crop damage (as an indicator of future rationing), and so γ_1 could reflect this effect rather than non-rational price expectations.[15]

Of course, this alternative interpretation of γ_1 is inconsistent with a competitive equilibrium since it assumes that storage agents had systematically failed to achieve their desired stock levels. Furthermore, if this alternative interpretation of γ_1 is preferred, then one must also maintain that δ, and hence γ_2, are positive. Either way, biases in expectations formation are indicated.

3.6 Markets and Government during the Famine

The above results also raise questions concerning the performance of government. By domestic procurement and its monopoly over imports, the Bangladesh government operates its own foodgrain buffer stock. During the period under study, injections from this stock into the economy mainly went through ration shops rather than the open market. This is likely to diminish their price stabilizing potential. But changes in the government's rice stock level are still likely to influence market prices, and this is confirmed by the results of Table 3.1. Thus, to form their expectations of the effects of pre-harvest crop damage on future prices, traders must make an assumption about the government's response to shared information. Here it can be hypothesized that stockholders' over-optimistic price expectations during the 1974 famine were premised on a belief that the government would be unable to implement a suitable stabilizing response to the reported damage to the future crop.

To test this hypothesis properly one should look not only at the actual stocking activities of government, but also at the way the government might have influenced the information sets of private traders. In forming expectations, traders' *beliefs* about what the government is capable of doing may well be more important than observations of what the government has actually done. This section will attempt to evaluate this aspect of the relationship between markets and government with the help of data from the Bangladesh newspapers. The data is discussed further in Appendix 3.2.

On a priori grounds one would expect a degree of interdependence between markets and governmental decision making; while governments can sometimes exert considerable influence on markets, the reverse is also true. News of action and promises to take further action are natural responses by government to shortages and unstable prices, and might be thought to yield quick results. This is because such news immediately conveys relevant information to traders. The effect on markets depends on the nature of that information and how it is used by traders in forming their price expectation. For example, if the news leads risk-neutral profit-maximizing stock holders to expect the future price increase to fall below their marginal storage cost, then the promise will increase current food availability. Of course, all this could occur before the date of the promised action.

Clearly, the success of a government's promise depends in part on the traders' belief that an action will follow. A survey of the newspapers and other historical evidence on the situation in Bangladesh in the first few years after Independence suggests that there had been a considerable and rapid deterioration in the Mujib government's credibility by the time of the famine (Ravallion and van de Walle, 1984). The government's threats against stockholders increased in number as the famine approached. The following is a typical example:

[The Minister for Food said today that] . . . the Government might adopt long term administrative measures for total liquidation of unscrupulous traders and businessmen engaged in hoarding and black marketeering of foodgrains . . .

The Bangladesh Observer 19 September 1974

By the autumn of 1974 it seems that the threats had become unbelievable. As one correspondent wrote (Lifschultz, 1974c, 29):

Each day, ministers issue public appeals to foodgrain merchants asking them to lower prices. The Government, by its own announcements, appears to be well aware who is in control of food stocks and prices. However, it also seems unprepared, or incapable of doing more than issue warnings.

The Bangladesh government's foodgrain stocks were unusually low during the first six months of 1974, due to a low procurement of the previous winter's rice, reductions in US food aid on foreign policy grounds, and to low imports (McHenry and Bird, 1977; Alamgir, 1980; Sobhan, 1980). And this appears to have been fairly common knowledge at the time.[16] No doubt, many agents in the rice markets had come to the conclusion that their government simply could not be trusted. By 1974, rumours and even documented reports of corruption within the ruling party, the Awami League, were common. For example, the low level of public foodgrain stocks in 1974 has been blamed, in part, on corruption:

On the whole, the 1974 procurement operation resulted in the farmers losing confidence in the program and the traders obtaining a greater control over food resources . . . This is because the levy committees were composed of the members of the ruling party and they reportedly allowed their sympathizers (who came largely from the surplus farmers) to escape compulsory levy. (Alamgir, 1980, 225)

Similarly, the government's use of military action against hoarders and smugglers in May 1974 was soon terminated when the army apprehended numerous members of the Awami League (Maniruzzaman, 1975). By late 1974, many observers, including the Finance Minister, Tajuddin Ahmed, claimed that the famine was as much the result of the government's activities as of bad weather.[17]

In the light of these criticisms it is of interest to examine the causes and effects of the Bangladesh government's activities during the famine. Clearly, this is a difficult thing to quantify and one can hope for little more than a crude idea of the government's role.

For this purpose a count was made of the incidence of newspaper articles in *The Bangladesh Observer* reporting the government's activities. Government actions (GA) actually taken (or, at least, reported to have been taken) and clearly intended to influence rice markets were distinguished from government promises (GP) to take such actions in the future. Appendix 3.2 discusses these data further.

Neither GA or GP appear to have had price stabilizing effects during the period. Neither variable added significantly to the explanatory power of the regressions reported in Section 3.4. This may partly reflect the endogeneity of GA and GP, although excluding them from the set of instrumental variables did not alter the conclusion.

However, the data do support the view that government activities were responsive to market conditions. The OLS regression of GA against current and recent prices and promises gives the following result:

$$GA = 0.31 + 0.055P - 0.043P_{-1} + 0.22GP_{-1} \qquad (3.22)$$
$$\quad (0.35) \quad (3.0) \qquad (2.3) \qquad (1.1)$$

$$R^2 = 0.33; \; SSR = 116; \; F(3,30) = 4.9; \; D-W = 2.19$$

There was no evidence of an autoregressive structure in this equation's residuals or in GA; the addition of GA_{-1} made negligible difference to the result. Higher lags on GP and P were also tested but were insignificant. An F-test did support acceptance of the following restricted form of equation (3.22) ($F(1,31) = 0.6$):

$$GA = 1.6 + 0.050\Delta P + 0.34GP_{-1} \qquad (3.23)$$
$$\quad (2.3) \quad (2.6) \qquad (1.6)$$

$$R^2 = 0.22; \; SSR = 134; \; F(2,21) = 4.4; \; D-W = 1.96$$

An instrumental variables estimate of this equation was also tested in which current price was excluded from the set of instrumental variables, but this made negligible difference to the above result.

Probably a more serious objection is that, since the dependent variable is discrete (taking integer values between zero and nine; see Appendix 3.2), the above model's error term will not be normally distributed. This leads one to question the efficiency of least squares regression, and also raises doubts about the inferential validity of standard tests.

Since this problem is intrinsic to the methodology of counting newspaper reports and using counts as dependent variables, it is worth investigating a more appropriate estimation procedure in this context. Probably the best approach here is the method of Poisson regression, based on the assumption that the counts are taken from independent Poisson distributions. This has been developed for the analysis of contingency tables based on classified counts (see, for example, Maddala, 1983). Maximum likelihood estimates of the model's parameters can then be obtained by an appropriate iterative procedure; in the present application, the Nelder and Wedderburn (1972) method of iterative weighted linear regression was used and the calculations were done using the GLIM programme (Nelder, 1975).

Re-estimation of equation 3.23 assuming Poisson errors gave the following result:

$$GA = 1.6 + 0.033P + 0.35GP_{-1} - 2L_{max} = 55 \qquad (3.24)$$
$$(3.2) \quad (2.4) \qquad (2.2)$$

In terms of the value of the log-likelihood function this is an improvement over the alternative hypothesis in which it is assumed that no systematic effects are present in the data:

$$GA = 2.7 - 2L_{max} = 65$$
$$(9.7)$$

(The gain in $-2L_{max}$ is approximately distributed as chi-square with 2 degrees of freedom and is significant at the 0.01 level.) The Poisson model also offers an impressive reduction in residual variance as compared to OLS; the residual variance of the Poisson estimator (equation 3.24) is 52, representing about 30 per cent of the variance of GA, as compared to 78 per cent for equation 3.23. The estimated standard error for the coefficient on lagged GP is also quite a lot lower, and so adds support to the conclusion that the government made some effort to fulfil past promises.

It is of interest to compare these results with the government's direct interventions on the supply side through changes in its own foodgrain stocks. Changes in the government's rice stock do appear to have had the expected positive effect on rice prices during the period, although this is not apparent for changes in its wheat stock holding. At the same time, the data do suggest that the government's stock decisions were influenced by past changes in rice prices, although the relationship varies between rice and wheat, being rather weak for the latter grain. There is also a mild one-month autoregressive effect in the series for stock changes (stocks do not fall close to zero at any time in the period for either grain). OLS gives the following estimates of the relationship (stock G in thousand tons and rice price in Taka per maund):

$$(\text{Rice}) \quad G = 6.2 + 0.36G_{-1} - 0.58P_{-1} \quad\quad (3.25)$$
$$\phantom{(\text{Rice}) \quad G = } (1.9) \quad (2.3) \quad\quad (3.7)$$

$$R^2 = 0.32; \ F(2,32) = 7.6; \ D-W = 2.05$$

$$(\text{Wheat}) \quad G = 11 + 0.21G_{-1} - 1.7P_{-1} \quad\quad (3.26)$$
$$\phantom{(\text{Wheat}) \quad G = } (0.75) \ (1.5) \quad\quad (2.4)$$

$$R^2 = 0.19; \ F(2,32) = 3.8; \ D-W = 1.81$$

In summary: the data and models tested suggest that the government's activities in rice markets—both those reported in the newspapers and the actual changes in its stock position—were influenced by events in those markets. Price increases induced government responses aimed at stabilization. But the effectiveness of those responses are open to serious question. The government's reported actions and promises do not appear to have affected rice markets. Changes in the government's rice stock holding did have such an effect, although this is not indicated for wheat. Both the qualitative evidence and the econometric analysis lend (qualified) support to the view that stockholders' inflated expectations of the effects of crop damage on future prices were correctly premised on a belief that, despite its pronounced aims, the government would not be able to deliver a successful stabilizing response to the impending scarcity.

3.7 Summary

An econometric model of rice price determination in Bangladesh has been formulated and shown to perform well in reproducing a monthly time series of rice prices for the period 1972–5, including the dramatic changes in the latter half of 1974. The results indicate that reports of future crop damage resulted in higher rice prices during the period, and that this effect existed independently of future prices.

The main interpretation offered for this empirical finding assumes that rice prices adjust competitively to clear markets. Although the adjustment need not be instantaneous, it is assumed that traders believe that future prices adequately reflect the future scarcities on which their storage decisions depend. This interpretation supports the conclusion that price forecasting errors were positively correlated with readily available information on damage to the future harvest. Thus, rice hoarding prior to anticipated production losses was excessive when compared to the likely outcome under competitive conditions with informationally efficient expectations.

In my view, it is not behaviourally implausible that stockholders had over-optimistic price expectations during the famine. But there is an alternative explanation: this assumes that stockholders also anticipated future quantity rationing. Although this could well be a rational expectation, it does suggest that markets failed in their primary function of equilibrating notional demands through price adjustment. By either interpretation of the results, rice markets in Bangladesh seem to have worked poorly.

The results also raise doubts about the performance of non-market food institutions. Rice prices in Bangladesh are influenced by changes in the government's foodgrain stock, itself determined by previous imports (including foreign aid) and internal procurement efforts. Thus, expectations of the effect of pre-harvest crop damage on future prices require an assumption about the government's response to shared information. The most plausible conclusion is that the stockholders' over-optimistic price expectations and/or anticipations of future rationing during the 1974 famine were premised on a belief that the government would be unable to implement a suitable stabilizing response to the reported damage to the future crop.

This may well be the most important lesson from Bangladesh's experience in 1974. And it is notable that, by at least one assessment, greater public confidence in the government's ability to stabilize food consumption was an important reason why Bangladesh was able to (narrowly) avoid further famines in 1979 and 1984 (Osmani, 1986).

Appendix 3.1

This appendix outlines from elementary principles the derivation of a number of the mathematical results used in the text.

(i) The derivation of equation 3.5 as the approximation to the solution of the storage problem given in equation 3.2 is as follows. The first-order condition for the problem in equation 3.2 is:

$$U_s(S,P) + P^e_{+1} - P - C - T.P = 0 \qquad (3A.1)$$

The second-order condition is that $U_{ss}(S,P) < 0$. By assumption, $U(.)$ is linear in P and quadratic in S within a neighbourhood of the optimum; in other words it can be written in the form:

$$U(S,P) = (b_1 S + b_2 S^2)P$$

where b_1 and b_2 are constant with $b_2 < 0$. Differentiating w.r.t. S, substituting into (3A.1), and then solving (3A.1) for S, one obtains equation 3.4 where $\alpha_0 = -b_1/(2b_2)$ and $\alpha_1 = -1/(2b_2) > 0$. Equation 3.5 is then obtained using the approximation:

$$(P^e_{+1} - P)/P \doteqdot \log(P^e_{+1}/P)$$

(ii) Equation 3.12 is derived as follows: the data collection agent is assumed to choose a recorded price $\log P$ that minimizes the expected value of the following loss function:

$$a(\log P^*/P)^2 + b(\log P/P_{-1})^2 \quad a,b>0$$

for which equation 3.12 is the first order condition with $\delta = b/(a + b)$. This derivation of the partial adjustment model is formally close to Griliches' (1967), although the interpretation is a little different.

(iii) Equation 3.18 is derived as follows:
By definition,

$$\text{cov}(\mu_t, \mu_{t-1}) = E(\mu_t \mu_{t-1}) \qquad (3.A5)$$

Using equation 3.17 to form the product $\mu_t\mu_{t-1}$ one obtains a string of nine terms in the three error processes ε_1, ε_2, and ε_3. However, seven of these vanish if ε_1, ε_2, and ε_3 are serially and contemporaneously independent, i.e.,

$$E(\varepsilon_{it}\varepsilon_{it-1}) = 0 \quad i = 1, 2, 3$$

$$E(\varepsilon_{it}\varepsilon_{jt}) = 0 \quad \text{for all } i \neq j.$$

This leaves two terms on the RHS giving equation 3.18.

Appendix 3.2

This appendix reports on a method of monitoring newspaper reports as a means of characterizing traders' *ex-ante* information sets. The method has generated the data used in the previous chapter and in Ravallion (1985a) for an assessment of the informational efficiency of rice markets in Bangladesh during the 1974 famine. This appendix discusses the peculiar methodological problems which arise in constructing and analysing these data, and in its applications. The appendix draws heavily from the results reported in Ravallion and van de Walle (1984).

Studies of foodgrain marketing in Bangladesh, India, and elsewhere have revealed that information acquisition is very important in trading activities.[18] Decisions concerning the timing and location of purchases and sales (and hence also storage) are influenced by the information gathered by traders from a variety of sources. Typically, personal contacts are the most important. During a recent survey of wholesale rice merchants in the main Dhaka market in Bangladesh, I found that most merchants had easy access to an information network linking markets throughout the country by telephone or via itinerate traders (Chapter 6 discusses the survey further). This confirms results from other studies; see, for example, Farruk (1972) for Bangladesh, and Lele (1971) for Tamil Nadu in India.

There can be little hope of measuring traders' *ex-ante* information from these sources. But newspaper monitoring can provide a practical and reasonably satisfactory alternative. For one thing, the newspapers are a source of information to traders, particularly about the activities of government. (Although literacy is very low in the aggregate in Bangladesh, this does not appear to be so in the main urban rice markets.) More importantly though, in a primarily agricultural economy such as Bangladesh, crop information is very newsworthy; the newspapers have an incentive to keep well informed about conditions in domestic agriculture. Both of the newspapers used in this study have an extensive network of reporters spread throughout Bangladesh (Eusuf and Currey, 1979). While no doubt there are delays in important information held by traders reaching the newspapers, my discussions with the traders suggest that these are unlikely to be longer than a week or two. And so an appropriate temporal partition of newspapers' reports—in the present case one month was used—should give a reasonable characterization of the information available to traders, even if their own source was not the newspapers.

Bangladesh's Newspapers.
Amongst the 40 or so daily newspapers in Bangladesh, *Daily Ittefaq* is widely viewed as the leading and most influential Bangla paper, while *The Bangladesh Times*, and the prominent government owned newspaper, *The Bangladesh Observer*, are the most widely read English language dailies.

Government censorship of the Press was common in the Post-Independence period, particularly during 1974/5 (Lent, 1982). The first major blow to the press came in July/August 1974 when Mujib's government set itself up as sole source of information and newsprint distribution. It also banned all news from foreign sources concerning Bangladesh (Maniruzzaman, 1975). A year later, in June 1975, the government cancelled many of the privately owned newspapers and took over publication of *The Bangladesh Times* and *Daily Ittefaq*. Under the first (short-lived) post-Mujib government, in September 1975, a few newspapers were returned to their previous owners.

The Bangladesh Observer was chosen to be monitored, in the belief that it is reasonably representative of the information which would have been available to traders at the time. The *Daily Ittefaq* was also monitored for crop damage stories by a Bangladeshi research assistant. The newspapers were read at the Bodleian Library (Oxford), the library of *The Bangladesh Observer*'s Offices (Dhaka), and at the library of the *Bangladesh Institute of Development Studies* (Dhaka).

The number of separate articles mentioning specific categories of information were counted. No satisfactory method was found for weighting different articles according to the severity of the reported event. It seemed that the prominence given to a story of, say, crop damage (for example, its page number) depended as much on journalistic and political consideration as on the actual severity of the damage. Also, counting separate articles rather than, say, mentions of damage, makes the final count more likely to be consistent over time and between different investigators. Problems of double counting are also avoided.

When attempting a rigorous monitoring of the Bangladeshi newspapers, quite a few potential pitfalls for the coder were found. It is important that the coder's reading of the newspapers is not biased by preconceptions of either their contents or the purposes of the research. The coder must rely solely on the information in the newspapers, and be exhaustive in documenting that information. It is easy to prejudice the counting by prior beliefs about the relative importance of different reports based on, for example, the prominence of their headlines, or their position in the paper. As was noted earlier, it was decided to avoid weighting reports in this way.

When more than one coder is involved it is a good practice to overlap coverage extensively, for example, the Bangladeshi coder spent some time reading *The Bangladesh Observer* over months that had previously been coded in Oxford. Initially, the Bangladeshi coder's count was consistently lower; on close scrutiny, it was found that this reflected a bias toward stories which had prominent headlines, or had crop damage as their sole topic. This was easily remedied.

Above all, the coder must have a thorough understanding of the definitions of each category of reports to be counted, and must stick to those definitions rigidly. In practice, the only sure way to achieve this is by intensive rehearsals, in close consultation with other investigators. If there is more than one coder then there are bound to be initial inconsistencies which will have to be ironed out prior to coding.

The remainder of this section will describe the definitions used in monitoring the Bangladeshi newspapers.

Four categories of articles were deemed to be of interest, and their occurrence in *The Bangladesh Observer* was counted from July 1972 to June 1975, with counts for the crop damage category extended to June 1976. A lengthy trial run of the monitoring exercise helped considerably in making the categorization of reports unambiguous; this often necessitated refinement of the initial definitions of each category. When the definitions had evolved enough to give a watertight classification, counting was started anew. After one complete count of the newspaper reports, about half the months were tallied a second time as a check. This included all of the famine year, 1974. The following definitions were settled on:

Crop Damage. The Crop Damage (CD) variable includes all accounts of adverse effects on current rice output or the time profile of future output. All stories mentioning damage to standing paddy or deleterious effects on the planting or growing cycle were tallied under this variable; causes of damage included flood, drought, excessive rainfall, cyclones, river erosion, salinity, crop diseases, and pests.

  The following points should be noted about CD:

(i) Not all stories referred directly to rice or paddy. Many described crop damage without naming the crop. Unless a non-rice crop was specifically named, all such reports were included. The predominance of rice cultivation in Bangladesh seems ample justification for this decision.

(ii) Other articles reporting submerged crops due to flooding without explicitly referring to damage were likewise included, since damage was presumed almost certainly to follow.

(iii) Relevant damage was for the current season or for up to a period of one year. In this way, theoretical articles about, for example, 'the yearly scourge of floods damaging food crops' were not counted. Editorials are often of this type.

(iv) *Daily Ittefaq* was found generally to have a greater number of articles about crop damage than the *Bangladesh Observer*; the former newspaper had a mean monthly CD of 30 (standard deviation of 11), while the latter had a mean of 13 (standard deviation of 10). However, the two series were found to follow a similar pattern of highs and lows, and there is a reasonably stable relationship between the two.[19]

Other Damage. Articles reporting bad weather with resulting damage to human life or property, but not to crops, were counted in a separate category, 'other damage' (OD). In many cases these reports were early information on CD before it was known that crops had been affected. Assessment of crop damage can rarely be made immediately, and so a delay often occurs before reference is made to loss of paddy in the newspaper. Thus, OD can provide important information for the formation of expectations about future output. In addition, it was hoped that this variable would help in gauging the extent of human hardship through the weakened physical and economic position of the Bangladeshi people during the sample period. Typical examples of OD are 'Flood victims facing paucity of drinking water' (9 July 1972) and 'Erosion of 34 square miles in Rajshahi, 500 families homeless' (29 Dec. 1973).

Government Actions and Promises. Reports were also counted of the government taking action (GA) or promising to do so (GP) with the likely intention of influencing the availability and price of rice. GP refers to a concrete promise to take a reasonably specific action within a maximum period of one year. GP's include laws shortly to be introduced, new internal procurement prices and dates advertised in advance, steps to procure foodgrains from abroad, changes in the ration rice quota or in ration prices soon to be introduced, intended acquisition of new farming equipment, plans for army involvement in foodgrain distribution or in anti-hoarding and smuggling campaigns, and promises to take direct action on the supply side to lower prices. GA's comprise all reports of the government actually taking such actions.

The following points should be noted:

(i) Articles concerning the government transacting a deal with another country for foodgrain aid were classed as promises rather than actions. They are interpreted as promises of future foodgrain arrival.

(ii) Every year, relief operations follow the April cyclones (Anderson, 1976). Similarly, other flood-relief services, consisting primarily of food distribution, first aid, and innoculation drives are a matter of course. These were not tabulated. More unusual, one-off events such as the opening of gruel kitchens in October 1974, were included.

(iii) In certain cases, a single nationally administered GA produces a newspaper report from each district. For example, the yearly launching of the nationwide procurement drive, or the opening up of 4300 gruel kitchens in October 1974, got media coverage in each locality. Beyond the one general story, the separate repetitions were not included.

(iv) Anti-hoarding and smuggling action stories were counted only when explicit reference was made to rice.

(v) Finally, it should be noted that GA by no means implies completion or success of government action.

By the rigorous monitoring of these categories of reports, a weekly history of the period was built up, and also by drawing from a more casual reading of other publications, particularly *The Far Eastern Economic Review* published in Hong Kong. This carried a number of critical reports on the situation in Bangladesh during the famine, which would probably not have been publishable within Bangladesh without heavy censorship. These qualitative historical data proved to be useful background information.

The Results. Table 3A gives the main results of the newspaper monitoring. It also gives some additional information on rice prices and a monthly summary of events during the period.

Table 3A.

	P	CD (*BO*)	CD (*DI*)	OD	GP	GA	Comments
1972							
July	62	9	34	14	6	2	
Aug	74	14	37	14	4	2	Protests against high prices (*BO*)
Sept	74	11	32	2	4	7	
Oct	73	10	29	2	4	2	Smuggling claimed (*BO*). Border trade suspended. UN asserts food situation is under control. Aman crop affected by drought.
Nov	70	8	32	1	2	3	More anti-smuggling measures.
Dec	65	7	20	0	5	0	Procurement of aman rice to begin on a voluntary basis (27 Dec).
1973							
Jan	72	19	19	3	1	3	Crop damage due to drought and failures of irrigation equipment (*BO*).
Feb	77	13	16	4	3	0	
Mar	84	5	20	4	2	0	Winter procurement has failed.

Table 3A. continued

	P	CD (BO)	CD (DI)	OD	GP	GA	Comments
							Massive electoral victory for Mujib's party, the Awami League. Quota of rationed rice is reduced. Food stocks claimed to be sufficient (*BO*).
April	96	11	31	17	5	1	Drought delays planting of aus crop. Army assists food administration and distribution.
May	96	19	43	10	2	3	Curfews along border. Further protests about prices.
June	91	15	38	5	1	2	Increased involvement of army is claimed to have ended hoarding (*BO*). Claims of armed attacks on police stations and political killings in countryside (Jahan).
July	87	19	39	9	4	2	
Aug	86	24	40	16	1	0	
Sept	89	14	36	14	0	2	
Oct	94	19	34	8	3	0	Mujib takes control of Information Ministry. Army law and order operations have indicted many Awami Leaguers and Mujib associates (Kamaluddin).
Nov	90	15	31	7	3	3	Some damage due to pests but generally good prospects for the aman harvest (*BO*). Procurement drive starts 15th with target of 5%. Legislation to bar traders from holding stock longer than one week.
Dec	81	12	25	2	1	2	Procurement drive reported to be failing. Restrictions imposed on interdistrict movement of foodgrains. Local elections in 450 centres indefinitely suspended due to political violence (Rahman and Hasan). President resigns in protest against govenment policies (Lifschultz, 1974*a*; Rahman and Hasan). Massive anti Awami League rally held in Dhaka (Lifschultz, 1974*a*). First hints of US intention to hold back 1974

Table 3A. continued

	P	CD (BO)	CD (DI)	OD	GP	GA	Comments
							food aid to protest Bangladesh trade with Cuba (Sobhan).
1974							
Jan	92	7	12	1	3	2	Further protests and strikes (Rahman and Hasan: Lifschultz, 1979). Meetings and rallies banned in Dhaka. Rice rations stopped for 6 months (*DI*). Reports of smuggling and hoarding (*DI*).
Feb	99	1	17	0	1	4	Procurement stopped (24 Feb). Failure is blamed on smuggling (*DI*), and on official corruption (Alamgir, 1980). Security police given further powers (Rahman and Hasan).
Mar	117	3	24	1	1	1	Good prospects for boro harvest. Minister of Food asserts that government's stock is sufficient. Hoarding Claimed (*DI*). Further demonstrations and confrontations with security police lead to Minto Road Massacre: 30 to 50 dead and wounded (Lifschultz, 1979; Rahman and Hasan). Widespread starvation begins in Rangpur (Alamgir, 1980).
April	137	13	37	14	1	4	Further claims by traders and government that rice stocks are sufficient. Rice wholesalers encouraged to sell directly to consumers. Flash floods in Sylhet. Rangpur leaders demand grain from government. Hoarding reported (*DI*). Claims that 'man-made famine' is in the offing (*DI*). Armed forces dispatched to stop smuggling and hoarding of foodgrains. Opposition parties form United Front with charter of demands (Maniruzzaman). Strikes and political gatherings forbidden for 3 months.
May	136	8	45	11	1	1	Irregular ration supplies (*BO*).

Table 3A. continued

P	CD (BO)	CD (DI)	OD	GP	GA	Comments
						Ration prices increased. Scandal: Army called off anti-smuggling operation after apprehending high ranking district officials belonging to the Awami League (Lifschultz, 1979; Maniruzzaman). Increased licensing and cordoning to help in boro procurement said to adversely affect supply of rice in Dhaka (*DI*).
June 139	19	37	12	1	2	Reports of starvation are denied by Food Minister (*BO*). Rice arrivals in Dhaka reported to be unusually low (*BO*). Government claims that stocks are adequate and that more will be imported (*BO*). Severe flooding toward end of month. Foreign reserves are reported to be low and Bangladesh importers are denied credit (Lifschultz, 1974*d*; Rahman and Hasan). Leaders of United Front arrested (29 June).
July 142	43	61	9	3	4	Further flooding damages aus and aman crops. Low supply of rice in markets (*DI*). Cholera and diarrhoea outbreaks. Nine ministers resign. Capital punishment for 'anti-social activities' is added to the Constitution. Further newspaper censoring and control by government (Maniruzzaman).
Aug 171	49	50	21	7	7	Damage to aman seedlings. Ten more ministers removed. Epidemics and lack of drinking water. Flood relief camps opened in Dhaka. Army on flood alert. Emergency seed procurement established.
Sept 213	16	24	6	5	3	Further flooding. Famine reports. Influx of people into Dhaka. Flood relief camps closed; official reason: flood waters have sufficiently

Table 3A. continued

P	CD (BO)	CD (DI)	OD	GP	GA	Comments
						receded, unofficial: to avoid too many incoming villagers and threat of food riots (Lifschultz 1974c). Mujib announces that 'Almost famine condition is prevailing' (24 Sept, BO). 4300 gruel kitchens to be opened. Government makes emergency appeal for foodgrain to international agencies (DI). Mass rally in Dhaka protests high prices (BO). Bloody conflicts between Awami League and opposition. US repeats threats to stop all food aid unless Bangladesh ends its jute trade with Cuba (McHenry and Bird). Mujib on aid seeking trip to Washington.
Oct	252 10	26	13	3	8	Gruel kitchens opening. Law is passed prohibiting traders from retaining rice over 20 days. Two tornadoes and one cyclone. Food minister places the food gap at 2.3 million tons. Quota of rationed rice and sugar reduced. Widespread complaints about gruel kitchen management (Alamgir, 1980). Dhaka charity group disposing of 20 abandoned bodies a day (Eusuf and Currey). Many famine reports. Finance Minister resigns in protest.
Nov	214 10	25	4	2	5	Compulsory procurement of aman crop announced. Minister for Food concedes that '. . . around 27,500 persons have died prematurely during the previous months' (DI). Nation wide strike observed (26 Nov, Maniruzzaman). Gruel kitchens closed.
Dec	189 4	20	2	2	1	At end of month, Mujib declares a State of Emergency.

Table 3A. continued

	P	CD (BO)	CD (DI)	OD	GP	GA	Comments
1975							
Jan	207	3	15	0	2	2	Public meetings banned. Arrests. Ration card scandal: Officials arrested (*BO*). Mujib declares new constitution and presidential system with himself as President amidst protests.
Feb	240	2	16	2	3	9	Rice traders arrested for high prices in Barisal (*BO*). Cordoning system partially lifted as procurement effort continues (*BO*). Ration rice quota to be raised (1 Mar). Ration cards confiscated from all Dhaka slum dwellers (McHenry and Bird). Mujib declares a one party state.
Mar	264	2	19	2	4	2	Limits on private stocks are relaxed. Cordoning is lifted. Mujib launches 'second revolution.'
April	245	11	32	9	7	2	Compulsory boro procurement is introduced. Movement across the border temporarily suspended. Ration rice quota to be raised again.
May	197	9	33	10	3	1	Taka devalued.
June	204	2	26	9	2	4	All but a few newspapers are banned and all remaining ones to be under government management. Army and Navy deployed to aid movement of goods.
July	205	18	38	11	–	–	Flooding during second half of month.
Aug	172	5	27	5	–	–	Assassination of Mujib (15 Aug). Khondakar Mushtaque Ahmed becomes President. The supply of rice is reported abundant and prices to be declining. Martial law regulations and clampdown on corruption. All political parties are banned.

Note: Price is retail, coarse quality in Taka per maund. Sources are only noted under 'Comments' if it is believed that the comment might be contentious. The abbreviations are *BO* (*The Bangladesh Observer*), and *DI* (*Daily Ittefaq*).

Appendix 3.3

There is a very different alternative explanation that may be offered for the rice price instability in Bangladesh during this period, drawing on the observation that grain prices were also highly volatile in world markets. Thus, in spite of the insulating effects of the Bangladesh government's policies, the conditions in Bangladesh markets may have been due to the influence (albeit a slow and imprecise one) of conditions in world markets.

Is this plausible? In Chapter 4, I shall demonstrate how hypotheses about spatial market integration can be formulated as testable restrictions on a distributed lag model of the form:

$$\log P_{it} = \sum_{j=1}^{n} a_j \log P_{it-j} + \sum_{j=0}^{n} b_j \log P_{t-j}^{w} + \mathbf{X}_t \mathbf{c} + e_t$$

where P^w denotes (in this application) the world price, and $\mathbf{X}$ is a vector of other relevant variables affecting domestic markets. Thus, the hypothesis that the domestic markets were segmented from world markets is testable as the joint parameter restriction $b_0 = b_1 = \ldots = b_n = 0$.

Following this approach, and using US No. 2 'hard winter' wheat prices as the foreign prices, the following OLS estimate was obtained for the 36 months from July 1972 to June 1975:

$$\log P = 1.2 \log P_{-1} - 0.631 \log P_{-2} + 0.231 \log P_{-3} + 0.52 \times 10^{-2} t$$
$$\quad (6.9) \qquad\quad (2.1) \qquad\qquad (1.1) \qquad\qquad\quad (0.41)$$

$$-0.12 H - 0.12 \times 10^{-2} \log P^w - 0.05 \log P^w_{-1}$$
$$\quad (2.3) \qquad (0.00) \qquad\qquad\qquad (0.17)$$

$$+0.21 \log P^w_{-2} - 0.13 \log P^w_{-3}$$
$$\quad (0.67) \qquad\qquad (0.64)$$

$$R^2 = 0.97; \text{SEE} = 0.085; Q(7) = 2.1$$

The joint market segmentation restriction performs very well; an F-test of the hypothesis gives $F(4,23) = 0.18$. The model was also estimated for $n = 6$, with segmentation continuing to perform well ($F(7,13) = 0.36$).

It appears, then, that domestic markets in Bangladesh were effectively segmented from world markets during this period. The domestic price instability is not attributable to conditions in foreign markets.

Appendix 3.4

This appendix examines price instability in the post-famine period. Chapter 2 demonstrated that the existence of informational inefficiency need not mean that prices are less stable than one would expect in a competitive equilibrium with rational expectations. As this appendix will show, the effect of biased expectations on the variability of prices will partly depend on the correlation between future price forecasting errors and current prices. If the correlation is negative then biased expectations can help stabilize prices. For example, the effect on storage decisions of a tendency to overestimate future prices when current prices are low, will (as long as the forecasting error is not too large) have a stabilizing influence on the spread of prices over time.

The effect of price forecasting errors on price variability will also depend on properties of the dynamic process generating observed prices. To see how, write the model outlined in Section 3.2 in the following simplified form:

$$\log P_t = \beta_0 + \beta_1 \log P_{t-1} + \beta_2 \log P_{t+1}^e + \mu_t \qquad (3A.1)$$

where μ_t is now a composite of the various non-price effects on the market; clearly, one can set $\mu = 0$ by appropriate choice of β_0. As before, let e_t denote the error in forecasting log price (equation 3.6). Then equation 3A.1 can also be written in the equivalent form:

$$\log P_t = b_0 + b_1 \log P_{t-1} + b_2 \log P_{t-2} + \varepsilon_t \qquad (3A.2)$$

where

$$b_0 = -\beta_0/\beta_2$$
$$b_1 = 1/\beta_2$$
$$b_2 = -\beta_1/\beta_2$$
$$\varepsilon_t = -e_t - \mu_{t-1}$$

This second-order autoregressive process will be stationary if $b_1 + b_2 < 1$, $b_2 - b_1 < 1$ and $|b_2| < 1$. When these conditions hold, it can be shown that:[20]

$$\mathrm{var}(\log P) = k\mathrm{var}(\varepsilon) \qquad (3A.3)$$

where

$$k = \frac{1 - b_2}{(1 + b_2)((1 - b_2)^2 - b_1^2)}$$

And so the variance of log price is related to the precision in price forecasting and the non-price stochastic effects according to:

$$\text{var}(\log P) = k(\text{var}(e) + 2\text{cov}(e, \mu_{-1}) + \text{var}(\mu))$$

For example, if price formation is nearly a random walk, so that b_2 is close to zero while b_1 is close to unity, then k will be large. And so even small imprecision in forecasting future prices may induce a large variance in realized prices.

Now consider the variance of log price when expectations are informationally unbiased. In this case, e will be orthogonal to μ_{-1} (since μ_{t-1} is contained in the time t information set). Assuming that the underlying parameters relating to storage costs, the preferences of storage agents, and the aggregate demand function are constant, it follows that

$$\text{var}(\log P^*) = k(\text{var}(e^*) + \text{var}(\mu))$$

where P^* and e^* denote prices and forecasting errors in a rational expectations equilibrium. Thus the difference between the variance of observed log prices and the variance of the log prices implied by informational efficiency is:

$$\text{var}(\log P) - \text{var}(\log P^*) = k(\text{var}(e) - \text{var}(e^*)) + 2\text{cov}(e, \mu_{-1})$$

The first term on the RHS must be non-negative, since informationally unbiased forecasts will minimize the variance of *ex-post* forecasting errors given *ex-ante* information for all possible expectations.

Thus, observed prices will be less stable than those implied by unbiased expectations if future price forecasting errors are positively correlated with μ. Also $\text{cov}(e, \mu_{-1}) = \text{cov}(e, \log P_{-1})$ since $E\mu = 0$. Thus a positive correlation between forecasting errors and known prices implies greater price instability than one would expect in the rational expectations equilibrium.

Previous sections have discussed the possible correlation between e and $\log P_{-1}$ in Bangladesh rice markets. Chapter 6 will also present more direct evidence on this question, indicating that the correlation is generally non-negative for a sample of Bangladesh rice traders. It follows that the pattern of forecasting biases is price de-stabilizing.

It is of interest to look more closely at the way in which price forecasting imprecision is translated into market price variability. This requires estimation of the parameter k. The results of Section 3.4 are of little use for this task since equation 3.1 has been estimated over a period in which the price formation process is non-stationary. For example, the first regression in Table 3.1 implies that $b_1 = 1.89$ and $b_2 = -0.85$ which (narrowly) violate the stationarity conditions for equation 3A.2. This is not surprising; the model has been intentionally estimated during a period of highly unstable prices in which it is hard to detect (finite) long-run tendencies.

The picture becomes a good deal clearer if the time period is extended. For this purpose, estimation must be done on a restricted data set; further newspaper monitoring was not feasible. Estimating equation 3A.2 by OLS over the 60 month 'post-famine' period January 1975 to December 1979, and including a time trend and dummy variable for the aman harvest, I obtained:

$$\log P = 0.30 + 1.13 \log P_{-1} - 0.20 \log P_{-2} - 0.071H + 0.92 \times 10^{-3}t$$
$$\quad (18) \quad (8.7) \quad\quad (5.7) \quad\quad (2.7) \quad\quad (1.7)$$

$$R^2 = 0.94; \text{ SEE} = 0.07; \; Q(13) = 8.5 \quad\quad (3.35)$$

The model's fit is satisfactory and the (15 month) residual correlogram comfortably passes the Box–Pierce Q test for randomness at the five per cent level.[21] The stationarity conditions are now satisfied, although $b_1 + b_2$ is still quite close to unity; a t-test of the hypothesis $b_1 + b_2 = 1$ gives $t = -2.0$, although this test is likely to be biased in favour of non-stationarity (Nankervis and Savin, 1985, have shown recently that this is so for an AR1 process).

This result indicates a high value of $k = 9.2$. Thus, price forecasting imprecision is magnified considerably in observed prices; a ten per cent increase in the variance of forecasting errors can be expected to result in about a 90 per cent increase in the variance of realized market prices. Clearly, under these conditions, even small departures from rational expectations can induce considerable price instability.

Notes

1. See Khan (1977), Alamgir (1978, 1980), Ahmed (1979), de Vylder (1982), Osmani (1982), and Hassan and Ahmad (1984). The latter paper reports a recent nutrition survey indicating further deterioration since 1974. This trend is usually attributed to a long period of agricultural stagnation and high population growth; on the causes of the former, see Januzzi and Peach (1980), de Vylder (1982), and Boyce (1986). The seasonal variability of prices within each year also tended to increase over the ten years or so prior to 1974 (Ahmed, 1979). Following the arguments of Chapter 2, this would also have contributed to a decline in survival chances.

2. For example see Baishya (1974), Hartmann and Boyce (1979), BRAC (1979), Sobhan (1980), Rashid (1980), Sen (1981*a,b*) Greenough (1982), Arnold (1984).

3. Aman rice rarely arrives in markets in any substantial quantity before the end of November and the crop was delayed during 1974. Rice traders I interviewed in Bangladesh (as part of the survey reported in Chapter 6) confirmed this, and also told me that falling prices before a harvest were common.

4. I do not know of any previous work using this approach. The usual method is to compare seasonal price differentials with storage costs, assuming that profits indicate market inefficiency; see Farruk (1972) and Alamgir (1980) for attempts to apply this method to Bangladesh rice price data. Spatial price differentials have also been used to test market performance, although the received method using bivariate correlations is fraught with inferential dangers; Chapter 4 offers an alternative approach and applies it to Bangladesh.

5. For recent examples see Newbery and Stiglitz (1981, 1982*a*) and Wright and Williams (1982).

6. The seminal contribution here is Working (1949*a*); for recent evidence see Gray and Peck (1981).

7. Although errors in approximating $\Delta P/P$ by $\Delta \log P$ are large for large $|\Delta P|$, very good piece-wise log linear corrections are possible over the range of price differences found in the present data. However, the main results are unaffected by using the simpler approximation and so I have omitted discussion.

8. For example, it is implied by the condition that static expectations, while not generally rational, should at least be consistent with stationarity in the autoregressive process of actual prices. (Noting that $\log P^e = \log P_{-1}$ implies that $\log P = (1 - \gamma_2)\log P_{-1} - \gamma_1 Z_{-1} - \varepsilon_2$).

9. For other examples, see Bowden (1978), Domberger (1979).

10. There is an important but subtle difference between McCallum's (1976) 'partly rational expectations' model and the present one.

McCallum estimates a model in the form: $P = \beta_1 P_{-1} + \beta_2 P^e_{+1} + \text{error}$ (or in log form as appropriate), and only variables from the assumed current information set should be used for predicting P_{+1} as the instrument for P^e_{+1}. The present method estimates a new equation which is derived from the one above under an *additional* assumption about the determinants of $e = P^e - P$. By McCallum's method one should not use I.V.'s correlated with e_{+1}; by my method one should not use I.V.'s correlated with the error term in the behavioural equation for forecasting errors. If one does, then estimates of β_2 will be inconsistent. As a precaution against this, all I.V.'s which were significant in an OLS regression of $\log P_{+1}$ were tested as possible additions to equation 3.1.

11. For further discussion see Ahmed (1979). Appendix 3.3 tests for international market integration. Restricted trade policies could well account for some of the significant urban–rural rice price differentials during this period, particularly between Dhaka and its rural hinterland; see Chapter 4 for further discussion. The price model was also estimated using a national price series excluding Dhaka but this made negligible difference to the results.

12. See Pitt's (1983) estimates of the rice demand cross-price effects with other foodgrains.

13. The Box–Pierce Q statistic for the correlogram in Table 3.2 is 1.0, distributed as chi-square with four degrees of freedom; for discussion of this test and the Breusch–Pagan LM test reported in Table 3.2 see Harvey (1981).

14. The following Poisson regression was used to construct an estimate of CD:

$$CD = 5.0 + 0.30 CD_{-1} + 0.24 OD_{-1} + 16D$$
$$ (5.7) \quad (3.3) \phantom{CD_{-1}} (1.8) \phantom{+ 0.24 OD_{-1}} (6.0)$$

$$-2L_{max} = 100; \text{ Chi-square (3)} = 139$$

where D is a seasonal dummy variable for the flood vulnerable months of July and August. (Section 3.6 discusses the use of Poisson regression in this setting).

15. Similarly, excessive storage can be due to existence of a government imposed price ceiling (Wright and Williams, 1984), although no such ceiling existed in Bangladesh at this time.

16. The failure of the 1973–4 winter procurement was widely reported in the Bangladesh newspapers in December and January. The curtailment of US aid early in 1974 on foreign policy grounds and various other delays to imports are thought to have been well known to foodgrain merchants (Sobhan, 1980); on the US aid issue see McHenry and Bird (1977).

17. Lifschultz (1974a), Davidson (1974), Maniruzzaman (1975), Hartman and Boyce (1979, 1983).
18. For example, see Lele (1971), Farruk (1972), Jones (1972), Alexander (1986).
19. A Poisson regression of Crop Damage reports in *Daily Ittefaq* (*DI*) against those in *The Bangladesh Observer* gave the following result (*t*-ratios in parentheses):

$$DI = 19 + 0.85BO \quad -2L_{max} = 61$$
$$(13) \quad (7.9)$$

Comparing this to the hypothesis of no relationship one obtains chi-square (1) = 72 which is highly significant. Nor did the introduction of heavy censorship in early August 1974 alter this relationship significantly; neither intercept nor slope dummies for post-July 1974 had coefficients exceeding their standard errors. (The use of Poisson regression with these data is discussed in Section 3.6 of this chapter).
20. Re-writing equation 3A.2 in mean deviation form and defining $p := \log(P/\bar{P})$ it follows that, on taking expectations:

$$E(p^2) = b_1 E(pp_{-1}) + b_2 E(pp_{-2}) + \text{var}(\varepsilon)$$

(Note that the LHS is the variance of log price and the first and second terms on the RHS are its first and second order autocovariances). Similarly (on multiplying equation 3A.2 by p_{-1} and p_{-2} alternatively and taking expectations):

$$E(pp_{-2}) = b_1 E(p^2)/(1-b_2)$$
$$E(pp_{-2}) = b_1 E(pp_{-1}) + b_2 E(p^2)$$

The following result can then be obtained by solving the last three equations for $E(p^2)$.
21. This ceases to be true if the famine period is included in the estimation; for the 84 months from January 1973 to December 1979 one obtains:

$$\log P = 0.33 + 1.26\log P_{-1} - 0.33\log P_{-2} - 0.08H + 0.28 \times 10^{-3}t$$
$$(2.5) \quad (13) \qquad (11) \qquad \qquad (3.5) \qquad (0.75)$$

$$R^2 = 0.95; \text{ SEE} = 0.07; Q(13) = 27$$

Clearly the famine period is adding considerable serially dependent noise to the model. The earlier results of this chapter can be interpreted as a model of the extra noise in the price formation process associated with the famine.

4

Market Integration during the Famine

4.1 Introduction

It is well-known that, under regularly assumed restrictions on preferences and technologies, a competitive equilibrium for a complete set of markets will exist and be efficient in the Paretian sense. In general this will also hold for the *spatial* competitive equilibrium of an economy consisting of a set of regions amongst which trade occurs at fixed transport costs (Takayama and Judge, 1971). Such an equilibrium will have the property that, if trade takes place at all between any two regions, then price in the importing region equals price in the exporting region, plus the unit transport cost incurred by moving between the two. If this holds then the markets can be said to be spatially integrated.

Much research has gone into testing spatial market integration in agriculture.[1] This is often viewed as a way of determining market efficiency. However, market integration is by no means sufficient for the Pareto optimality of a competitive equilibrium, and so the conclusion that markets are well integrated does not, of itself, imply an efficient allocation (see, for example, Newbery and Stiglitz, 1981, 1984). Nonetheless, one can be interested in testing empirically for spatial market integration, without wishing to rest the case for or against Pareto optimality on the outcome. Measurement of market integration can be viewed as basic data for an understanding of how specific markets work.

In the present setting, a study of the dynamics of market integration should throw some light on one of the oldest questions concerning famines in market economies: how long can an initially localized scarcity be expected to persist? Policies of non-intervention with markets during famines have often been advocated or defended along the following lines: given that the necessary transport infrastructure exists, the unaided response of grain traders to the induced spatial price differentials will eliminate quickly any localized scarcity. For example, this assumption was a cornerstone of the Indian government's famine relief policy during much of the nineteenth and early twentieth centuries (Bhatia, 1967; Ambirajan, 1978). Against this view, it has often been argued that markets will be too slow to respond; for example, Ambirajan reports that during the severe famine of the mid-1870's, the local government in Madras rebelled against the government of India's policy, arguing that '. . . if time were given to the market, the necessary grain would eventually come, but time was what could not be given' (Ambirajan, 1978, 95).[2] Since Independence, governments of India and other countries in the sub-continent have tended to adopt highly interventionist policies concerning foodgrain markets (see, for example, Bhatia, 1967, ch. 12; George, 1984). An empirical assessment of the speed of market adjustment to spatial price differentials may help resolve this long standing debate.

Though much maligned, static price correlations remain the most common measure of spatial market integration in agriculture.[3] By this method, bivariate correlation or regression coefficients are estimated between the time series of spot prices for an otherwise identical good or bundle of goods at different market locations.[4] There are a number of inferential dangers in bivariate modelling of this sort. The following example expands on an important point made elsewhere in the literature on market performance in agriculture (Blyn, 1973; Harriss, 1979). Suppose that trade is infinitely costly between two market locations, but that the time series of prices at the two locations are synchronously, identically, and linearly affected by another variable. Possible examples include the price of a related third good traded in a common market, or a shared dynamic seasonal structure in production. Then one can readily express price in one market as a linear function of price in the other market, with slope unity, even though the markets are segmented. Of course, stochastic elements or omitted variables in the true models would yield imprecision in a test equation based on the static bivariate model. But it remains that, under these conditions, the received method fails hopelessly as a test for market integration. The likelihood of serial dependence in the residuals obtained from a static model calibrated to non-stationary time series, also leads one to be suspicious of the conclusions drawn from this method (Granger and Newbold, 1974).

However, with the same data, the static bivariate method can be extended readily into a dynamic model of spatial price differentials. By permitting each local price series to have its own dynamic structure (and allowing for any correlated local seasonality or other characteristics), as well as an inter-linkage with other local markets, the main inferential dangers of the simpler bivariate model can be avoided.[5] Most importantly, the alternative hypotheses of 'market integration' and 'market segmentation' can then be encompassed within a more general model and so tested as restricted forms.

A dynamic model also has the advantage that one can distinguish between the concepts of instantaneous market integration, and the less restrictive idea of integration as a long-run target of the short-run dynamic adjustment process. This distinction seems important. In many settings it will be implausible that trade adjusts instantaneously to spatial price differentials, and so one would be reluctant to accept short-run market integration as an equilibrium concept. But, given enough time, the short-run adjustments might exhibit a pattern which converges to such an equilibrium. If short-run integration is rejected, then it would be nice to know if there is any long-run tendency toward market integration. By permitting the investigator to answer this new question, a dynamic model can extract more information about markets from the same data used by the static model.

This chapter offers an approach to testing agricultural market integration along these lines and illustrates it using data on the interregional price differentials for rice in Bangladesh during the turbulent post-Independence period, 1972–75. The period of analysis has been chosen to include the substantial regional price shocks which occurred during the 1974 famine (Seaman and Holt, 1980; Alamgir, 1980; Sen, 1981a). Section 2 outlines a reasonably general dynamic model of spatial market structure, which Section 3 applies to the Bangladesh data. Section 4 discusses the results.

4.2 A Dynamic Model of Spatial Market Structure

The specification of an econometric model of spatial price differentials will depend, in part, on assumptions about spatial market structure. Here I shall assume that there exists a group of local (rural) markets and a single central (urban) market. While there may be some trade amongst the local markets, it is trade with the central market which dominates local price formation. Depending on the number of local markets and their sizes, one can also posit that the central market price is influenced by various local prices.

Thus, the static pattern of price formation amongst N markets, where market 1 is the central market, may be summarized by a model of the form

$$P_1 = f_1(P_2, P_3, \ldots, P_N, \mathbf{X}_1) \tag{4.1}$$

$$P_i = f_i(P_1, \mathbf{X}_i) \ (i = 2, \ldots, N) \tag{4.2}$$

where $\mathbf{X}_i$ $(i = 1, \ldots, N)$ is a vector of other influences on local markets. The functions f_i $(i = 1, \ldots, N)$ can be thought of as solutions of the appropriate conditions for market equilibrium, taking account of the main spatial choices and the costs of adjustment facing traders when deciding where to sell. The derivation of these functions does not seem to pose any new theoretical problems or insights, and so I shall take them as given.

At first sight, this model only seems well suited to a simple 'radial' configuration of markets, in which each local market is directly linked with the central market. In most applications (including Bangladesh) a more plausible configuration is one in which some local markets only trade with the central market *via* other markets. However, provided one is willing to forgo identification of at least some of the non-radial linkages, the radial model given by equations 4.1 and 4.2 can often provide a useful characterization of more complex market structures. By subsuming linkages between intermediate local markets, an (implicit) binary relation can be obtained between each local market and the central market, and so the radial model is preserved.

Clearly this approach has its limitations. Since spatial price differentials become more aggregated, it produces inferential difficulties when investigating the linkage location of any revealed impediment to trade. Indeed, if there is a large number of local market linkages, then (depending on what other local non-price variables are relevant) it may become impossible to identify even the indirect radial linkage. As always the merits of the model need to be judged in its specific applications.

Since the main aim in estimating the model is to test alternative hypotheses to do with market integration, its econometric specification should not prejudice the outcome. This is most easily assured if the alternative hypotheses can be nested within a more general model, and so tested as restricted forms. For estimation, it is also convenient to assume that the functions f_i ($i = 1, \ldots, N$) can be given a linear representation by introducing an appropriate stochastic term.

The econometric version of equations 4.1 and 4.2 should also embody a suitable dynamic structure; as is well known, dynamic effects can arise from a number of conditions in the underlying behavioural relations, including expectations formation and adjustment costs (for a survey of the possibilities see Hendry, Pagan, and Sargan, 1984).

Combining these considerations, the following econometric model of a T period series of prices for N regions is assumed:

$$P_{1t} = \sum_{j=1}^{n} a_{ij} P_{1t-j} + \sum_{k=2}^{N} \sum_{j=0}^{n} b_{1j}^{k} P_{kt-j} + \mathbf{X}_{1t}\mathbf{c}_1 + e_{1t} \qquad (4.3)$$

$$P_{it} = \sum_{j=1}^{n} a_{ij} P_{it-j} + \sum_{j=0}^{n} b_{1j} P_{1t-j} + \mathbf{X}_{it}\mathbf{c}_i + e_{it} \ (i = 2, \ldots N) \ (4.4)$$

where the es are appropriate error processes, and the as, bs, and cs are fixed.

A wide range of possible hypotheses about inter regional trade can be formulated and tested as parameter restrictions on equations 4.3 and 4.4. In discussing these, I shall concentrate on equation 4.4 since, in many applications, equation 4.3 will be underidentified. (I shall return to this point later.)

In terms of the parameters of equation 4.4, the following hypotheses will usually be testable:

1. *Market segmentation*: Central market prices do not influence prices in the ith local market if

$$b_{ij} = 0 \ (j = 0, \ldots, n) \qquad (4.5)$$

in which case the data would be better described by the corresponding restricted form of equation 4.4.

2. *Short-run market integration*. A price increase in the central market will be immediately passed on in the ith market price if

$$b_{io} = 1 \qquad (4.6)$$

Of course there will also be lagged effects on future prices unless, in addition to equation 4.6:

$$a_{ij} = b_{ij} = 0 \quad (j = 1, \ldots, n) \tag{4.7}$$

If both equations 4.6 and 4.7 are accepted as parameter restrictions, then one can say that market i is integrated with the central market within one time period. A weaker form of market integration will also be tested in which the lagged effects need only vanish on average:

$$\sum_{j=1}^{n} a_{ij} + b_{ij} = 0 \tag{4.8}$$

3. *Long-run market integration.* A 'long-run equilibrium' is one in which market prices are constant over time, undisturbed by any local stochastic effects. So consider the form that equation 4.4 takes when $P_{it} = P_i^*$, $P_{1t} = P_1^*$ and $e_{it} = 0$ for all t; then

$$P_i^* = \frac{P_1^* \sum_{j=0}^{n} b_{ij} + \mathbf{X}_{it} \mathbf{c}_i}{1 - \sum_{j=1}^{n} a_{ij}} \tag{4.9}$$

It can be seen that market integration now requires that:

$$\sum_{j=1}^{n} a_{ij} + \sum_{j=0}^{n} b_{ij} = 1 \tag{4.10}$$

If this parameter restriction is accepted then the short-run process of price adjustment described by the model is consistent with an equilibrium in which a unit increase in central price is passed on fully in local prices. Notice that acceptance of the short-run restrictions implies long-run market integration but that the reverse is not true.

If the long-run market integration restriction is accepted, then more efficient estimates of the remaining parameters and more powerful statistical tests will be possible if the model is re-estimated with long-run integration imposed. For example, under long-run integration, equation 4.4 can be written in the following equivalent form:

$$\Delta P_{it} = (a_{i1} - 1)(P_{it-1} - P_{1t-1}) + \sum_{j=2}^{n} a_{ij}(P_{it-j} - P_{1t-j}) + b_{io}\Delta P_{1t}$$

$$+ \sum_{j=1}^{n-1} (b_{io} - 1 + \sum_{k=1}^{j} a_{ik} + b_{ik})\Delta P_{1t-j} + \mathbf{X}_{it}\mathbf{c}_i + e_{it} \qquad (4.11)$$

This is a member of the class of 'error correlation models' discussed by Hendry and Richard (1983) and Hendry, Pagan, and Sargan (1984). By interpretation, changes in local prices are attributed to changes in central prices *and* past spatial price differentials; the latter variables allow for the possibility that the markets are not observed in an integrated equilibrium at a given point in time, and so there is feedback from prior disequilibria.[6]

There are a number of possible variations around these three main hypotheses, particularly to do with the non-price influences on each local market. The existence of significant localized market characteristics also indicates that arbitrage is imperfect in eliminating price differentials. Thus, stronger integration conditions can be formulated by adding $\mathbf{c} = 0$ to the above restrictions. I shall return to this point in discussing the results for Bangladesh.

One problem that may arise when applying the above approach is multicollinearity amongst the regressors of the unrestricted model given by equation 4.4. The inferential difficulties that can arise are well known; a high standard error on, for example, the coefficient for central market price may be due to its high correlation with lagged local prices, rather than weak market integration. However, such collinearity is a poor reason for adopting a more restrictive model specification. The bias induced by omitting relevant variables is well known. Also, the removal of such variables from a model can actually worsen the precision in estimation of the remaining regressors, even when the two sets of variables are highly (albeit imperfectly) correlated (Davidson *et al.* (1978) give an example). Rather than impose parameter restrictions to reduce collinearity, a better approach in this setting is to test first for long-run integration; since this restriction involves all of the price variables, a good deal of the collinearity danger is avoided (possible correlations with $\mathbf{X}_i$ remain). If long-run integration is accepted, then it should be imposed on the model with subsequent tests based on a restricted form such as equation 4.11, for which the collinearity problem is likely to be a good deal less severe. If long-run integration is rejected then this avenue is best closed off, and so one should apply extra caution in rejecting the short-run integration conditions.

4.3 Spatial Price Differentials in Bangladesh

In this section the general approach outlined above will be applied to monthly district-level data on rice prices (coarse quality) for Bangladesh in the post-Independence period, as monitored by the Bangladesh Directorate of Agricultural Marketing. A 36-month series was used, from July 1972 to June 1975. This period was chosen for its unusual price turbulence; there were numerous localized scarcities (particularly during the famine year 1974) and disturbances to trade and communications (see Chapter 3, Table 3A). Certainly this should be a hard (but important) test for the market integration restrictions.

The demand for rice in Dhaka, the capital and (by far) the largest city, would appear to be the dominant influence on inter-district rice trade in Bangladesh. And this is reflected in the country's heavily monocentric transport system. Aside from the old transport linkages to Calcutta in West Bengal (the colonial capital of Bengal prior to Partition in 1947), the main road, rail, and water routes are focused on Dhaka. The radial model seems well suited to this setting.

It was decided to concentrate on Dhaka's trade linkages with the main surplus districts of its rural hinterland: Mymensingh, Bogra, Rangpur, Dinajpur, and Sylhet. During 1974 these five contiguous districts of northern Bangladesh had the five highest levels of foodgrain production *per capita* among the 19 districts of Bangladesh, while the neighbouring district of Dhaka had one of the lowest (rank 16).[7] Table 4.1 gives summary data for these districts. Even taking first differences, the correlation coefficients between Dhaka and local prices are quite high and reasonably significant. The average price differentials also accord roughly with the distances to Dhaka, although their standard deviations are very high indeed. It is hard to believe that transport costs could vary so much. This alone leads one to doubt the existence of reasonably stable price differentials determined by transport costs, and so the picture given by the correlation coefficients may well be spurious.

Table 4.1 *Summary data for main Bangladesh surplus districts 1972–5*

	District				
	Mymensingh	Bogra	Rangpur	Dinajpur	Sylhet
Distance to Dhaka	120	150	200	250	200
Mean monthly price differential	12	20	19	22	14
Standard deviation of price differential	20	32	44	39	22
Simple correlation of price with Dhaka	0.97	0.93	0.81	0.87	0.96
Correlation of first differences	0.79	0.57	0.43	0.43	0.48

Note: Distances in road miles, price differentials (Dhaka–Mymensingh etc.) in Taka per maund, $n = 36$.

Three variables were selected as likely non-price influences on local markets, aiming to capture the seasonality in rice production, any localized effects of the 1974 famine, and any local time trend. The main 'aman' harvest is from mid-November to early January, and seems to be quite adequately described by a single dummy variable for November and December. It is widely agreed that the worst months of the 1974 famine were August, September, and October; a single dummy variable was included for these months.

As has been noted, there will often be difficulties in identification of the parameters of equation 4.3. But equation 4.4 will not generally pose such problems. The simultaneity in the system can easily be dealt with using an appropriate instrumental variables estimator, such as the least squares estimate of equation 4.4, obtained by replacing P_{1t} by its predicted values from the reduced form equation obtained by using equation 4.4 to eliminate P_{jt} ($j = 2, \ldots, N$) from equation 4.3. This is the method of estimation used here. Reduced form estimates of P_{1t} were obtained from a regression of this variable against its own lagged values, the lagged values of prices in all other districts, and the seasonality, famine, and time trend variables. All seventeen districts of Bangladesh in the data set were used, although, because of the number of degrees of freedom needed, only one month lags were included.

The way transport charges are levied offers a guide to appropriate model specification in this setting. During the winter of

1983/4, I asked a number of wholesale rice merchants at Badamtali in Dhaka how the rice was transported and how much it cost to do so. I was told that by the main modes of rice freight transport (road and ferry), the transport cost for any trip largely depends on the number of trucks involved. And so, when comparing given markets, transport cost can be treated as fixed per unit quantity, rather than an *ad valorem* charge.[8] Thus, an equilibrium in which price differentials depend solely on transport costs would fix the unit price difference rather than, say, the percentage (log) difference. For the econometric model to be at least consistent with the possibility of such an equilibrium under linear parameter restrictions, it should itself be linear in nominal prices.

Any lagged effects in the model are likely to arise from sluggishness in price adjustment, delays in transportation, and expectations formation under price uncertainty. On a priori grounds, maximum lags greater than six months due to these causes seem highly implausible, and also strain the data in terms of degrees of freedom.

The unrestricted model (equation 4.4) was estimated for $n = 6$ assuming an AR1 error. This gave an excellent overall fit and a

Table 4.2 *Tests for the spatial integration of Bangladesh rice markets*

Hypothesis	District				
	Mymensingh	Bogra	Rangpur	Dinajpur	Sylhet
1. Market segmentation	18	7.0	14	13	16
2. Short-run integration	60 (52)	56	236	63	15 (12)
3. Short-run integration (weak form)	7.1	33	99	25	6.0*
4. Long-run integration	5.4*	16	184	32	9.1*
5. No local seasonality	13	21	9.5	12	0.50*
6. No local famine	11	23	117	31	16
7. No local time trend	2.3*	20	92	0.45*	8.4*

Note: The unrestricted model is equation 4.4 for $n = 6$ with an AR1 error. The table gives F-tests of the linear restrictions on this model implied by each hypothesis. 1, 2 and 3 are distributed as $F(7,13)$, $F(13,13)$ and $F(2,13)$ respectively while the rest are $F(1,13)$. All restrictions are rejected except * (at 0.01). The figures in parentheses in row 2 are the values of F when long-run integration is imposed.

reasonably flat residual correlogram over six lags for each district.[9] Residual variance *F*-tests were then applied to the three main restricted forms described in the previous section. The significance of the two postulated non-price influences was also examined. Whenever the long-run integration restriction was accepted, the model was re-estimated in the form of equation 4.11, and short-run integration was then re-tested.

The test results are given in Table 4.2.

4.4 Summary and Discussion

To summarize the results:

(i)   Market segmentation performs poorly as a restricted form of the general model for all districts.

(ii) At the other extreme, short-run market integration within one month cannot reasonably be accepted for any districts except Sylhet, and in this case only for the weaker form. For all other districts, residual variances are increased considerably by assuming short-run market integration, and so the assumption is hard to justify for these data.[10]

(iii) The parameter restriction implied by long-run market integration performs slightly better, but is still difficult to accept for three of the five districts. Short-run integration continues to be weak when long-run integration is imposed for the other two districts.

(iv) Local seasonality is in evidence for four districts. For each of these, winter harvest prices were significantly lower than Dhaka prices.

(v)   The price series for all districts exhibit quite strong localized effects of the 1974 famine. In all cases, local prices were (*ceteris paribus*) significantly *higher* than Dhaka prices. Indeed, for two districts (Mymensingh and Rangpur) the price differential actually changed direction briefly during the famine.

(vi) There is evidence of a local (positive) time trend for two districts, Bogra and Rangpur.

These results suggest some quite significant impediments to trade between Dhaka and its main rural supply areas, with the possible exception of the north-eastern district of Sylhet. The north-western trade corridor to Rangpur and Dinajpur seems highly restricted. While these are relatively remote areas, it is also notable how poorly the short-run market integration restrictions perform for the much closer district of Mymensingh.

It should be emphasized that such test results do not reveal the sources of spatial price differentials. In particular, it cannot be concluded that the markets are non-competitive; the Bangladesh government is also known to exert considerable influence on the private grain trade. For example, having first observed that Dhaka prices were not falling during the 1983–4 winter harvest period, I asked a number of the wholesale rice merchants at Badamtali why this was so. (This was done during a related survey reported in Chapter 6.) I was told that government officials and police were 'cordoning' rural markets to prevent trade with Dhaka. The government was thought to be doing this so that rice could be obtained at the government's procurement price, at that time below the Dhaka price, allowing for transport costs.[11]

Of course, government procurement is only one of the risks facing inter-district trade. Most years see quite heavy flooding in Bangladesh, and in 1974 it was very bad. This is certain to have added to transport costs. Also, it adds the risk of losing all or part of the trader's consignment *en route*, and, given that rice traders in Bangladesh are unlikely to be able to insure against such a loss, this will also reduce expected returns from trade at given prices.

Notes

1. For surveys see Harriss (1979) and Helmberger, Campbell, and Dobson (1981). Harriss includes critical discussion of a number of studies of foodgrain market integration in South Asia. Also see Rudra (1982, chapter 3).
2. The assumption that a localized shortfall will be reflected in spatial price differentials has also been questioned. For example, Sen (1981) has pointed to the possibility that the shortfall may be associated with a fall in incomes and, hence, demand (due to, for example, the effect of a drought on employment) and that this will mitigate the upward price response needed to encourage imports. Elsewhere I have tested this argument for famines in British India (Ravallion, 1986*b*).
3. Another, less common, method of testing for market integration is to calculate the spatial variance of prices and test for long-run convergence to zero or close to it (for an example, see Hurd, 1975). How-

ever, it can be readily shown that if prices at different markets are generated by identical but *independent* stationary autoregressive processes then they will asymptotically converge to zero variance. Thus, nothing can be inferred about the interlinkage of markets from the results of such tests.

4. A statistically significant coefficient is sometimes taken to imply market integration. Of course, if testing for a non-zero result, the null hypothesis being (invariably) rejected is market segmentation, i.e., the absence of any relationship between the two price series. One could easily reject this without accepting that the markets are integrated in the sense of having a reasonably stable price differential. This problem can be readily solved by changing to the appropriate null hypothesis for market integration, as some studies have done.

5. Spurious correlations can also be avoided by filtering the price series prior to calculating pairwise correlations; this can be done by testing for residual cross correlations amongst univariate ARIMA models of each price series (Haugh, 1976; Fase, 1981, applies the method to international share prices) or by similar Granger-causality methods (Uri and Rifkin, 1985). Rather than follow this approach here, I have preferred to formulate and test market integration conditions as nested hypotheses within a multivariate model of spatial market structure. As will be seen, this permits a much greater range of null hypotheses of economic interest. However, the pre-whitened bivariate correlation method is likely to be useful in some applications, particularly if one has no a priori basis for identifying a model of market structure.

6. See Salmon (1982) for a control theoretic interpretation of the error correction model. Also see Nickel (1985).

7. See Alamgir (1980, table 6.29) and Sen (1981a, table 9.7) for details. Also see Thomas (1980).

8. For example, transport cost from Rajshahi to Dhaka was reckoned to be Taka 22–25 per maund. This is the cost of hiring a truck for one day (about Taka 4000) divided by the quantity of rice carried (about 76 bags, at 2.25 maund per bag).

9. All residual correlograms comfortably passed the Box–Pierce test at the five per cent level (for further discussion of this test see Harvey, 1981).

10. Nor do collinearity problems appear to be the reason. One check for this is to examine the significance of individual coefficients in the unrestricted model. Over all unrestricted equations, 14 of the 30 coefficients on lagged 'own price' had absolute t-ratios over 3.0 while this was the case for 12 of the 35 coefficients on Dhaka price and its lagged values. Clearly, quite a high degree of resolution is possible in spite of multicollinearity.

11. This was later reported in the Bangla newspaper *Daily Ittefaq* (12 December 1983), although apparently the cordoning was not government policy at the time (*The Bangladesh Observer*, 28 December 1983). It had been policy in other years including 1974; for example, see the entry for May in Table 3A.

5
Agricultural Wages
before and after the Famine

5.1 Introduction

The food purchasing power of agricultural work fell dramatically in Bangladesh during the 1974 famine, and landless agricultural workers, part-time farmers and village artisans were the famine's main victims (Alamgir, 1980; Sen, 1981a). This is typical of other famines in the sub-continent and elsewhere.[1] Since the decline in the food wage rate coincided with a substantial increase in rice prices it is natural to look at conditions in rice markets for an explanation of the famine. Indeed, the results of Chapter 3 suggest that the rice markets could have performed much better in transfering rice from the relatively successful harvests prior to the famine to the lean months. However, one can also question the way labour markets performed. Certainly the nominal wage rate responded very little to the high rates of rice price inflation during the famine and most other prices remained relatively stable.[2] Was this because money wages in Bangladesh generally respond very little to changes in rice prices or was the famine associated with a disturbance to the equilibrating mechanisms of money wage adjustment?

The experience of rural labour markets in Bangladesh during the famine also provides an interesting test case for theories of agricultural wage determination. A good deal of recent literature has elaborated Leibenstein's (1957) views on the influence of individual food consumption levels on work effort in poor countries into a popular model now known as 'efficiency wage theory'.[3] A strong implication of this theory is that the food wage rate should be invariant to the price of food. This property is shared by the well-known models of Lewis (1954) and Fei and Ranis (1964) in which the real wage is fixed at a predetermined 'subsistence' level. Such theories appear to be at odds with Bangladesh's experience of considerable real wage flexibility during the 1974 famine. Against this view it may be argued that fixity of the real wage is a long-run property. This begs the further question: Was there also a fall in the long-run real wage rate following the events of 1974?

This chapter reports an econometric investigation of the dynamic adjustment of agricultural wages to rice prices in Bangladesh. Monthly data is used for the period mid-1972 to mid-1976, including the dramatic changes in rice prices which occurred during the second half of 1974. Figure 5.1 gives the natural logarithms of agricultural wages and the retail price of coarse quality rice, both in mean deviation form. (The data are discussed further in Section 5.3.) Casual inspection of Figure 5.1 suggests some tentative observations:

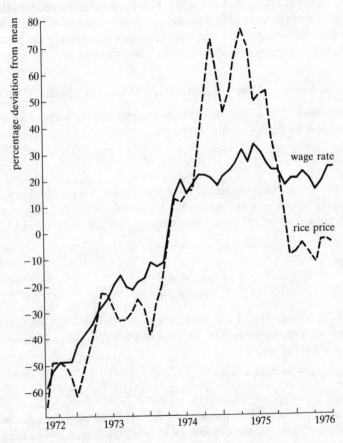

Fig. 5.1

(i) Up to mid-1974 wages roughly kept up with rice prices.
(ii) The relationship broke down considerably after this point.
(iii) The short-run response of wages to prices is asymmetric; while there is some suggestion of an upward response to price increases, there is little impression of downward flexibility.

The following sections investigate whether these observations are supported by a more careful econometric modelling, taking account of the main seasonal influences on labour demand and the possible simultaneity between wages and prices. Section 2 outlines the theoretical model. Section 3 estimates the model for the full sample period, while Section 4 gives the results obtained when the period is split into two at July 1974. Finally, Section 5 examines the influence of the pre-famine model on wage expectations after the famine and demonstrates that this influence can explain the peculiar long-run properties of the post-famine model.

5.2 A Dynamic Model of Asymmetric Wage Adjustment

It is assumed that the time series of agricultural wages can be described by the following model:

$$W_t = a_0 + a_1 W_{t-1} + a_2^t P_t + a_3^t P_{t-1} + \mathbf{X}_t \mathbf{a}_4 + e_t \ (t = 1, \ldots, T) \tag{5.1}$$

where W and P denote the natural logarithms of wages and prices respectively, $\mathbf{X}$ is a vector of other relevant variables and e is an appropriate error process. The as are invariant to time except for

$$a_i^t = \delta_t a_{i0} + (1 - \delta_t) a_{i1} \quad (i = 2, 3) \tag{5.2}$$

where

$$\delta_t = 1 \text{ if } P_t > P_{t-1}$$
$$= 0 \text{ otherwise}$$

Thus, the response of the wage rate to a price increase need not equal its response to a fall in price. Equation 5.1 can be written in the equivalent form:

$$\Delta W_t = a_0 + (a_1 - 1) RW_{t-1} + a_2^t \Delta P_t$$
$$+ (a_1 + a_2^t + a_3^t - 1) P_{t-1} + \mathbf{X}_t \mathbf{a}_4 + e_t \tag{5.3}$$

where $RW = W - P$ is the log of the real food wage rate. Using equation 5.2 the model can also be written in a form which is linear in the time invariant parameters, namely:

$$\Delta W_t = a_0 + (a_1-1)RW_{t-1} + a_{20}\delta_t\Delta P_t + a_{21}(1-\delta_t)\Delta P_t$$
$$+ (a_1+a_{21}+a_{31}-1)P_{t-1} + (a_{20}+a_{30}-a_{21}-a_{31})\delta_t P_{t-1}$$
$$+ \mathbf{X}_t\mathbf{a}_4 + e_t \tag{5.4}$$

There is a restricted form of equation 5.1 of special interest. Consider a long-run equilibrium in which W and P are constant for a given value of $\mathbf{X}$. If equation 5.1 holds in such an equilibrium then

$$RW = (a_0 + (a_1+a_{21}+a_{31}-1)P + \mathbf{Xa}_4)/(1-a_1) \tag{5.5}$$

and so

$$a_1 + a_{21} + a_{31} - 1 = a_{20} + a_{30} - a_{21} - a_{31} = 0 \tag{5.6}$$

given that RW must also be constant and noting that it is arbitrary whether one defines δ to be 0 or 1 when $P = P_{-1}$. Thus, if equation 5.1 is constrained (on a priori grounds) to be consistent with long-run equilibrium then equation 5.3 becomes

$$\Delta W_t = a_0 + (a_1-1)RW_{t-1} + a_2^t\Delta P_t + \mathbf{X}_t\mathbf{a}_4 + e_t \tag{5.7}$$

In the special case of a symmetric wage response to a price change ($a_2^t = a_2$, $a_3^t = a_3$, say) one obtains:

$$\Delta W_t = a_0 + (a_1-1)RW_{t-1} + a_2\Delta P_t + \mathbf{X}_t\mathbf{a}_4 + e_t \tag{5.8}$$

This form has been proposed and estimated using wage and price data for some developed countries by Sargan (1964) and others.[4] Of course, the restrictions embodied in equations 5.7 and 5.8 are testable by first estimating the unrestricted version given by (5.4).

It may be worth noting at least one possible a priori justification for the econometric model given by equation 5.1. This assumes that, while the labour market need not be in a Walrasian stable competitive equilibrium at any one instant, it does tend to converge on such an equilibrium conditional on other prices. Unemployment at time t is assumed to be a function of the wage rate at time t, current and lagged rice prices, and a vector of other relevant variables $\mathbf{X}$. Thus unemployment (Walrasian supply less demand) is

$$U_t = U(W_t, P_t, P_{t-1}, \mathbf{X}_t) \quad U_w > 0 \tag{5.9}$$

with the sign of U_w implied by Walrasian stability. Of course, this does not tell us how wages adjust out of equilibrium. A common assumption in the dynamic analysis of markets is that:[5]

$$W_t - W_{t-1} = f(U_t) \quad f' < 0, f(0) = 0 \tag{5.10}$$

Combining equations 5.9 and 5.10, the wage at date t can be written as

$$W_t = g(W_{t-1}, P_t, P_{t-1}, \mathbf{X}_t) \quad 0 < g_w < 1 \tag{5.11}$$

The restriction on g_w is implied by $U_w > 0$ and $f' < 0$. Equation 5.1 can be interpreted as a log linear approximation of (5.11).

5.3 Agricultural Wages in Bangladesh, 1972–6

Monthly rice prices are monitored at markets throughout Bangladesh by the Bangladesh Directorate of Agricultural Marketing. Also the Bangladesh Directorate of Agriculture compiles a comparable, although probably less accurate, series for the average daily cash wage of agricultural labourers.[6] Alamgir *et al.* (1977) have compiled these data for the period July 1972 to June 1976 which is the source of the data used here.

As is common, monthly data is not available on agricultural employment and labour supply in Bangladesh. The omission of employment, particularly at harvest time, is likely to bias estimates of the wage response to prices at given employment (via the likely negative correlation between harvest employment and harvest price). An attempt has been made in the present study to take account of the seasonal variation in labour demand using monthly dummy variables. All regressions initially included 11 monthly dummy variables, although highly insignificant ones were subsequently eliminated. On the basis of the typical crop calendar for Bangladesh, one would expect the main seasonal peaks in labour demand to be April–May which is simultaneously the time of sowing the aus rice and harvesting the boro rice and the period mid-November to mid-January which is the harvest of the main crop for the year, the aman rice (Clay, 1981). Other regressors described important atypical events during the four year period, the most important being a dummy variable for the 1974 famine. In view of the possible simultaneity in wage and price formation, current prices in the wage equation were treated as endogenous. This was done by replacing current prices by predictions based on predetermined variables including lagged prices and seasonal dummy variables. (The instruments are given in Ravallion, 1982.)

The corresponding IV estimates of a_{21} and $a_{20} + a_{30} - a_{21} - a_{31}$ in equation 5.4 were found to be highly insignificant (t-ratios of 0.001 and 0.35 respectively). On setting these coefficients to zero, the following result was obtained:

$$\Delta_w = 0.05 - 0.31RW_{-1} + 0.35\delta\Delta P - 0.23P_{-1}$$
$$\quad (0.78) \quad (3.5) \qquad (4.7) \qquad (3.4)$$

$$\quad - 0.06FAM74 + 0.07MAY - 0.02OCT + 0.03DEC$$
$$\qquad (2.6) \qquad\quad (3.9) \qquad\quad (1.5) \qquad\quad (2.0)$$

$$\quad + 0.06t \tag{5.12}$$
$$\qquad (2.6)$$

$$SEE = 0.030; \text{Mean}W = 1.95; n = 46; D - W = 1.63$$

The dummy variable for May was set to zero for 1973 in view of the drought and subsequent flooding which occurred at the time and the consequent drop in employment (particularly in harvesting the much depleted 1973 boro crop). The drop in wages in October reflects the usual lean period between transplanting and harvesting the aman rice. The wage increase in December reflects the extra demand for labour at the aman harvest. The decline in rural employment and weakened bargaining position of workers resulted (*ceteris paribus*) in a rate of wage decline of six per cent per month during the 1974 famine.

The above results indicate a strong autocorrelation in the wage series ($a_1 = 0.69$, with a t-ratio of 18). However, the 'random walk' restriction ($a_1 = 1$) is firmly rejected and so the dynamic wage adjustment process is stationary, converging on a positive finite nominal wage, conditional on the price of rice. In the short run, wages respond to prices with an upward elasticity of 0.35 but with zero downward elasticity. However, the short-run dynamic adjustment of wages is not consistent with the assumed conditions for long-run wage and price equilibrium. The following sections will attempt to explain why.

5.4 Wage Adjustment before and after the Famine

It seems plausible that the 1974 famine could have (at least temporarily) displaced the short-run wage adjustment process. In addition to its identified effects on food prices, the famine is likely to have considerably weakened workers' bargaining power. For example, Clay's (1976) survey of labourers at the harvesting of the 1975–6 aman crop in the Joydebpur area suggests that the labour market at the time was in a state of transition due in part to the influence of the new migrant labour after the famine.

To test this proposition, table 5.1 gives the estimates of equation 5.4 obtained by splitting the sample into two periods:

1. The 'pre-famine' period; up to and including July 1974 ($n = 23$).
2. The famine and post-famine period; August 1974 on ($n = 22$).

Table 5.1 *Wage adjustment before and after the 1974 Famine*

Variable	Parameter	1 Pre-famine (to July 1974)	2 Famine and post-famine
1	a_0	−0.85 (4.0)	0.91 (4.9)
RW_{-1}	$a_1 - 1$	−0.31 (4.0)	−0.55 (5.3)
$\delta \Delta P$	a_{20}	0.63 (5.6)	0.35 (5.4)
P_{-1}	$a_1 + a_{21} + a_{31} - 1$	0	−0.50 (5.2)
Error$_{-1}$		0.49 (2.1)	−0.59 (2.6)
SEE		0.024	0.017
Mean W		1.77	2.19
n		23	22
SSR		0.098	0.0033
$D-W$		1.60	2.40
$\chi^2(6)$		84	n/a

Note: IV estimates of equation 5.4; absolute *t*-ratios in parentheses.
Specification 1 included dummy variables for May, December, and July, while 2 included February, April, May, July, September, October, and FAM74.

The cut-off point was decided on the basis of the history of the famine period and a visual inspection of Figure 1. (The corresponding price instruments are given in Ravallion, 1982.)

Comparison of the two equations indicates that the famine was associated with a clear structural break in the wage adjustment process. This is indicated by the chi-square test using the pre-famine model's post-sample predictive errors (Table 5.1) and was also revealed using a Chow test based on the sum of squared residuals of the unrestricted models. As was found in the full-sample model, the short-run wage response is asymmetric in both sub-periods (both estimates of a_{21} were highly insignificant). However, the implied elasticity of wages to a rice price increase (a_{20}) is substantially greater in the pre-famine model,[7] as is the wage autoregression coefficient ($a_1 = 0.69$ with a t-ratio of 9.0 in the pre-famine model while $a_1 = 0.45$ with $t = 4.3$ in the second period). Unlike the full-sample model, reasonably strong first-order auto-regression of the errors was found in the two sub-periods (of opposite signs) and this has been modelled explicitly in the estimates in Table 5.1. However, no significant time trend remained in the wage series for either sub-period.

In contrast to the post-July 1974 model, the short-run adjustment process in the pre-famine model is consistent with the conditions for long-run equilibrium. (The estimate of $a_1 + a_{21} + a_{31} - 1$ had a t-ratio of 0.07). The long-run real wage rate is estimated by solving for $RW^* = W_t - P_t = W_{t-1} - P_{t-1}$ with $\Delta W_t = \Delta P_t = 0$ and is given by:[8]

$$RW^* = -2.74 + 0.06MAY + 0.04JY + 0.07DEC \qquad (5.13)$$
$$(51) \quad (2.6) \qquad (2.5) \qquad (4.0)$$

The implied value of the long-run real wage rate in units of coarse quality rice is 5.3 pounds per day in the lean months (i.e., excluding May, July, and December). The actual real wages during the months of August, September and October of 1974 were 4.2, 3.3, and 2.8 pounds of rice per day respectively. Thus, by October 1974 the real wage rate had fallen to 52 per cent of its long-run value, as predicted from the conditions found prior to August 1974.

It is of interest to compare the actual wage rates during the famine with the wages one would have expected if there had not been a structural break in the wage equation. Table 5.2 gives the predicted values of ΔRW during August, September, and October

Table 5.2 *Predicted changes in the rice wage during the Famine based on the pre-famine model*

Month in 1974	Actual ΔRW (%)	Pre-dicted ΔRW (%)	Components of predicted ΔRW			
			$-\Delta P$	$a_{20}\Delta P$	$a_0+(a_1-1)$RW$_{-1}$	p error$_{-1}$
Aug.	−16	−5	−19	12	2	0
Sept.	−23	−6	−22	14	7	−5
Oct.	−18	0	−17	11	14	−8

Note: Predicted values assume that the previous month's wage rate is known. Dynamic forecasting using only the wage rates prior to August gives higher forecasting errors in all months.

of 1974 based on the pre-famine model in Table 5.1. The rice wage rate actually fell by almost sixty per cent during the quarter. However, the pre-famine model predicts a fairly stable rice wage over the period. This is due both to the higher elasticity of the money wage to rice price and the higher wage autocorrelation found under the pre-famine conditions.

5.5 Seasonality in Wages

If the parameters of equation 5.1 vary across seasons such that wages are relatively sticky in the lean months then this could explain the poor post-sample predictive ability of the pre-famine model in Table 5.1. Thus, the model's predictive errors for the relatively lean months of August, September, and October of 1974 could reflect model misspecification rather than a structural break.

To test this explanation, suppose that a_{20} is a linear function of a variable AUT which takes the value one in August, September, and October, but is set to zero otherwise. (One might also suppose that a_1 has a similar seasonal component. However this effect did not prove to be significant.)

The corresponding estimate of the pre-famine model is as follows:

$$\Delta W = -0.96 - 0.34\text{RW}_{-1} + (0.71 - 0.46\text{AUT})\delta\Delta P + 0.07\text{MAY}$$
$$\quad (4.7) \quad (4.7) \quad\quad (6.4) \quad (2.0) \quad\quad\quad (3.0)$$
$$+ 0.04\text{JY} + 0.07\text{DEC} + 0.48\text{error}_{-1} \quad\quad\quad (5.14)$$
$$\quad (2.5) \quad\quad (4.5) \quad\quad (2.3)$$

$$\text{SEE} = 0.022; D-W = 1.64$$

A mildly significant seasonal dimension in the short-run wage response is obtained and this permits a slight improvement in the model's within-sample performance. Not surprisingly, the new model has lower post-sample predictive errors for the months of August, September, and October of 1974. (The predicted changes in the real wage corresponding to Table 5.2 are -9, -7 and -2 per cent.) However, the predicted real wage is still over 50 per cent higher than the actual by October 1974 and the chi-square test on the post-sample errors continues to indicate a significant structural break. (For example, $\chi^2(3) = 99$.) The structural break cannot be plausibly attributed to misspecification of the seasonal dimension in wage adjustment.

5.6 The Influence of the Pre-Famine Model on Post-Famine Wage Expectations

There is one possible explanation for the peculiar long-run behaviour of the wage equation after the famine. Geographic mobility and other forms of social disruption in the period would have left many workers in unfamiliar settings. Furthermore, there is little unionization amongst rural workers in Bangladesh. Thus it can be safely assumed that it was unusually costly for individual workers to obtain information about the new wage adjustment process during and probably for some time after the famine.

In this case, a considerable time is likely to have elapsed before wage expectations had adjusted to conform with the new model. Then wages in the post-famine period will also depend on wage expectations formed using the pre-famine model but based on current prices. Failure to consider this effect would produce omitted variable bias in the main parameters including the error correction coefficient.

Following this explanation suppose that:

$$W_t = a_0 + a_1 W_{t-1} + a_2^t P_t + a_3^t P_{t-1} + a_4 W_t^* + a_5 W_{t-1}^* + \mathbf{X}_t \mathbf{a}_6 + e_t \tag{5.15}$$

where W^* denotes the expected value of the wage rate on the basis of the current price information but using the pre-famine model. On separating out the error correction term:

$$\Delta W_t = a_0 + (a_1 - 1)\text{RW}_{t-1} + a_2'\Delta P_t + (a_4 + a_5)\text{RW}_{t-1}^* + a_4\Delta W_t^*$$
$$+ (a_1 + a_2^t + a_3^t + a_4 + a_5 - 1)P_{t-1} + \mathbf{X}_t\mathbf{a}_6 + e_t \quad (5.16)$$

The following result was obtained by applying the same estimation methods as in the previous section:

$$\Delta W = 1.17 - 0.80\text{RW}_{-1} + 0.14\delta\Delta P$$
$$(6.4) \quad (6.8) \quad\quad\quad (2.1)$$
$$+ 0.44\text{RW}_{-1}^* + 0.46\Delta W^* + 0.05\text{MAY}$$
$$(6.7) \quad\quad\quad (7.1) \quad\quad\quad (4.8)$$
$$- 0.02\text{JY} - 0.04\text{FAM74} - 0.02\text{OCT} - 0.49\text{error}_{-1} \quad (5.17)$$
$$(1.5) \quad\quad (3.1) \quad\quad\quad (1.4) \quad\quad\quad (2.1)$$

SEE = 0.014; Mean $W = 2.19$; $n = 22$; $D-W = 2.4$.

Under this specification, the long-run wage elasticity is now unity (The coefficient on P_{-1} had a t-ratio of 0.2). Predictions of the current wage rate based on the pre-famine model have a significant effect on post-famine wages and, once an allowance is made for this effect, the short-run wage adjustment process is found to be consistent with the condition for long-run equilibrium.

5.7 Summary

Past assumptions about the short-run elasticity of nominal wages to rice prices in Bangladesh have varied widely. For example, Ahmed (1981) considers a figure of 0.9 to be reasonable, while Mahmud (1982) prefers 0.35 or zero. A number of choices about development policy depend quite crucially on the value of this parameter and it is clearly an important determinant of the vulnerability of the rural poor to food crises such as the 1974 famine.

The results of this chapter indicate a significant structural break in the short-run wage adjustment process in Bangladesh before and after the 1974 famine. For the data prior to August 1974, the short-run elasticity with respect to a price increase is estimated to be 0.63, while the figure is 0.35 when estimated on an identical basis for the second period. However, when an allowance is made for the likely influence of the pre-famine model on post-famine wage expectations, the short-run elasticity for the post-famine data is 0.14, rising to 0.43 once wage expectations have adjusted to the price increase. Without this structural break in the model, the real wage rate in units of rice would have been almost twice as high during the worst months of the famine.

The famine appears to have been associated with a sizeable shock to rural labour markets. There were a number of possible sources of this disturbance. The heavy flooding is likely to have resulted in sharp (localized) falls in demand for labour (B.R.A.C., 1979; Alamgir, 1980; Sen, 1981*a*). Substantial increases in land-lessness in areas hit badly by the famine have also been reported (Alamgir, 1980; Currey, 1981), although, as an explanation for the changes in labour market conditions, this begs the question of who bought the land and how much extra demand for hired labour resulted. Nonetheless, there seems little doubt that the famine resulted in an increase in the excess supply of rural labour. This will lead to a fall in the competitive wage (in a stable market) and so the revealed fall in the long-run real wage rate can be explained. The attendant drop in the *short-run* response of the nominal wage to rice prices suggests that the famine was also associated with a change in the way the labour market adjusts dynamically towards its long-run equilibrium. A plausible explanation for this is that the famine disrupted social customs, including payment systems, within local labour markets. This may have been due to the appearance in many local areas of new workers, having migrated from flood-affected areas.[9]

Notes

1. See Das (1949), Bhatia (1967), Dandekar and Peth (1972), Alamgir (1980), Sen (1981*a*), Greenough (1982), Oughton (1982).
2. Salt was the main exception, due to a short lived monopoly. The problem seems to have passed by the time the famine arrived in full force (Alamgir, 1980).
3. See Mirrless (1975), Stiglitz (1976), and Bliss and Stern (1978).
4. See Hendry and Richard (1983), Hendry, Pagan, and Sargan (1984) for a detailed discussion of econometric models using error correction mechanisms.
5. For further discussion of this assumption see Arrow and Hahn (1971, chapter 11) or Varian (1978, chapter 6). Booth and Sundrum (1985) use a similar model to equations 5.9 and 5.10 in analysing unemployment in rural labour markets and also suggest some alternatives to equation 5.10 as an interpretation of the negative effect of unemployment on wages.

6. Bose (1968) discusses the methods of collection and limitations of these data. Sampling biases are thought to be large in the underlying district and sub-district level data, but this is less of a problem in the national series. There does not appear to be any good reason for rejecting the assumption that errors in the wage series are white noise (in which case they will not bias estimation), although one might speculate that the (unobserved) meals given to many agricultural workers will be diminished in time of rice shortage. This is another reason for instrumenting current price in the wage equation.

7. The t statistics for the null hypotheses that the estimate of $a_{20} = 0$ for each sub-period are 2.5 and 4.3 respectively and both hypotheses are rejected at the 5 per cent level.

8. The general formula for long-run real wage rate given $\mathbf{X}^*$ is $RW^* = (a_0 + \mathbf{X}^* \mathbf{a}_4)/(1 - a_1)$. The standard error of $a_0/(1 - a_1)$ and other non-linear functions of parameters have been estimated by taking a first-order linear approximation in the neighbourhood of the parameter estimates using the TSP programme (Hall and Hall, 1980).

9. For evidence of this see Clay (1976), van Schendel (1981). For a theory of the role of social customs in labour markets see Akerlof (1980).

6

Inside a Present-Day
Bangladesh Rice Market

6.1 Introduction

Previous chapters have used aggregate time series data in examining market performance; there is little choice for data when looking at events ten or more years ago. But, in the light of the results of previous chapters, it is of interest to take a close look at a present day Bangladesh rice market. This will permit use of a much richer data source, being survey evidence (collected for this purpose) on the quoted prices and expectations of individual traders replicated over many trading days. The specific questions addressed are:

(i) Is there much variation within the market in the prices quoted for a given grade of rice on a given day? Are the quoted prices consistent with competitive equilibrium?

(ii) Is there evidence of price inflexibility in the market? Does observed sluggishness of average prices reflect price fixing by individual traders?

(iii) Is there much variation in traders' expectations about future prices? Do they tend to converge in the long run?

(iv) How well do the traders forecast future prices? Are their forecasts consistent with rational expectations? What are the likely sources of any informational inefficiency?

(v) How do the traders form their expectations? Is there evidence of learning from past observations, including past forecasting errors?

The following section describes the setting and the data. Section 3 tests for price and expectations variability within the market, while Section 4 tests for price flexibility. Section 5 presents the main results obtained in testing for short-term forecasting bias. Section 6 shows that conventional multiple tests for rationality of expectations can be nested within a more general framework which permits further interpretation of the results of Section 5. Section 7 examines forecasting performance over a longer time span. Section 8 looks at the way the traders' expectations were formed. Finally Section 9 summarizes the results and their implications for storage and market stability.

6.2 The Setting and Data

Typically, the main agents in a large Bangladesh rice market are either itinerate traders (called 'Beparies' and 'Farias') or 'Aratdars'. The latter are established wholesale merchants with their own shop and storage facilities. The Aratdars are found only in the larger markets, particularly those in the main urban areas, although small merchants with similar functions (called 'Dalals') are found in most other markets. For this study, 20 Aratdars were interviewed at the main wholesale rice markets of Dhaka at Badamtali~on each trading day over three months during the winter of 1983/4.

For many reasons, the Aratdars are the group of most interest. Aratdars are popularly viewed as the dominant people in the Bangladesh rice trade. They have often been personally blamed for shortages and high prices, although the accusations rarely seem to have been well considered. Their prominence in the markets makes them a natural scapegoat.

There is some mystery about what Aratdars actually do. When asked by a stranger they will usually say that they are only brokers. For this job they receive a fixed commission per unit quantity from both parties. However, there is little doubt that they also trade on their own right. Popular opinions, 'anti-hoarding' laws, hostile police and governments and (probably to a lesser extent) fear of jeopardising their brokerage business, have made them rather evasive about this aspect of their work. And it is also very difficult for an observer to distinguish physically the two activities. Certainly an Aratdar's shop is a good base for pure trading activities in terms of access to information and legal storage facilities. Farruk (1972) claims that their own trading is as important to the Aratdars as brokerage. However, it is difficult to say whether this remains true today.

The Aratdars are clearly the market's most knowledgeable participants. They usually have easy access to an impressive network of traders in other markets linked by telephone or via itinerate traders, moving between markets. Of the twenty Badamtali Aratdars interviewed for this study, all but two had contacts at least every day or two in other markets; these involved between two and ten traders (with an average of five) spanning two to seven different markets (an average of four). All had telephones or easy access to them.

In both their brokerage and trading activities, the Aratdars have an incentive to be well informed about the market. This is obvious for trading. As brokers they compete for trade according to the quality of their brokerage services, including their information, rather than their brokerage fee. The latter is fixed by their professional society.

The Aratdars also have an important function as a source of credit. Many of them told me that they often give large advances in transactions with individual traders. (Some of the figures quoted for individual advances were in excess of ten times the annual GDP per capita of Bangladesh!) Credit facilities are used mainly to attract customers rather than as a separate source of income, although (again) the Aratdars are a little evasive on this point. (Naturally, interest on credit is an uncomfortable topic in Islamic countries.)

All Aratdars are members of a single professional society, which charges its members a small fee. The society seems to survive by having good relations with government; if an Aratdar does not join the society then he has less chance of getting a government licence. The society fixes brokerage fees, but it does not appear to limit other forms of competition between the traders such as over rice price and quality of brokerage services. Relative newcomers to the Badamtali Aratdars told me that their entry into the market was fairly easy, although all had either been in the same business elsewhere or had previous contacts in the trade, usually family. Nonetheless, the number of Aratdars in the market has grown at a considerable rate since Bangladesh's Independence, certainly exceeding by a wide margin the (high) rate of growth in Dhaka's population.[1] Thus, while it is probably hard for a complete outsider to enter the rice trade, there does not appear to be any significant restriction on entry into the market.

For the purpose of this study, twenty-eight traders in the main wholesale rice market at Badamtali were interviewed at about the same time on each day the market was open for three months, giving 70 days' data. The survey began about two weeks before the main winter ('aman') harvest of 1983–4. In addition to the twenty Aratdars, four retailers were interviewed. These are one-man businesses set up on the sidewalk but in the middle of the whole-sale market. The remaining four were itinerate traders, called 'Beparies', who are rarely in the same market on consecutive days. So different Beparies were interviewed on different days. One of the retailers disappeared half way through the study and one of the other retailers was often absent. Thus, only two retailers were kept in the sample used for analysis, giving panel data for a total of twenty-two traders, together with non-panel data for the Beparies.

The main daily questionnaire was kept short. Each trader was asked the day's price for a specific quality of rice, namely 'IRRI' (or a comparable grade of good 'Paizzum' on the occasional day when IRRI was not available). The trader was then asked what price he expected for this rice by this time tomorrow and what price he expected by mid-February, the end of the study period. This was done by first asking 'do you think the price will go up, go down, stay the same?' and then asking 'by how much?' All inter-views were done in Bangla by a single interpreter under reason-ably close supervision, particularly in the early stages. The interviewer built up a good rapport with a number of the Aratdars during the study who became useful sources of qualitative information.

There was no obvious source of sample bias. In terms of appear-ances, the sampled Aratdars' shops seemed a reasonable cross-section of the market. A check was made to see if they tended to be less busy than average: the entire market was surveyed in a one and a half hour period, making a count of whether or not the shop had a customer at that moment. Of the 138 Aratdars counted, 36 were busy. This was true of five of the sample and so the propor-tions are very close indeed.

Although a good deal of care was exercised in collecting these data, it seems likely that the results overstate the level of agree-ment amongst the traders. The interview process can act to trans-mit information between traders. This is produced by the tendency of an interviewer to form expectations of the answers on the basis of previous interviews which are then used as prompts. The inter-viewer was told to try to avoid this. Unintended transmission of information through the interviewing process may also lead to strategic biasing of quoted expectations, although it was my impression that none of the traders had sufficient influence to do this successfully.

An overview of the results
The following comments give an overview of the survey results, prior to their detailed analysis.

Figure 6.1 plots the mean wholesale price (averaged over the 20 Aratdars) for each day and the mean expected price for that day.[2] Price increased by about 16 per cent during the period, although certainly not monotonically. It can be seen from Figure 6.1 that expectations track prices fairly well; the standard deviation of the forecasting error is about two per cent of mean price. But the variance is quite high; the coefficient of variation is about 1.9. And

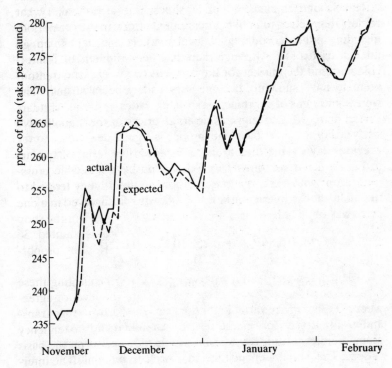

Fig. 6.1

a tendency to underestimate is apparent, particularly in December and early January, the period when the new harvest arrives.

Of course, it is not hard to achieve quite precise forecasting of the day-to-day movements of a highly autocorrelated variable; static expectations will often do the trick. But they will rarely be informationally efficient, and could yield substantial biases in storage decisions (relative to a rational expectations storage rule) if prices become highly unstable.

There are two days when the forecasting error is unusually high, namely days 8 (November 28) and 16 (December 11). On both days there was a sharp unanticipated price increase. The first coincides with large scale political demonstrations in Dhaka against the government which had unexpectedly turned quite violent, ending in a number of deaths and a 24-hour curfew. This marked the beginning of a period of many weeks during which it seemed more difficult to get rice into Dhaka from the rural areas.

The second unexpected price shock was attributed by the traders themselves to public procurement efforts in the rural areas, including police cordoning of local markets and harassment of inter-district trade. Although there had been rumours of this sort going around the market for the previous two weeks, the rumours seem to have suddenly become very widely believed and there were some signs of shortage for specific grades.

As Figure 6.1 also suggests, average prices in the market were fairly sticky; on most days, mean price is a good deal closer to the previous day's value than to more distant prices. The price series in Figure 6.1 is reasonably well described by a first-order autoregression; with some obvious additions to describe its trend and the main shocks to the market, the following OLS estimate of log price was obtained:

$$\bar{P}_t = 0.76 + 0.86\bar{P}_{t-1} + 0.25\times10^{-3}t + 0.042D_t \qquad (6.1)$$
$$\phantom{\bar{P}_t = } (2.7) \quad (17) \qquad (2.7) \qquad (7.6)$$

$$R^2 = 0.96; \text{ SEE} = 0.0071; \text{ Durbin } h = 1.2; Q(14) = 9.9$$

where D is a dummy variable for the price shocks on days 8 and 16 and $Q(14)$ is the Box–Pierce test for a random residual correlogram. Neither test for residual autocorrelation suggests misspecification. The serial dependence in prices is high, although the coefficient is significantly less than unity by a conventional t-test

$(t = 2.7)$.[3] Nonetheless, allowing for the two shocks, a random walk performs well $(F(3,60) = 3.2)$ as a simplification of equation 6.1:

$$\Delta \bar{P}_t = 0.046 D_t; \; R^2 = 0.52; \; SEE = 0.0074; \; Q(15) = 7.0$$
$$(8.7)$$

This can be interpreted as saying that 'normally' $(D = 0$ and at mean error) average price in the market does not change from one day to the next.

However, there are a number of interesting questions about this market which cannot be answered by looking solely at the averages; these require a closer investigation of the *deviations* about the mean points plotted in Figure 6.1. Following sections turn to the data on individual prices and expectations.

6.3 Homogeneity of Prices and Expectations within the Market

In a non-stochastic competitive equilibrium with zero search costs for buyers the prices quoted by different sellers of the same product will be equal. Similarly, while there may be price differentials between traders at any one point in time if the equilibrium is stochastic, a sufficiently large number of observations will reveal that such differentials vanish on average. Thus, a testable implication of stochastic competitive equilibrium is that each trader's quoted price is an unbiased estimate of the average price in the market.

A similar test can be used to determine if, on average, different traders agree on their price expectation. Expectations dispersion will arise if traders have diverse information sets, in which case prices will serve the function of transmitting information in addition to their usual allocative role (for an example, see Grossman and Stiglitz, 1980).

Appendix 6.1 (Column 1) gives test results for the unbiasedness restriction $a_0^i = a_1^i - 1 = a_2^i = 0$ in the model:

$$\bar{P}_t^i = a_0^i + a_1^i P_t^i + a_2^i t + u_t^i \qquad (6.2)$$

$$u_t^i = \varrho^i u_{t-1}^i + v_t^i$$

where P_t^i is the price quoted by trader i on date t and $\bar{P}_t^i$ the sample mean, excluding that trader. Column 2 of Appendix 6.1 gives the results for the corresponding test using price expectations rather than observed prices.

In both cases the results indicate that, for about half of the Aratdars, the quoted prices and expectations are statistically unbiased estimates of the corresponding averages in the market (at the five per cent level; at the one per cent level the proportion increases to about two-thirds). But even when bias is indicated, its magnitude turns out to be small on average. For both prices and expectations the largest difference between the average figure quoted by an individual trader over the study period and the average for the market as a whole is less than 0.2 per cent of the latter. Thus, although systematic biases are indicated for a number of traders, there appears to be a high level of agreement about both prices and expectations within the market.

It is of interest to also ask if the observed price dispersion is likely to be a long-run phenomenon. This may reflect unidentified differences in the quality of service or product. Equilibrium price dispersion is also possible for a homogeneous product if buyers incur search costs (Rothschild, 1973; Rob, 1985).

As a test for long-run price dispersion, the coefficient of variation in traders' quoted prices (CV^p) was calculated for each day in the series. Dynamic models of the CV^p series were then estimated and their long-run properties examined. OLS estimation of a first-order autoregression for CV^p (as a percentage) gave:

$$CV^p = 0.11 + 0.44CV^p_{-1}$$
$$\quad\ (1.1)\quad (14)$$

$R^2 = 0.75$; Durbin $h = 0.10$; $Q(14) = 12$; $\bar{CV} = 1.4$; SEE $= 0.41$

(In terms of overall fit, this model performed as well as a second-order autoregression including a time trend and so was preferred; an F-test of the restricted form gave $F(2,61) = 1.2$). Since the intercept is not significantly different from zero, the model's long-run equilibrium implies zero price variance. Thus, these data are consistent with an equilibrium in which all traders charge the same price.

There is evidence of significant dispersion of price expectations in the long-run. Using the CV of expectations (CV^e), OLS estimation gave the following result:

$$CV^e = 3.0 + 0.052(CV^e_{-1} + CV^e_{-2}) - 0.034t$$
$$\quad (10) \quad (2.4) \qquad\qquad\qquad (5.8)$$

$R^2 = 0.54$; Durbin $h = 0.45$; $Q(14) = 6.9$; $\bar{CV} = 2.0$; SEE $= 0.74$;
Linear restriction $t(60) = 0.8$.

The intercept is highly significant. However the long-run equilibrium is non-stationary, declining through the study period. By the end of the study period, the total of the intercept and the component due to the time trend has declined to 0.66, although it remains significantly positive ($t = 3.5$). Thus the long-run CV of expectations declines from 3.4 to 0.74 per cent over the study period. As was noted in section 6.2, at least some of the convergence of expectations is likely to have arisen from the interviewing process. Other explanations will also be offered later when discussing expectations formation.

However, there is an important caveat on the interpretation of these results, particularly concerning price dispersion. As has been emphasised, while it is implied by competitive equilibrium, price homogeneity does not of itself imply that markets are competitive. For example, a tendency towards homogeneity is possible even if individual traders fix their prices independently of each other; all that is required is that they set their prices in a sufficiently similar way.[4] Further tests which may help distinguish competitive price adjustments from independent price fixing require a closer look at price formation at the individual level. This is the task of the following section.

6.4 Price Flexibility

In published price series, it is common to observe sluggishness in the form of a high positive autocorrelation. Published prices are generally sample averages of some sort, such as modelled by equation 6.1. It may be thought that the price stickiness revealed by equation 6.1 is inconsistent with competitive conditions. Indeed, it is often assumed that the more competitive a market is the more flexible its prices will be; see, for example, Means (1972).[5]

It is worth investigating further the source of the autocorrelation in average prices. In principle, it could arise from one or both of two very different causes:

(1) Inflexibility of the prices quoted by individual traders. Average price stickiness in a market can arise if individual traders tend to fix their prices independently of the prices set by other traders.

(2) An equilibrium in which competitive arbitrage has eliminated expected spatial price differentials in the market. This assumes that each trader is uncertain of the prices charged by others on a given day, so that equilibrium only requires that each trader's quoted price is arbitraged against the *expected* price charged by other traders on that day. In drawing out the implications of this argument, I shall also assume that (i) the expectation is formed on the basis of the previous day's information which includes that day's average price and that (ii) each trader expects the average price to follow an AR1 process such as equation 6.1. (This is not inconsistent with rational expectations although it does not imply it.)

Thus one can think of equation 6.1 as the mean across all traders of the following model of each trader's quoted prices:

$$P_t^i = a_0^i + a_1^i P_{t-1}^i + a_2^i \bar{P}_{t-1} + a_3^i t + a_4^i D_t + u_t^i \qquad (6.3)$$

The first explanation of the inflexibility in average prices assumes that $a_2^i = 0$ so that the autoregression coefficient in equation 6.1 is simply $\sum a_1^i / N$. By contrast, the second explanation assumes that $a_1^i = 0$, so that the average price autoregression is $\sum a_2^i / N$.

Table 6.1 gives the distribution of the absolute t-ratios on OLS estimates of a_1 and a_2 in equation 6.3 while Appendix 6.1 (columns 3 and 4) give the estimated t-ratios for each trader. (The OLS

Table 6.1 *Decomposition of aggregate price stickiness*

Coefficient on:	Absolute t-ratio			
	<1	1–2	2–3	>3
Lagged own price	13	6	1	0
Lagged mean price	0	3	6	11

Note: See Appendix 6.1 for detailed results.

residuals passed both the Durbin–Watson and Box–Pierce tests for serial independence at the five per cent level for all traders.)

Overall, the results suggest that each trader's quoted price is highly responsive to the prices previously quoted by other traders. And this effect generally dominates any sluggishness in own price. Indeed, this holds for 18 of the 20 Aratdars. Thus the strong autoregressive tendency in the market's average price does not appear to reflect price fixing at the level of most of the individual traders. Indeed, these results suggest considerable price flexibility at the individual level.

6.5 Forecasting Bias

The key testable implication of informationally unbiased forecasting is that the resulting forecasting errors should be uncorrelated with costlessly available information.[6]

Forecasting bias can be tested by regressing realizations against their forecasts and then testing the appropriate unbiasedness restrictions using the calculated regression coefficients and residuals. For example, if price forecasts are observed for one time unit ahead then one can estimate the following equation (letting P_t^e denote the expectation held at time $t - 1$ of P_t, the price to prevail at time t):

$$P_t = \alpha_0 + \alpha_1 P_t^e + \varepsilon_t \qquad (6.4)$$

for each trader and test the joint hypothesis that $(\alpha_0, \alpha_1) = (0, 1)$ and ε_t is a zero mean white noise error.[7]

Figure 6.1 suggests a time dependence of forecasting errors, with underestimation indicated in the early period but gradually decreasing. So, for these data, a better starting point than equation 6.4 is a model of the form

$$P_t = \alpha_0 + \alpha_1 P_t^e + \delta t + \varepsilon_t \qquad (6.5)$$

Durbin–Watson tests on OLS residuals from this model for a subsample suggested serial dependence in the error term and so an AR1 estimator was used on the complete sample.

The detailed results are given in Appendix 6.2. They show a quite striking similarity in the structure of price forecasting bias between the traders. Without exception, estimates of α_0 are found to be significantly positive (at the one per cent level) while the estimates of α_1 are significantly positive (as one would expect) but also significantly less than unity. In testing the null hypothesis, $\alpha_0 = 0$, t-ratios range from 3.6 to 9.7 while for $\alpha_1 = 1$ they range from 3.5 to 9.6. Estimates of the time-dependence of forecasting errors (δ) are significantly positive for about half of the traders. The joint restriction $\alpha_0 = \alpha_1 - 1 = \delta = 0$ is convincingly rejected by an F-test for all traders.

Two modifications to the test procedure were also tried on a random sub-sample of five traders: (i) Equation 6.5 was re-estimated including dummy variables for Days 8 and 16 when (as noted in Section 6.2) forecast errors were unusually high. It would be worrying if inferences depended on these extremes. However, estimates of both α_0 and $\alpha_1 - 1$ remained highly significant for all traders. (ii) Any measurement errors in the expectations series (such as due to the problems of interviewing noted in Section 6.2) will impart a downward bias on estimates of α_1. So equation 3 was re-estimated by an instrumental variables method, in this case by replacing P_t^e with a predicted series formed by an AR1 regression on P_{t-1} and t. Again, significant estimates of α_0 and $\alpha_1 - 1$ were obtained.

The bias test was also performed using each day's mean price and composite price forecasts formed by linearly weighting the individual forecasts for each date. This test is of interest because a linearly weighted combination of a set of diverse forecasts will generally have improved forecasting properties (Bates and Granger, 1969). While it is not known how the market aggregates information, three *ad hoc* weighting schemes were considered: equal weights, weights determined by each trader's storage capacity, and weights determined by the number of years the trader has been working in the market. These gave very similar results and the unbiasedness conditions were rejected for all three. (The result for equal weights is given in Appendix 6.2.)

To summarize these results: forecasting errors (expected minus actual) are found to be positively correlated with expectations. Thus at any point in time (and given that α_0 is positive) there is a critical value of each trader's price expectation, above which future price will be overestimated and below which it will be underestimated. The turning point in the direction of bias varies quite a lot amongst the traders; when evaluated at the beginning of the sample period and at $\varepsilon = 0$ the price at which bias changes sign ranges from 188 to 320, with a mean of 260 Tk/md. For most traders, these figures are contained within (or are reasonably close to) the range of the data, although underestimation is more common than overestimation for all traders. As has been noted, this seems most marked during the harvest period. At the same time there is a universal tendency to *overestimate* price changes and, in this sense, expectations tend to be more volatile than realizations.

As an aside, it may be of interest to note that this finding is contrary to the well-known tendency of forecasts to underestimate changes. However, I think one should be wary of this comparison. For one thing, the recent literature contains numerous exceptions to the underestimation tendency (see, for example, Friedman, 1980; Bailey *et al*, 1984; and Struth, 1984). Also, many of the earlier bias tests were misspecified in that expectations (rather than realizations) were used as the dependent variable (Evans and Gulamani, 1984). Indeed, as Muth (1961) points out, OLS estimation of such a specification for the bias test actually implies that changes will appear to be underestimated when the rational expectations hypothesis is valid.

6.6 Forecasting Efficiency

In the recent empirical studies of expectation surveys and futures prices, the bias test outlined above has usually been accompanied by tests for the orthogonality of forecasting errors to past realizations of the forecasted variable. For example, in the present setting, one might suppose that

$$P_t^e - P_t = \beta P_{t-1} + \varepsilon_t \tag{6.6}$$

Then, as long as the information set used in forming P_t^e includes P_{t-1} (as is definitely the case here since the traders reported P_{t-1}), unbiased forecasting implies that $\beta = 0$. This is often referred to as the test for *efficiency* in forecasting (see, for examples, Mullineaux, 1978; Friedman, 1980; Evans and Gulamani, 1984) while the test based on equation 6.4 is termed *unbiasedness*.

The sign of β in equation 6.6 also indicates whether price forecasting errors tend to have a de-stabilizing influence on the market (see Chapter 2, Section 2.7). If $\beta > 0$ then future price is overestimated when current price is high. The effect on storage will then lead to a further increase in price. On the other hand, if $\beta < 0$ then the effect will tend to be price stabilizing.

At mean points and including a time trend, OLS estimation of equation 6.6 yields:

$$\bar{P}_t^e - \bar{P}_t = -1.4 + 0.25\bar{P}_{t-1} - 0.21 \times 10^{-3}t \qquad (6.7)$$
$$\phantom{\bar{P}_t^e - \bar{P}_t = }(4.3) \quad (4.4) \qquad (2.0)$$

$$R^2 = 0.34; \text{ SEE} = 0.0075; \ Q(14) = 9.9.$$

The coefficient on lagged price is significantly positive indicating a tendency for price forecasting errors to be price de-stabilizing.

However, the practice of estimating equations 6.4 and 6.6 separately is unappealling. Both are tests for the orthogonality of forecasting errors with available information; that information is P_t^e in the case of equation 6.4,[8] while it is P_{t-1} in the case of equation 6.6. By nesting the two tests within a single equation, one is in a better position to distinguish the sources of forecasting bias.

Applying this idea, the following composite model (embodying both bias and efficiency tests) was estimated for each trader:

$$P_t = \alpha + \beta P_{t-1} + \gamma_0 P_t^e + \gamma_1 P_{t-1}^e + \delta't + \mu_t \qquad (6.8)$$

Sargan's Common Factor (COMFAC) restriction:

$$\beta\gamma_0 + \gamma_1 = 0$$

was then tested for each regression and was accepted (quite convincingly) for all except one trader.[9] Under the COMFAC restriction equation 6.8 can be simplified to equation 6.5 with an AR1 error:

$$P_t = \alpha_0 + \alpha_1 P_t^e + \delta t + \varepsilon_t \qquad (6.9)$$

where

$$\varepsilon_t = \beta\varepsilon_{t-1} + \mu_t$$

and the parameters of the two models correspond according to:

$$\alpha_0 = (\alpha - \beta\delta)/(1-\beta)$$
$$\alpha_1 = \gamma_0$$
$$\delta = \delta'/(1-\beta)$$

So, provided that the error structure is properly specified and the COMFAC restriction is valid, the bias test is also a test for 'forecasting efficiency'; the error autocorrelation coefficient measures the correlation between forecasting errors and lagged realizations. Since it has fewer parameters to estimate, the model based on equation 6.9 is a more powerful test than equation 6.8.

As can be seen from Appendix 6.2, the estimates of β vary quite a lot amongst the traders; considerably more so than α_0 or α_1. Estimates of β are significantly positive for nine traders and either insignificant or weakly negative for the rest.

Thus, when the two sources of forecasting bias are nested within one model, it is found that forecasting errors are more consistently correlated with forecasts than with past realizations. This suggests that the traders hold a commitment to their prior expectations. Such behaviour is consistent with the explanation of non-rational expectations in terms of cognitive dissonance theory, as mentioned in Chapter 1.

6.7 Terminal Price Expectations

A further implication of informationally unbiased forecasting is that changes in the expectations of the price to prevail at a fixed future date should be unpredictable on the basis of current information.[10]

In the present setting, suppose that an unbiased expectation is formed at time t of the price to prevail at the terminal date T of the study period. Then $E(e_t|I_t) = 0$ where $e_t = {}_tP_T^e - P_T$ is the forecasting error and I_t is the information set. But, of course, I_t includes I_{t-1}, so e_t must also be orthogonal to I_{t-1} in which case $\Delta e_t = \Delta_t P_T^e$ also has this property. Hence, if ${}_tP_T^e$ is an unbiased forecast then it is also a martingale i.e., $E({}_tP_T^e|I_{t-1}) = {}_{t-1}P_T^e$.

Clearly, this argument applies equally well to higher order differences; in particular, unbiasedness implies that the ith difference of e_t is orthogonal to I_{t-i}. Then a further testable implication of unbiasedness is that $\alpha = 0$ in the following model:

$$\Delta_t^i P_T^e = \alpha P_{t-i} + \mu_t \qquad (6.10)$$

Unbiasedness also implies restrictions on the error term. In the special case $i = 1$, μ_t should be serially independent. More generally, μ_t should be serially independent of μ_{t-k} for all $k > i$.

The null hypothesis $\alpha = 0$ was tested for $i = 1$ (first differences) and $i = 2$ (second). For $i = 1$, OLS was initially used for all traders but the Durbin–Watson test indicated significant (negative) first-order error autocorrelation for seven traders and so an AR1 estimator was used for these. Of course, for the $i = 1$ model, first-order autocorrelation of the error term is inconsistent with unbiased forecasting. For the $i = 2$ model (positive) error autocorrelation is to be expected, even with unbiased forecasting, and so in this case AR1 estimation has been used for all traders.

To summarize the results: the terminal price forecasts for a majority (but not all) of the traders turn out to be inconsistent with informationally efficient forecasting. The martingale property can be reasonably rejected for either first or second differences for 14 traders. Appendix 6.1 gives the detailed test results.

As another aside, this finding seems to be in marked contrast to the results of numerous tests of the efficient markets hypothesis for futures and other speculative prices in developed countries (see, for example, Labys and Granger, 1970; Praetz, 1975). While this comparison suggests greater informational inefficiency in Bangladesh rice markets, one should note that it is probably a good deal easier to find such inefficiency at the individual level than in futures market prices, since the latter will improve forecasting performance by aggregation. Thus, the present results do not imply that, if an organized futures market for rice existed in Bangladesh, it would be inefficient. Rather, the results suggest that relevant allocative decisions made in the existing spot market will depart significantly from those based on informationally efficient price expectations.

6.8 Expectations Formation

The above results beg the question of how the traders' biased expectations were actually formed.

Following common practice it is assumed here that expectations are formed by linear extrapolation from past realizations:

$$P_{t+1}^e = \sum_{i=0}^{n} \pi_i P_{t-i} + e_t \tag{6.11}$$

As is well-known, if the weights attached to past observations decline exponentially as $\pi_i = \lambda(1 - \lambda)^i$ then this model is equivalent to the popular 'adaptive' or 'error learning' model due to Cagan (1956) and Nerlove (1958):

$$\Delta P_{t+1}^e = \lambda(P_t - P_t^e) + e_t \qquad (6.12)$$

If, instead, $\pi_i = \lambda_1^i \lambda_2$, $\lambda_1 + \lambda_2 \neq 1$, then one obtains the less restrictive form (used by Jacobs and Jones, 1980, and Nerlove, 1983):

$$P_{t+1}^e = \lambda_1 P_t^e + \lambda_2 P_t + e_t \qquad (6.13)$$

Rather than assume the error learning process implied by exponential smoothing, I shall treat this as a testable restriction on the more general distributed lag specification given by equation 6.11. The key testable implication of the error learning model is that $\lambda_3 = \lambda_4 = \ldots = 0$ in the regression:

$$P_{t+1}^e = \lambda_0 + \lambda_1 P_t^e + \lambda_2 P_t + \sum_{i=1}^{n} \lambda_{2+i} P_{t-i} + e_t \qquad (6.14)$$

Adding time to pick up any trended non-price information, the following AR1 estimate was obtained using the series of mean prices and expectations for Badamtali:[11]

$$\bar{P}_{t+1}^e = 0.20 + 0.17\bar{P}_t^e + 1.18\bar{P}_t - 0.39\bar{P}_{t-1} + 0.19 \times 10^{-3}t \qquad (6.15)$$
$$\quad\; (0.74)\;\; (1.2)\qquad (12)\qquad (3.3)\qquad\;\; (2.4)$$

$R^2 = 0.98$; SEE = 0.0055; Durbin $h = -0.07$; $Q(14) = 9.0$.

Both the significant effect of lagged price and the insignificant effect of lagged expectations are inconsistent with the error learning model. Dropping $\bar{P}_t^e$ one obtains an estimate of equation 6.11 for $n = 1$:

$$\bar{P}_{t+1}^e = 0.18 + 1.20\bar{P}_t - 0.23\bar{P}_{t-1} + 0.21 \times 10^{-3}t + 0.15\text{error}_{-1}$$
$$\quad\; (0.65)\;\; (16)\qquad (3.6)\qquad\;\; (2.3)\qquad\qquad (1.2)$$
$$\qquad\qquad\qquad\qquad\qquad\qquad\qquad\qquad\qquad\qquad (6.16)$$

There is clearly a strong static element in expectations formation. (As one would expect, noting that the coefficient on expected price in the estimates of equation 6.5 in Appendix 6.1 is very close to the autocorrelation coefficient of realized prices in equation

6.1.) However, the coefficient on $\bar{P}_t$ is significantly greater than one ($t = 2.7$). The joint parameter restriction that $\lambda_0 = \lambda_2 - 1 = \lambda_3 = 0$ is rejected ($F(3,58) = 7.5$). On the other hand, the restriction that $\lambda_2 + \lambda_3 = 1$ does perform very well ($t = 0.7$), suggesting the more parsimonious model:[12]

$$\bar{P}^e_{t+1} - \bar{P}_t = -0.73 \times 10^{-2} + 0.26\Delta\bar{P}_t + 0.16 \times 10^{-3}t \qquad (6.17)$$
$$\quad\;\;(4.4) \qquad\qquad (4.0) \qquad\quad (4.0)$$

$$R^2 = 0.33; \; SEE = 0.0055; \; D-W = 1.80; \; Q(14) = 7.6.$$

Summarizing these results, the traders' expectations appear to have been formed using the following 'rules':

(i) At the beginning of the period ($t = 0$) and at a given price (so that $\Delta P_t = 0$) traders expected tomorrow's price to fall relative to today's by about $\frac{3}{4}$ per cent. This amount was reduced through the period of analysis, reaching zero by day 45 ($= 0.73/0.016$) with price rises expected after that day.

(ii) However, observed price changes did have a significant influence on expectations formation. Prices were expected to continue moving in the same direction; about one quarter of an observed price increase since yesterday was added to the expected increment of tomorrow's price over today's. This will have a de-stabilizing influence on the market.

It is interesting to note that the turning point at day 45 roughly coincides with the end of the (aman) harvest period. Thus price expectations appear to have been strongly influenced by the traders' prior assumptions about the seasonality of production which explains point (i) above. As a rule of thumb, rice prices throughout Bangladesh tend to fall sharply in late November and through December, then rising in January. The price fall starts just before the aman harvest (which rarely arrives in Dhaka markets before December) and continues through most of the harvest period.

In most years, the aman harvest has less effect on Dhaka prices than elsewhere, but the seasonal pattern is still in evidence (see Chapter 4 for further discussion of spatial market integration during the aman harvest). The survey period did not conform to this pattern. Despite a good harvest, December prices were relatively high and this seems to have persistently surprised the traders. The high price appears to have been due to two relatively unusual factors in the survey period:

(i) The apparent success of the government's official procurement efforts in some areas, involving non-compulsory procurement at a fairly high procurement price to producers.
(ii) A degree of police cordoning of local rural markets and harassment of inter-district grain movements, particularly in areas where the official procurement price was below the market price.

A testable implication of this explanation is that forecasting bias should vanish after the aman harvest. This is generally agreed to be the middle of January. To test this, the bias test based on equation 6.5 was repeated for the last twenty-five days of the study period starting from mid-January. This time the *F*-test implied acceptance of the unbiasedness restrictions for all except two traders (at the five per cent level). This is consistent with the above interpretation of the revealed forecasting biases during the harvest.

Of course, this does not explain the persistence of the traders' belief that the harvest would bring prices down. One answer might be that the traders were poorly informed about the two factors mentioned above leading to higher prices. On the whole, the traders seemed to be very well informed about the activities in rural markets of the government and police, although there was doubt (seemingly well founded in past experience; see Chapter 3) about the effectiveness of public procurement efforts in supporting the harvest price. But the psychological interpretation is more appealing; this postulates that the traders felt a commitment to their prior expectations, a commitment which could result in the short-term suppression of dissonant information.

6.9 Summary and Discussion

The overall picture of this market which emerges is one of a reasonably large number of similar traders with individually flexible prices which are responsive to market conditions and converge in equilibrium. The observed sluggishness of average prices in this market is more plausibly attributed to lags in competitive price adjustment at the individual level than price fixing.

However, there is little sign of informational efficiency. The restrictions implied by the unbiasedness of one-day-ahead price forecasts are convincingly rejected on the basis of residual variance tests at the individual level. The martingale model of price forecasts for a terminal date is also rejected as a generalization of traders' forecasting behaviour. Overall, the rational expectations hypothesis is a poor characterization of expectations formation in this market.

A striking result of the bias tests is the universal tendency of the traders to overestimate price changes; forecasting errors (expected minus actual) are positively correlated with forecasts. There exists a critical level of expectations below which future prices are underestimated and above which they tend to be overestimated.

The corresponding bias in profit expectations suggests that private stocks will be insufficient (relative to those implied by rational expectations) when expectations are low, while storage will be excessive at times of high expectations.[13] Thus storage will tend to be excessive (relative to a rational expectations equilibrium) during lean periods of sufficiently high prices.

A number of interesting points emerge when one looks at how the traders formed their price expectations. In keeping with the assumptions usually made in expectations modelling, the traders do appear to have extrapolated from recently observed prices, with largest weight attached to the most recent observation. But there is little sign of 'error learning'; the traders' day-to-day expectations were not influenced much by recent forecasting errors. Thus, while a distributed lag of past prices does give a fair representation of expectations formation, exponential smoothing does not. The most parsimonious model appears to be a 'rule of thumb', according to which the traders expected price to fall during the harvest (in line with past years), while modifying their expectations as the harvest progressed and in accordance with recent day-to-day price movements. While this rule offers a good characterization of how expectations were formed, it did not work well (relative to unbiased forecasting) during the seemingly unusual harvest period included in the present survey. But it did perform a good deal better after the harvest and, arguably, may have worked well in 'normal' years.

It is interesting to note that this conclusion is in sympathy with some recent work by psychologists. The use of such rules of thumb (also called 'heuristics') has been inferred from experimental results on how people deal with uncertainty.[14] A common conclusion of this work is that the heuristics used result in over-reaction to new information. This is borne out in results of the present study suggesting that the forecasting rules used by traders in Bangladesh led them to place too high a weight on the most recent price observations when forming their expectations. The persistence of the forecasting rule in the light of conflicting information appears to reflect a more strongly held commitment to prior beliefs than is allowed by the rational expectations hypothesis.

Notes

1. There were 17 Aratdars at Badamtali in 1973, now the figure is about 150. Dhaka's population has almost doubled in the same period.
2. Sixty-four days are plotted for the expectations series; only the expected direction of change was asked for the first five days.
3. Although it should be noted that the t statistic has low power in small samples when the autocorrelation is close to unity (Nankervis and Savin, 1985).
4. Indeed, traders' prices will converge asymptotically (to zero variance) if they follow identical but independent autoregressive processes.
5. Although the theoretical grounds for this assumption are, as yet, poorly understood. Nor has it been well supported by empirical tests; see Domberger (1979).
6. To see why this is so, let $_{t-n}P_t^e$ denote a forecast of the price P_t to prevail at time t conditional on the information set I_{t-n} available at $t-n$. The corresponding forecasting bias $_{t-n}B_t$ is defined as the mean forecasting error conditional on I_{t-n}:

$$_{t-n}B_t = E(_{t-n}e_t|I_{t-n})$$

where

$$_{t-n}e_t = {}_{t-n}P_t^e - P_t$$

denotes the forecasting error. By the properties of conditional expectations unbiased forecasting ($_{t-n}B_t = 0$) implies that $_{t-n}e_t$ is orthogonal to all random variables in I_{t-n}. In general (for r.v.s formed by $f:R_N \rightarrow R$):

$$E[_{t-n}e_t \cdot f(I_{t-n}) \mid I_{t-n}] = f(I_{t-n}) \cdot {}_{t-n}B_t$$

which yields the orthogonality property of unbiased forecasting. Clearly, the validity of test procedures based on this result depends crucially on correct identification of the available information sets (see, for example, Minford and Peel, 1984). The problem is avoided here since only information supplied by the traders is used in testing for bias. The use of individual data also avoids the problems raised by Dietrich and Joines (1983) in response to Figlewski and Wachtel (1981).

7. This test appears to be due to Theil (1966). It has since been used by Turnovsky (1970), Friedman (1980), Figlewski and Wachtel (1981), Evans and Gulamani (1984), de Leeuw and McKelvey (1984), and Struth (1984), amongst others.

8. Noting that equation 6.5 is equivalent to

$$P_t - P_t^e = \alpha_0 + (\alpha_1 - 1)P_t^e + \mu_t$$

and that, of course, P_t^e is contained in I_{t-1}.

9. For discussion of COMFAC restrictions, see Sargan (1980) and Hendry and Mizon (1978). For ease of computation I have tested COMFAC using the TSP programme for the analysis of non-linear parameter restrictions rather than the sequence of Wald tests proposed by Sargan.

10. Thus Working (1949) characterized an 'ideal futures market' as one in which price changes were unpredictable. The idea has evolved into the well-known 'efficient markets hypothesis'; see Fama (1970).

11. Notice that n is set to one arbitrarily. However, there is little sign of misspecification due to this from the residual autocorrelation diagnostics which follow. The residual correlogram is reasonably flat (absolute t-ratios less than 1.5) up to 14 lags.

12. It may be of interest to note that the following model was one of the early attempts to improve upon the 'naive' expectations assumption embodied in the cobweb theorem; see Goodwin (1947). For an exposition of the dynamic properties of markets under this model of expectations see Gandolfo (1971, chapter 5).

13. In particular, assuming that private stock at time t is a stable and increasing function of $P_{t+1}^e - P_t$ and that expectations are biased such that $\alpha_1 < 1$ in equation 6.5, it follows that actual storage will be greater (less) than perfect foresight storage when price is greater (less) than $\alpha_0/(1-\alpha_1)$.

14. In particular see the various experiments reported by Kahneman, Slovic and Tversky (1982). Also, see Arrow's (1982) survey and Heiner's (1983) interesting rationale for the use of rules of thumb.

Appendix 6.1   Test Statistics

Trader	1 Homogeneity test	2	3 Price flexibility	4	5 Bias test	6 Martingale test	7
	Prices $F(3,60)$	forecast $F(3,60)$	own $t(60)$	mean $t(60)$	$F(3,58)$	$i=1$ $F(5,57)$	$i=2$ $F(5,55)$
(Aratdars)							
1	3.8**	1.7	0.27	3.0*	9.4*	4.4*	7.3*
2	3.2**	3.7**	2.2**	1.5	8.3*	4.6*	9.5*
3	1.7	0.87	1.2	1.9**	9.0*	4.4*+	7.3*
4	5.8*	1.5	1.0	3.7*	9.4*	1.3	3.7*
5	5.9*	1.1	0.19	2.2**	5.4**	2.4**	4.3*
6	2.7	4.9*	1.8**	1.7**	8.2*	1.6	2.3
7	6.0*	7.8*	0.46	3.2*	7.6*	2.0	3.7*
8	4.7*	8.6*	1.4	4.2*	13*	2.5**	6.3*
9	0.68	0.54	0.12	2.7*	13*	1.8	1.9
10	2.4	2.3	0.92	2.9*	15*	0.55	0.66
11	0.97	4.0**	0.54	2.2**	6.8*	0.67+	0.29
12	1.8	5.2*	0.26	3.4*	8.6*	3.3*	3.5*
13	2.5	2.5	0.78	3.2*	7.8*	2.7**	2.9**
14	0.07	1.9	0.41	3.7*	7.3*	3.5*	2.7**
15	10*	2.4	1.2	3.7*	11*	3.0**+	4.7*
16	7.6*	3.6**	1.1	3.7*	15*	2.2+	1.4
17	1.5	9.1*	0.60	3.2*	14*	1.5+	1.5
18	2.9**	5.6*	0.69	2.1**	13*	0.53+	0.47
19	4.3**	1.1	0.61	3.3*	11*	2.0	7.4*
20	1.7	4.6*	1.7**	2.5*	10*	4.0*	9.1*
(Retailers)							
21	n/a	n/a	n/a	n/a	12*	1.6+	1.4
22	n/a	n/a	n/a	n/a	19*	1.5	4.2*

* Rejected at 1%; ** rejected at 5%
\+ First-order residual autocorrelation at 5%

Appendix 6.2   Forecasting bias test*

Trader	1 α_0	2 α_1	3 $1-\alpha_1$	4 $\delta(\times 10^3)$	5 β	6 SEE $\times 10^2$ R^2
1	1.2	0.78	0.22	0.18	−0.064	0.83
	(3.9)	(14)	(3.9)	(1.6)	(0.49)	0.98
2	1.5	0.74	0.26	0.27	−0.061	0.97
	(4.3)	(12)	(4.2)	(2.1)	(0.46)	0.98
3	1.8)	0.68	0.32	0.34	−0.054	1.1
	(4.5)	(9.5)	(4.4)	(2.4)	(0.37)	0.96
4	1.0	0.82	0.18	0.094	−0.25	0.85
	(3.6)	(16)	(3.5)	(0.97)	(1.9)	1.0
5	1.1	0.79	0.21	0.23	−0.088	0.85
	(3.7)	(14)	(3.8)	(2.1)	(0.67)	0.99
6	4.0	0.28	0.72	1.01	0.65	1.0
	(7.8)	(3.1)	(7.8)	(4.1)	(6.7)	1.0
7	2.1	0.63	0.37	0.46	0.18	1.0
	(5.0)	(8.3)	(4.9)	(3.0)	(1.4)	0.99
8	2.8	0.50	0.50	0.62	0.51	0.88
	(6.5)	(6.4)	(6.4)	(3.3)	(4.6)	1.0
9	2.3	0.59	0.41	0.51	0.43	0.69
	(6.3)	(8.9)	(6.2)	(3.6)	(3.7)	1.0
10	1.7	0.69	0.31	0.25	0.035	0.86
	(4.9)	(11)	(5.0)	(2.0)	(0.27)	0.93
11	2.1	0.63	0.37	0.46	0.48	0.72
	(4.8)	(8.1)	(4.7)	(2.9)	(4.0)	1.0
12	1.5	0.74	0.26	0.31	−0.098	0.91
	(4.6)	(13)	(4.5)	(2.7)	(0.70)	0.99
13	1.4	0.74	0.26	0.30	0.14	0.81
	(4.0)	(11)	(4.0)	(2.3)	(1.1)	0.99
14	1.3	0.76	0.24	0.23	0.006	0.88
	(3.7)	(12)	(3.7)	(1.8)	(0.046)	0.93
15	1.4	0.74	0.26	0.22	−0.22	0.89
	(4.7)	(13)	(4.7)	(2.1)	(1.7)	1.0
16	2.0	0.64	0.36	0.33	0.12	0.89
	(5.4)	(9.6)	(5.4)	(2.4)	(0.89)	0.97
17	3.7	0.33	0.67	0.92	0.63	0.87
	(8.8)	(4.4)	(8.8)	(4.4)	(6.5)	1.0
18	2.9	0.48	0.52	0.70	0.56	0.81
	(7.1)	(6.5)	(7.0)	(3.9)	(5.1)	1.0

Appendix 6.2   Forecasting bias test* (*continued*)

Trader	1 α_0	2 α_1	3 $1-\alpha_1$	4 $\delta(\times 10^3)$	5 β	6 $\text{SEE} \times 10^2$ R^2
19	1.7	0.70	0.30	0.26	0.29	0.82
	(4.0)	(9.3)	(4.0)	(1.7)	(2.4)	1.0
20	2.0	0.64	0.36	0.46	0.27	0.78
	(5.6)	(9.9)	(5.5)	(3.4)	(2.1)	1.0
21** retail	1.0	0.82	0.18	0.20	−0.34	0.79
	(3.6)	(16)	(3.5)	(1.9)	(2.8)	1.0
22 retail	4.6	0.82	0.18	1.4	0.67	0.91
	(9.7)	(9.6)	(2.1)	(5.6)	(7.1)	1.0
Mean	1.3	0.75	0.25	0.23	0.08	0.75
(excluding	(4.4)	(13)	(4.3)	(2.1)	(0.67)	0.94
retailers)						

* Natural logs; *t*-ratios in parentheses, $N = 62$, mean $(\log P) = 5.5$.

** COMFAC rejected $\beta v_0 + v_1 = 0.31$ $(t = 4.0)$ The unrestricted estimate for this trader is:

$$P_t = 2.2 \quad + 0.38\,P_t^e \quad + 0.77(P_{t-1}^e - P_{t-1}) - 0.39 P_{t-1} \quad + 0.00055t \quad + 0.48\,\text{error}_{-1}$$
$$\quad (3.9) \quad\quad (3.1) \quad\quad\quad (4.3) \quad\quad\quad\quad\quad (3.9) \quad\quad\quad\quad (2.5) \quad\quad\quad (4.3)$$

$R^2 = 0.55$; $\text{SEE} = 0.0071$.

Note: Estimates used the TSP maximum likelihood programme. (This uses the Beech–MacKinnon method of incorporating the stationarity condition $|\beta| < 1$ in the likelihood function. On the advantages of this method see Beech and MacKinnon (1978) and Harvey (1981).)

7

Policy Issues

7.1 Introduction

This chapter draws together and explores further a number of policy issues raised by the results of this study. I shall assume that the policies concerned are aimed at reducing famine mortality; specifically, the objective is to minimize mortality in some target group up to some future date, given aggregate food availability.

The intuitive appeal of this objective in this setting is strong. There can be little doubt that famine mortality is a very important criterion for judging an economy's performance in allocating food consumption. It is probably the overriding objective of those people vulnerable to famine; there is unlikely to be much else they might strive for which would conflict with it. The protection of individuals from policies or other actions which threaten their survival has been an important principle of many of our most respected legal institutions at both national and international levels.[1] Any relief policy which can reasonably be expected to result in more deaths than necessary is abhorrent to that principle. Of course, governments and relief agencies may often find that the available aid is simply not enough to keep everyone alive; typically there is a positive probability that, no matter how the food is allocated, at least someone will die from lack of it. Nonetheless, one can legitimately strive for relief policies which minimize that probability.

The first policy issue discussed concerns the interpersonal distribution of relief aid. There are some important but poorly understood (and rarely discussed) problems facing relief agencies in deciding how limited amounts of emergency aid should be allocated between famine victims. These involve questions to do with both the objectives of famine relief and the information available to the agency in allocating aid. Section 2 examines these issues.

The second main concern of this chapter is stabilization. Public storage of foodgrains is one of the oldest known famine relief policies.[2] The basic idea is familiar: the government raises its stocks when aggregate availability is high and lowers them when availability is low. But surprisingly little is known about how grain markets are likely to react; indeed, many advocates of public buffer stocks seem to ignore the very existence of private storage.[3] Section 3 of this chapter will examine some of the implications of this study's results on market performance for public buffer stock policies. Sections 4 and 5 discuss alternative stabilization policies using foreign grain trade and publicly supplied information.

Finally, Section 6 discusses some potentially important caveats on famine relief policies in market economies. Aid is too often thought of solely in partial equilibrium terms; in other words, an income transfer is assumed to leave all prices and other sources of incomes unchanged. This is a very difficult assumption to accept when considering wide-spread transfers of income in market economies. For example, rural public works have been a popular alternative to direct food handouts as a means of famine or poverty relief. Partial equilibrium analysis suggests that the recipient's income gain will be the same either way. This ceases to be true when income from other sources is affected.

7.2 Emergency Relief Aid

Governments and agencies involved in the relief of famines and other disasters often face the problem of how to allocate a fixed quantity of emergency food aid between people. Probably the most common means of doing so is by giving each person an equal share. Food allocation according to 'need' has been advocated and occasionally used as an alternative policy.[4] In practice this means that handouts are based on readily observed individual or group attributes such as assessments of age, height and weight.[5]

The same problem is faced by donors allocating food aid between regions or countries. Spatial inequality is common and will persist if mobility and trade are restricted. Here 'need' may be measured by, for example, the local price of grain.

The objective of food aid in this setting is assumed to be to maximize the number of people who survive to an (arbitrary) future date or, equivalently, to minimize mortality. In doing so, the relief agency is faced with uncertainty about the effects of aid on life expectancy. In keeping with the model of Chapter 2, the most important source of uncertainty is the existence of unobserved determinants of personal constitution. This creates imprecision in assessments of the effects of alternative food hand-outs (x) on health. However, to make the model more realistic, the relief agency is now assumed to be able to observe a health-relevant vector of measurable 'needs' (z); these are predetermined characteristics relevant to the individual's health experience.[6]

The relief agency then faces the question: Observing only x and z, but knowing that these are 'noisy' determinants of health, what is the probability of an individual surviving? In the spirit of the model in Chapter 2, one can imagine assigning a number e_0 to the unobserved error made in estimating y which is exactly enough to guarantee that the minimum health needed for survival is achieved. The probability of the individual surviving with x and z is then given by the probability that the error made in assessing y exceeds e_0. So, with the information contained in z, the agency estimates personal constitution to be, say, $k(z)$. The error it makes is $e = y - k(z)$ and has density function f and distribution function F. As in Chapter 2, y and (hence) e are assumed to have unimodal distributions such as depicted in Figure 2.1.

The probability of individual i surviving when consuming x_i and having observed health characteristics z_i is:

$$s(x_i, z_i) = 1 - F(e_{0i}) \tag{7.1}$$

where $e_0 = g(x) - k(z)$ is the value of e such that $\phi(x, k(z) + e_0) = h_0$, the (fixed) minimum health needed to survive. Without loss of generality, one can define 'needs' such that k is strictly decreasing in z. Thus, $s_z = f(e_0)k'(z) < 0$. Given the information contained in $\mathbf{z} = (z_1, \ldots, z_N)$ and, of course $\mathbf{x} = (x_1, \ldots, x_N)$, the number of people who can be expected to die is:

$$M(\mathbf{x}, \mathbf{z}) = N - \sum_{i=1}^{N} s(x_i, z_i) \tag{7.2}$$

I shall assume that, when optimally allocated, the available food is enough to give all affected individuals a positive quantity. This means that one can concentrate on interior solutions to the problem of choosing $\mathbf{x}$ to minimize $M(\mathbf{x}, \mathbf{z})$ subject to aggregate avail-ability. Furthermore, following Chapter 2, I shall assume that individual survival functions are strictly concave in consumption in a suitable neighbourhood of the optimum.[7]

It is clear that, under these conditions, there will be survival gains from equalizing redistributions of a fixed aggregate food stock, $\sum x_i$, between people with the same needs. If there is no variation in needs within the population then these gains will persist until consumption is equalized. Then the equal shares policy will minimize mortality.[8]

This will also be true if observed 'needs' are uninformative in that all possible errors in assessing personal constitution are equally likely. For then the distribution function F will be linear (since its density is uniform) and so the survival function given by equation 7.1 and, hence, aggregate mortality given by equation 7.2 will be additively separable between consumption and needs. The effect of extra food on survival chance will not vary with observed needs and so neither will the mortality minimizing food handout.[9]

More generally, however, the optimal allocation of food $\mathbf{x}^*$ equalizes the consumption slope of the survival function:

$$s_x(x_i^*, z_i) = -f(e_{0i})g'(x_i) \qquad (7.3)$$

across all i at a value s_x^* which gives the maximum number of lives that can be expected to be saved by increasing total food aid by one unit. For large N, one can treat this expression as a constant. The optimal handout to individual i is then implicitly a function of z_i only, $x_i^* = h(z_i)$ say, although it is not necessarily an increasing function. The appendix to this chapter shows that more food should go to those in greater need if and only if the minimum value of the unobserved attribute needed to guarantee survival is less than the mode of its distribution. But, in practice, one need not know anything about the distribution of the unobserved attribute to determine if more food should go to those in greater need. The survival function's second cross partial derivative, s_{xz}, is sufficient for determining the sign of $f'(e_0)$, and s_{xz} is, in principle, estimatable from observable data. If e_0 is less than the mode then a higher value of z will be associated with a higher consumption slope of the survival function, in which case allocations which give more food to those in greater need will yield lower mortality than those which do not.

The survival chance of each individual when handouts are optimal is $s^*(z_i) = s(h(z_i), z_i)$ and is (monotonic) decreasing in z (see the appendix). Thus, when mortality is at its minimum, survival chance will be lower for those in greater need. This holds irrespective of whether or not more food should go to those in greater need.

Figure 7.1 illustrates the case in which the optimal food handout is an increasing function of need; when need increases from z_0 to z_1, the consumption slope of the survival function s_x increases and survival chance falls for each $x > x_0$. Figure 7.2 illustrates a case in which $s_{xz} < 0$ for all x in the interval (x_0, x_1). Then the survival optimal policy entails smaller food handouts to those in greater need. The reason is plain: if those in greater need also tend to be the people for whom changes in consumption have a relatively

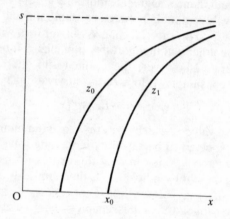

Fig. 7.1

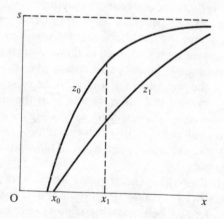

Fig. 7.2

small impact on their survival chance then it will be preferable, from the point of view of aggregate mortality, to give the food to someone in less need but with a better chance of surviving after the handout.

The pattern of recent shifts over time in the international cross-section relationship between life expectancy and national income provides an example. Preston (1975) presents strong evidence of concavity in the relationship between life expectancy at birth and national income per head. His results also suggest that, for all except relatively high incomes, the slope of the relationship was higher during the 1960s than the 1930s. In fact, Preston's results look quite a lot like Figure 7.2. Later results in Preston (1980) do not confirm this picture; at given income, the slope is found to be lower in 1970 than 1940. However, Fuchs (1980) has shown that this result hides considerable variation between LDC's and other countries. When Preston's (1980) sample is stratified, Fuchs finds that the income slope increased considerably between 1940 and 1970 for LDCs while it showed an even more impressive drop for developed countries. Thus, at least for LDC's, the international cross-sectional evidence suggests a negative correlation between vertical shifts over time in the survival function and its income slope. Since the same results support the concavity assumption, equalizing redistributions will lower aggregate mortality at a given point in time. However, for low income countries ($x_0 < x < x_1$), income transfers from the first period to the second would also have lowered mortality, even though survival chance was lower during the first period at each income level.

How applicable is the theory outlined above? It is certainly feasible to estimate survival functions defined on food consumption and needs (or in a dual form defined on prices and incomes). The data may be in the highly aggregated cross-section form used by the above authors or in the aggregate time series form used in Chapter 2 of this study. Dissaggregated data on individual deaths in a relief camp, for example, might also be used, provided that food consumption and need characteristics have been monitored carefully. As long as the functional form used is flexible enough to permit estimation of the survival function's second cross-partial derivative between 'food' and 'needs', such research will throw light on how food should best be allocated to minimize famine mortality. There appears to be considerable scope for future empirical research on this important question.

7.3 Buffer Stock Policies

A theoretical case for consumption stabilization over time as a means of famine relief follows straightforwardly from the arguments of Chapter 2. It was also noted there that the desirability of stabilizing consumption over time does not necessarily mean that price stabilization is also desirable. Nonetheless, a priori considerations and the empirical evidence of Chapter 2 support a case for foodgrain price stabilization during famines. But this conclusion does not, of itself, imply that government intervention is called for.

It is now known that the effectiveness of stock policies as price stabilizers depends crucially on the response of private storage decisions.[10] By stabilizing prices, buffer stock policies will reduce the incentives for private speculation. And so, changes in the government's stock level will displace private storage. Indeed, as will be demonstrated below, the displacement will be one-to-one in perfectly competitive markets; in this case public buffer stocks will be ineffective as price stabilizers.

This prompts the question of how effective buffer stocks may be in imperfect markets. The effects of informationally biased expectations on the formulation of buffer stock policies have received little attention.[11]

To help clarify the issues involved, consider first the familiar two period model of competitive markets for a storable good under perfect arbitrage and perfect foresight. The level of private storage is exactly enough to equalize prices p_t ($t = 1,2$) over time net of unit storage cost c:

$$p_2 = p_1 + c \qquad (7.4)$$

Aggregate consumption in the first period is $H - S^p - S^g$ where H is production in the first period and S^p and S^g are the levels of carryover to the second period by private traders and the government respectively. Consumption in the second period is $S^p + S^g$. The (inverse) demand functions are $p_t = f(x_t)$ ($t = 1,2$) for which $f' < 0$. Thus the level of private storage implied by perfect arbitrage is the solution for S^p of:

$$f(H - S^p - S^g) - f(S^p + S^g) = c \qquad (7.5)$$

Plainly this solution will depend on the values taken by S^g, H and

c; but it will do so in a special way, implied by the fact that S^p and S^g only enter equation 7.5 in the form of their sum $S^p + S^g$. Thus market equilibrium fixes the level of aggregate storage conditional on H and c, and so exogenous changes in public storage will displace private storage on a one-to-one basis when comparing equilibria.

Perfect arbitrage is crucial to this argument. For suppose instead that there are significant fixed costs in setting up storage facilities so that positive profits are possible in equilibrium, $p_2 > p_1 + c$. It will be assumed that the level of private storage is an increasing function of unit profit from holding stock (it does not matter here whether this is net or gross of unit storage cost):

$$S^p = g(p_2 - p_1 - c) \quad g' > 0$$
$$= g(f(S^p + S^g) - f(H - S^p - S^g) - c) \quad (7.6)$$

Private storage will no longer displace public storage on a one-to-one basis; the solution of equation 7.6 for S^p is implicitly a function of S^g with slope between -1 and 0 (see the appendix to this chapter).

How is the result affected by informational inefficiency? Following the analysis of Chapter 6, suppose that expectations and realizations are related as:

$$p_2^e = h(p_2) \quad (7.7)$$

So, the results of Chapter 6 imply a bias such that $h' > 1$. Analogously to equation 7.5, the level of private storage is now:

$$S^p = g(p_2^e - p_1 - c)$$
$$= g(h(f(S^p + S^g)) - f(H - S^p - S^g) - c) \quad (7.8)$$

Again, there is potential for stabilization using public storage. Holding other things constant, the displacement effect will be greater (less) with informational inefficiency whenever h' is greater (less) than unity (see the appendix). Thus the pattern of forecasting bias revealed by Chapter 6 suggests that public storage will be *less* effective as a stabilizer than would be the case with perfect foresight under otherwise identical conditions. So, at least for these data, the existence of informational inefficiency does not enhance the case for the use of changes in public buffer stocks to stabilize prices.

There is a straightforward way of comparing the displacement effect with and without the informational inefficiency. Using the results of Chapter 6 and taking a linear approximation of the demand functions the appendix shows that the absolute value of the displacement effect for the Badamtali data is at most 17 per cent higher than its value with informationally efficient forecasting. Thus, although the results of this study weaken the stabilization case for public storage relative to an informationally efficient market, the difference is probably small.

The Possibility of Perverse Displacement Effects.
One of the conclusions of Chapter 3 was that information that public stocks and future imports were likely to be low had a bullish effect on private storage in Bangladesh during the 1974 famine. There appears to have been a fairly widely held belief that the Bangladesh government would be unable to implement a suitable stabilizing response to the effect of crop damage on future output. This led to high expectations of future prices and, hence, high current prices. It was also seen that many of the Bangladesh government's announcements at the time appear to have been aimed at raising public confidence in the government's stock position as a means of lowering current prices.

However, the results of Chapter 3 also suggest that lack of confidence in the government (combined with crop damage information) led to systematic overestimation of future prices during the famine. This conclusion has some interesting implications for buffer stock policy.

It seems plausible that, while the forecasting bias may be high at low levels of public storage, it will vanish at sufficiently high levels of stock. Thus one can characterize the relationship by the assumption:

$$p_2^e - p_2 = \psi(S^g) \quad \psi' < 0 \tag{7.9}$$

Analogously to equation 7.6, the level of private storage is now determined by

$$S^p = g(f(S^p + S^g)) - f(H - S^p - S^g) + \psi(S^g) - c \tag{7.10}$$

However, the displacement effect is no longer bounded below by -1 (see the appendix). In particular,

$$\frac{dS^p}{dS^g} \gtreqless -1 \text{ as } g'\psi' \gtreqless -1 \qquad (7.11)$$

The aggregate level of storage in the economy need no longer have a monotonic relationship with the level of public storage. With some further restrictions on the functions g and ψ one can show that there exists a positive value of $S^g = S^*$, below which aggregate stock is *decreasing* in S^g. See the appendix to this chapter for details.

This suggests that the usual policy of selling from buffer stocks at times of high prices, may fail at sufficiently low levels of public storage. Indeed, at times of high prices, if public stocks are believed to be so low as to generate highly inflated expectations of future prices in response to supply shocks then a further reduction in the public stock will be price de-stabilizing. The Bangladesh government's efforts to raise public confidence in its stock and trade position during 1974 may well have been a sound (albeit unsuccessful) response to a plausible form of informational inefficiency in rice markets.

7.4 Famine Relief by Trade

Unrestricted international trade has recently been advocated as an alternative stabilization policy to buffer stocks.[12] The essence of the argument is simple: by raising the local food price relative to prices elsewhere, shocks to domestic consumption opportunities should be at least partly offset by an increase in imports or fall in exports. Thus free trade should help buffer aggregate domestic consumption from random shocks to, for example, price expectations or production possibilities.

Of course the effects of trade on the interpersonal distribution of consumption are also of concern here; while the results of this study suggest that famine mortality can be reduced by stabilizing consumption over time, trade is also likely to affect mortality via its effects on interpersonal distribution. If (as is common) restrictions on trade are used to keep domestic grain prices below world prices then free trade could well have sufficiently adverse effects on interpersonal distribution to mitigate its stabilizing influence on intertemporal distribution.

Lessons from British India's Experience.

The experience of British India around the turn of this century provides a rare opportunity for studying a famine vulnerable economy with easy access to foreign markets. British India had virtually unrestricted external trade for many decades prior to the First World War *and* highly variable aggregate foodgrain production.[13] The sub-continent was a net exporter of foodgrains (particularly rice) for most of the period, which included a number of severe famines (Bhatia, 1967; Ghose, 1982).

Thus free trade in foodgrains is likely to have reduced British India's aggregate grain consumption. To the extent that price elasticities of (net) demand for staple food grains tend to decline with the amount consumed, higher grain prices are also likely to have adversely affected interpersonal distribution.[14] But did it help stabilize consumption over time? Sluggishness in trade's response to domestic scarcities can arise from, for example, domestic price stickiness, the existence of long term contracts and delays due to transport.

The stabilizing performance of trade can be tested by regressing exports against output; a positive coefficient indicates that trade helped buffer domestic availability from output fluctuations. Allowing for dynamic effects and using Blyn's (1966) estimates of foodgrain output (Y) and net trade flows (X) for British India (excluding Burma) over the period 1892 to 1914, I obtained the following result (both quantities in million tons):

$$X = -6.9 + 0.49X_{-1} + 0.071Y + 0.079Y_{-1}$$
$$(4.5)\quad(3.4)\qquad(2.5)\qquad(3.1)$$

$$R^2 = 0.67; \text{ Durbin } h = 0.34 \tag{7.12}$$

The following restricted form of this equation performs well ($t = -0.2$):

$$X = -6.9 + 0.51X_{-1} + 0.075(Y + Y_{-1})$$
$$(4.7)\quad(4.0)\qquad(5.0)$$

$$R^2 = 0.67; \text{ Durbin } h = 0.34 \tag{7.13}$$

A significant positive marginal rate of export is indicated, although the effect is small in the short-run; only 7.5 per cent of a fall in output would have been passed on to trade. Export sluggishness is also indicated by the significantly positive effect of lagged exports.

And so the long-run marginal rate of export of about 30 per cent is higher than the short-run figure. Nonetheless, even in the long run, the stabilization of aggregate availability by free trade was far from complete.

While these results are not encouraging, there may be scope for government intervention using trade taxes aimed at enhancing the responsiveness of external trade to domestic prices.[15] A stabilizing tax on trade is one in which exports are taxed (imports subsidized) when output is below normal while otherwise exports are subsidized (imports taxed).

The main drawback of such policies is thought to be the induced instability of tax revenue (Reutlinger, 1982). To get an idea of the likely magnitude of the policy's revenue instability, suppose that the exporter-importer faces post-tax domestic price $(1+\tau)_p$ when pre-tax price is p. The tax rate τ is proportional to the mean deviations of domestic output (and so raises zero revenue on average):

$$\tau = \log(1+\tau) = \eta(\bar{Y}-Y) \tag{7.14}$$

where the parameter η is chosen to achieve stable net grain availability to the domestic economy. Suppose also that exports respond linearly to the log of the domestic/foreign relative price (Ravallion, 1986b):

$$X = a_0+a_1\log((1+\tau)p/p^w) \tag{7.15}$$

for world price p^w. The pre-tax domestic price is assumed to be a function of aggregate domestic availability alone and so it can be treated as fixed when the tax policy is chosen to fully stabilize availability. This requires $dX/dY = 1$ and so the stabilizing tax rate has $\eta = 1/a_1$.

Latham and Neal (1983) have compiled series of domestic and foreign rice prices and rice exports for British India which permit estimation of a model based on equation 7.15. Using their data I estimated the following equation for British India's rice exports (including Burma) over the period 1892–1914:[16]

$$X = 1.7 - 2.0 \log(PI/PL) + 0.057t \tag{7.16}$$
$$(11) \quad (3.6) \qquad\qquad (6.0)$$

$$R^2 = 0.53; \ D-W = 1.58; \ t \text{ (homogeneity)} = 1.4$$

where PI is the average price of rice in India and PL is the London price of Burma rice cargoes.

Using this estimate for a_1, I have calculated the revenue of the stabilizing tax $\tau = 0.5(\bar{Y} - Y)$ for each year in the series. Of course, (by design) revenue is zero on average. However, the variation is considerable. As a percentage of the total budget of the government of India in 1900, tax revenue would have ranged from -73 to 66, with a standard deviation of 34.

While these simulations are only intended to give a rough idea of the possible magnitudes that may be involved, they do confirm the view that revenue instability of a stabilizing trade tax is likely to be large. This suggests that some form of monetary buffer stock, such as the IMF's food financing facility, may be essential for the future success of such policies.[17]

7.5 Public Information

There are conditions under which the prices observed in a rational expectations equilibrium will fully reveal all relevant inside information to market participants.[18] Then governmental activities aimed at information dispersal will be futile.

However, the existence of informational inefficiencies in the markets studied in this book suggests that there may be a useful role for government in providing better information.[19] Since the existing informational inefficiencies in Bangladesh rice markets tend to be price de-stabilizing, suitable public information may also have a role as a stabilization policy.

What information should be collected? The government of Bangladesh now monitors market price as a famine predictor.[20] The survey discussed in Chapter 6 has established the feasibility of monitoring rice traders' expectations about future prices in Bangladesh. A suitable aggregate of individual expectations can be thought of as a convenient summary measure of the information held by traders. Of course, since the surveyed expectations turned out to be biased, there will exist price forecasts based on the same information with greater precision than the traders' own expectations. Nonetheless, even biased expectations can improve upon the predictive ability of current and past prices, provided the expectations embody relevant non-price information.

To get some idea as to whether it may be possible to improve upon the Bangladesh government's price forecasting performance using surveyed expectations, I have re-estimated the simple autoregressive price model for the Badamtali data (Chapter 6, equation 6.1), including the previous day's sample mean of each day's expected price as an additional regressor. This gave:

$$P_t = 0.58 + 0.096P_{t-1} + 0.80P_t^e + 0.11 \times 10^{-3}t + 0.037D$$
$$\quad (8.0) \quad (1.0) \qquad (8.0) \qquad (1.6) \qquad\qquad (9.7)$$

$$R^2 = 0.98; \text{SEE} = 0.0049; Q(14) = 15. \tag{7.17}$$

The expectations series is clearly significant and permits quite a sizeable drop in within-sample residual variance when compared with equation 6.1. For forecasting purposes, the variance of the model's *post-sample* forecasting error is also of interest. To check this, I re-estimated equations 6.1 and 7.17 leaving out the last ten days of the series. The mean square forecasting error (MSR) dropped considerably when the expectations series was included; the model based on equation 6.1 gave a MSR $= 0.20 \times 10^{-4}$ for the last 10 days while that based on equation 7.17 gave MSR $= 0.037 \times 10^{-4}$, an impressive 80 per cent drop in forecasting error variance.

This suggests that there are likely to be sizeable gains in price forecasting precision using traders' expectations monitored on a regular basis. Since actual prices are already monitored by public authorities at weekly intervals in numerous markets in Bangladesh, the marginal cost of also surveying expectations is unlikely to be large. Of course, the effectiveness of such public information will depend crucially on the credibility of the survey results; governmental censoring or interference with the published results may be tempting at times of impending food crises but would seriously undermine the longer term success of such a policy.

7.6 Caveats on Food Aid as an Income Supplement

Many famine victims are likely to have suffered a complete collapse of their exchange entitlements; aid will be their sole source of income. However, this is unlikely to be true for all potential famine victims or at all times during a famine. When aid is a supplement to the income from other sources, its effects on prices and other income can have considerable bearing on the recipient's survival prospects. This section examines those effects.

Past discussions of aid policy have often ignored market responses to redistribution. Aid can certainly alter relative prices. Adverse price effects have been identified as a constraint on redistributive policies within low-income countries (Griffin and James, 1981; Sen, 1981a, appendix B).

The effects of food aid on the prices facing recipients depend crucially on the extent of integration between the markets which donors and recipients face. As the following arguments will show, if the aid is a transfer of goods between segmented markets then it is likely to have a very different effect on the recipient's welfare to that resulting from a transfer between markets which are well integrated by trade.

If donor and recipient are located in different markets (in the sense that there is no trade between them) and markets facing the recipient are competitive and stable then the food transfer will act like an increase in aggregate supply and so lower the prices for food facing the recipient. Thus, recipients for whom the aid is a supplement to their market purchases will gain in two ways: they will have higher incomes (which now include an imputed money value of the aid) and they will face lower food prices.

The outcome is likely to be different when the aid is a transfer within an integrated free-trade economy. It is readily demonstrated that in a stable and competitive exchange economy for two goods with continuous excess demand functions, the interpersonal transfer of a commodity will raise (lower) its relative price if the donor has a lower (higher) marginal propensity to consume that good than the recipient. The rural poor in low-income countries tend to have very high marginal propensities to consume (mpc) food from their incomes; indeed, an mpc of unity for food amongst the rural poor is quite plausible during famines. Their mpc for food is very likely to exceed that of the aid donor. And so, in a market economy, supplementary food aid to the rural poor will result in them paying higher prices for the rest of their food. Thus, and in contrast to the case of transfers between segmented markets, price effects will mitigate the benefits from the aid.

In a stable competitive economy with only two income groups, the aid recipient will be better off. But doubts exist about even this, seemingly innocuous, conclusion under more realistic conditions.[21] Suppose there are two goods, food and a 'luxury' good, and three income groups, one of which (the third group) is not directly involved in the redistribution. The 'donor' can be thought of as a high income country, the 'recipient' as the rural poor in a low income country and the third group as the rich in the low income country. The two countries trade freely. Ravallion (1983) shows that the aid recipient will only gain when comparing general equilibria of the economy described above if:

$$\begin{pmatrix} \text{Donor's} & \text{Third group's} \\ \text{mpc} & - \text{mpc} \\ \text{luxury} & \text{luxury} \end{pmatrix} \begin{pmatrix} \text{Third group's} \\ \text{excess supply} \\ \text{of luxury} \end{pmatrix} > \begin{matrix} \text{Aggregate} \\ \text{compensated} \\ \text{substitution} \\ \text{effect} \end{matrix} \quad (7.18)$$

However, the recipient will only be worse off if the above inequality is reversed. For example, suppose that

(i) the aid donor has a higher mpc for the luxury good than the rich in the low income country,

(ii) the rich in the low income country are net demanders of the luxury good (for example, they are rich peasants who trade their food surplus for a manufactured good), and

(iii) compensated substitution effects between food and the luxury good are small.[22]

Then the adverse effects on the prices facing the aid recipient will actually leave the recipient *worse off* after the transfer is made and markets have responded. Since the first two of the above conditions are plausible, it can be seen that the size of the aggregate substitution effects in consumption may be quite crucial in determining the effects of food aid on survival chances when it supplements market exchange.

Relief Works.

Aid can also affect income from other sources of which wages are likely to be an important part for the rural poor. Government intervention in labour markets has often been advocated and used as a means of relieving poverty and famines in South Asia. Relief works were a prominent part of the Indian Famine Codes which emerged in the late nineteenth century (Aykroyd, 1974, chapter 5); governments of British India were a good deal less reticent to intervene in labour markets than in grain markets. Similar policies have been followed in Post-Independence India; for example, the government of Maharashtra has offered guaranteed employment on rural public works, and their policy has been widely praised (for recent discussions see Herring and Edwards, 1983; Lieberman, 1985; Dreze, 1986). In Bangladesh, the World Food Programme has initiated a growing 'Food for Work Programme' along similar lines. Recent surveys have suggested that the policy has had success in raising the incomes of the very poor, although the effects on their employment appear to have been less than expected (Chowdhury, 1983; Osmani and Chowdhury, 1983).

How much can rural incomes be raised by relief work? Ignoring any effects on wages, other employment or other sources of income, an extra job on rural works projects will raise rural incomes by the amount of the wage rate. More plausibly, both wages and other employment will change, although probably with opposite effects on rural incomes; an increase in public works employment is likely to put upward pressure on the agricultural wage rate leading to a reduction in demand for agricultural labour. Both effects have been observed in Bangladesh's Food for Work Programme (Osmani and Chowdhury, 1983). Thus the gain in rural income from an extra job could be above or below the wage rate.

A simple model can help clarify the issue.[23] The model includes a prominent feature of this setting, namely the existence of unemployment associated with labour market dualism between the traditional (rural) sector and the modern (urban) sector in which real wages are relatively rigid. Large scale migration from rural to urban areas is common during famines. The appendix outlines a model of dual labour markets incorporating the (Harris–Todaro) assumption of unrestricted mobility between the urban and rural sectors. It is shown that the marginal effect on employment in the agricultural section (N_a) of an aid financed change in rural public works employment (N_g) is given by:

$$\frac{dN_a}{dN_g} = \frac{-\varepsilon}{\varepsilon + N_u/N_a} < 0 \qquad (7.19)$$

where $-\varepsilon$ is the wage elasticity of demand for agricultural labour and N_u is the size of the urban workforce (including unemployed workers). Thus an increase in rural public works employment will displace at least some employment in agriculture. When the level of urbanization (N_u/N_a) is low the outcome will resemble a full employment equilibrium in which the displacement will be close to one-to-one; total rural employment will be invariant to the size of the public works programme. For a country such as Bangladesh, the level of urbanization (as defined above) is about 20 per cent, while the elasticity of demand for agricultural labour is probably in the region -0.7 to -0.2.[24] Thus, using the formula in equation 7.19, the displacement effect will be between 50 and 80 per cent; the increase in total employment will be between 20 and 50 per cent of the increase in rural public works employment. While these numbers are only intended to be a rough guide to the orders of magnitude involved, they do suggest that the displacement of other employment by relief work need not be negligible.

Turning to wages and rural incomes, the appendix also shows that, when the modern sector wage is institutionally fixed, the marginal effect of an increase in public works employment on total rural income

$$Y = w_a(N_a+N_g) \qquad (7.20)$$

is identical to its effect on the agricultural wage; both are positive. Furthermore, dY/dN_g is greater (less) than the wage if $\varepsilon N_a + N_u$ is less (greater) than unity (where N_a and N_u are the proportions of the country's total workforce in the agricultural and urban sectors).

The range of figures considered plausible above for Bangladesh imply that the marginal effect of an extra job on rural income will exceed the wage rate, and it will do so by quite a wide margin whenever the level of urbanization is low and/or agricultural labour demand is fairly wage inelastic. To give a numerical example, suppose that $\varepsilon = 0.25$, $N_a = 0.8$ and $N_u = 0.2$. Then an extra job in the rural sector will raise rural income by a factor of 2.5 times the wage rate for that job.

As long as the elasticity of demand for rural labour does not exceed unity, the rural income gain will exceed the wage rate (see the appendix). The intuition behind this result is clear: inelastic labour demand guarantees that the exogenous increase in aggregate demand as a result of the relief work will *raise* income from non-relief work since, although the amount of such work will fall, the wage rate will increase by a greater proportion. Hence total

rural income will increase by more than the wage from the relief
work alone.

7.7 Summary

In the same way that a drop in aggregate food availability need not
cause a famine, an increase in availability need not stop one.[25] The
effect of an increase in aggregate food supply on famine mortality
will depend crucially on how that food is distributed over time and
between people. This chapter has attempted to evaluate critically
alternative policies affecting food distribution.

In examining interpersonal distribution, it is assumed that the
relief agency can monitor 'needs', interpreted as noisy indicators
of personal constitution. The optimal food handout is a function of
need. And its properties are in principle estimatable. However, in
aiming for minimum mortality one must admit the possibility that
this need not imply more food for those in greater need. Exceptions arise if there is a negative correlation between need and the
food consumption slope of survival chance. While there may be
serious moral objections to an aid allocation which did not give
more food to those in greater need, one should not lose sight of the
fact that, under the above condition, alternative allocations will
result in more deaths than necessary. Empirical research is clearly
called for on the relationship between existing need indicators and
the consumption slopes of the survival functions of famine victims.

Turning to intertemporal distribution, although the results of
this study suggest a case in favour of foodgrain price stabilization,
the most appropriate form of policy intervention remains unclear.
The case for public storage rests on the nature of the distortions to
markets; buffer stocks will not be able to stabilize a competitive
market with rational expectations. Nor can it be presumed that the
existence of distortions associated with informational inefficiency
will enhance the case in favour of buffer stocks. Indeed, the
specific pattern of price forecasting bias revealed by the results of
this study implies that the displacement of private stocks by public
stocks will be greater than one would expect (under otherwise
identical conditions) in an informationally efficient market.

At the same time, the risk of letting public stocks fall too low in
such markets should be appreciated. Bangladesh's experience
clearly suggests that greater confidence about the government's

stock position could have gone a long way towards diffusing excessive speculative activity in rice markets during the 1974 famine.

There are a number of alternatives or supplements to conventional buffer stock policies. This chapter has discussed two of these, namely external trade and public information policies.

British India's experience with free trade during famines around the turn of this century does little to support the case for famine relief by this means. However, there may well be good prospects for enhancing trade's response to domestic scarcities using stabilizing tax policies, coupled with an appropriate monetary buffer stock to deal with the policy's likely revenue instability.

The informational inefficiencies revealed by this study also suggest that there may be potential for policies aimed at improving the information of traders and relief agencies pertaining to future food availability. One feasible means of doing this in a systematic way is by monitoring traders' future price expectations in conjunction with realized prices. Bangladesh data suggest that this could achieve considerable gains in price forecasting precision, relative to forecasts based solely on observed prices.

There are other policy options to public buffer stocks. Intervention can also be aimed at expanding *individual* opportunities for buffering consumption from market uncertainties. As was noted in Chapter 2, the very existence of trade entitlement failure as a cause of the sharp increase in mortality observed during a famine presupposes that famine victims have either had non-rational expectations of income changes *or* restricted access to storage and credit. There are policy initiatives which could improve the latter. Government loans or subsidies may be offered to encourage private but co-operatively used storage facilities. There also appear to be a number of relatively unexplored possibilities for intervention in rural credit markets. For example, the introduction of a government backed financial asset with guaranteed food purchasing power could offer an attractive alternative to storage and would avoid the familiar problem of declining real asset prices in terms of food during famines. But again it should be emphasised that such policies will be of little help if potential famine victims hold biased expectations of their future consumption opportunities.

This chapter has also examined the caveats that are called for when aid is only an addition (albeit an important one) to other income. It has been argued that the recipient's benefit from food aid as a supplement to market exchange depends crucially on who the donor is. If the donor does not trade in the same markets as the recipient then the price effects of aid are likely to be to the recipient's advantage; the aid will be worth more than its value at the initial prices. On the other hand, when donors and recipients do trade in the same markets and the recipient has the higher marginal propensity to consume food, the value of the aid to the recipient will be diminished. Indeed, it could even be negative. Whether it is or not depends on the market behaviour of third parties not directly involved in the transfer. This chapter has noted a simple test for checking whether or not food aid will have at least a positive net benefit to the recipient when it supplements market exchange in a competitive economy.

An interesting implication of the above argument is that aid policies which are combined with trade liberalization may well be self-defeating; the aid is likely to be worth more to the recipient if it is combined with restrictions on trade between donor and recipient.

The value to the recipient of aid given in the form of relief work will also be affected by the response of markets and in this case the effects on labour markets are likely to be important. Under seemingly plausible conditions, the gain in rural income from an extra job will exceed the wage from that job. This suggests that 'food for work' programmes may provide an effective alternative to direct food handouts as a means of raising the incomes of the rural poor.

In short, while poor performance by markets indicates a potential for successful government intervention, the difficulties in achieving effective famine relief must not be underrated. It is often the case that well intentioned policy initiatives have unexpected or even perverse effects in market economies. Famine relief is no exception. The causation of famine involves a lot more than bad weather and its relief requires much more than aid.

Appendix 7.1.

(i) The following argument substantiates claims made in Section 7.2. For large N, the optimal allocation of food $\mathbf{x}^*$ is such that

$-f(e_{0i})g'(x_i)$ is a constant for all i. The implicit solution has $x_i^* = h(z_i)$ with slope (dropping subscripts):

$$h'(z) = \frac{f'(e_0)k'(z)g'(x)}{f'(e_0)g'(x)^2 + f(e_0)g''(x)} \gtreqless O \text{ as } f'(e_o) \lesseqgtr O \qquad (7A.1)$$

(Noting that strict concavity of s in x implies that $f'(e_0)g'(x)^2 + f(e_0)g''(x) > 0$). Since f is assumed to be unimodal, it follows that $h'(z) > 0$ if and only if e_0 is less than the mode, as claimed in Section 7.2. The corresponding survival chance of a person with 'needs' z when handouts are optimal is $s^*(z) = s(h(z),z)$ and

$$s^{*\prime}(z) = \frac{f(e_0)^2 k'(z)g''(x)}{f'(e_0)g'(x)^2 + f(e_0)g''(x)} < 0 \qquad (7A.2)$$

(ii) The following results are used in Section 7.4. Implicitly differentiating equation 7.6 with respect to S^g and solving, it is clear that:

$$-1 < \frac{\mathrm{d}S^p}{\mathrm{d}S^g} = \frac{g'(f_1' + f_2')}{1 - g'(f_1' + f_2')} < 0 \qquad (7A.3)$$

Proceeding similarly from equation 7.8:

$$-1 < \frac{\mathrm{d}S^p}{\mathrm{d}S^g} = \frac{g'(f_1' + h'f_2')}{1 - g'(f_1' + h'f_2')} < 0 \qquad (7A.4)$$

Comparing equations 7A.3 and 7A.4 it can be verified that the $\mathrm{d}S^p/\mathrm{d}S^g$ will be greater (less) with perfect foresight whenever h' is greater (less) than unity. Letting $(\mathrm{d}S^p/\mathrm{d}S^g)^*$ denote the value of the displacement effect with perfect foresight, it can readily be shown that (for $f_t' = f'$ for both t):

$$\frac{\mathrm{d}S^p}{\mathrm{d}S^g} \bigg/ \frac{\mathrm{d}S^{p*}}{\mathrm{d}S^g} = \frac{1 + h'}{2 + (1 - h')\mathrm{d}S^{p*}/\mathrm{d}S^g} \qquad (7A.5)$$

The results of Chapter 6 imply (at mean points; see Table 6.2) a value of $h' = 1/0.75 = 1.33$. Then the RHS of equation 7A.5 is strictly increasing in $\mathrm{d}S^{p*}/\mathrm{d}S^g$; in the limit as $\mathrm{d}S^{p*}/\mathrm{d}S^g$ approaches zero, the ratio of the two displacement effects approaches its maximum of 1.17. Implicitly differentiating equation 7.10 with respect to S^g one obtains

$$\frac{\mathrm{d}S^p}{\mathrm{d}S^g} = \frac{g'((f_1'+f_2')+\psi')}{1-g'(f_1'+f_2')} < 0 \qquad (7A.6)$$

from which equation 7.11 follows by inspection. Sufficient conditions for the existence of S^* such that $\mathrm{d}S^p/\mathrm{d}S^g < -1$ for $S^g < S^*$ are that g is linear, and that ψ has the properties $\psi'' > 0$, $\psi'(0) = -\infty$ and $\psi(\infty) = 0$. These properties imply that there exists a unique $S^* > 0$ such that $g'\psi'(S^*) = -1$. The inequalities in equation 7.11 then imply that S^* yields a unique minimum of the aggregate stock $S^g + S^p$.

(iii) The following argument proves the claims made in Section 7.6 concerning the effects of relief work on rural incomes under labour market dualism. The model is:

$$w_i = f_i(N_i) \quad f_i' < 0, i = a, m \qquad (7A.7)$$

$$N_a + N_u + N_g = 1 \qquad (7A.8)$$

$$w_a N_u = w_m N_m \qquad (7A.9)$$

where w_i is the real food wage in sector i, which can be either agriculture ($i = a$) or manufacturing ($i = m$) and N_i is the number of workers in sector i. N_u denotes the number of workers in the urban sector comprising those employed (N_m) and those unemployed ($N_u - N_m$). N_g workers are employed on public works projects and their wage bill is financed by aid. The possibility of unemployment arises because the wage in the manufacturing sector is assumed to be fixed. The model is closed by the assumption (following Harris and Todaro, 1970) of free mobility between urban and rural sectors which, under risk neutrality, implies equality of the agricultural wage rate with the expected urban wage, $w_m N_m/N_u$.

Fixity of w_m implies that N_m and, hence, $w_a N_u$ are also fixed (7A.9). Then,

$$w_a \mathrm{d}N_u + N_u f_a' \mathrm{d}N_a = 0 \qquad (7A.10)$$

Also, from equation 7A.8:

$$\mathrm{d}N_u + \mathrm{d}N_a + \mathrm{d}N_g = 0 \qquad (7A.11)$$

The solution of the last two equations for

$$\mathrm{d}N_a/\mathrm{d}N_g = \frac{-w_a}{w_a - N_u f_a'} = -k\varepsilon N_a < 0 \qquad (7A.12)$$

as claimed, where $k = 1/(\varepsilon N_a + N_u)$ and $1/\varepsilon = f'_a N_a / w_a$. From equation 7A.7, the corresponding effect on the agricultural wage of an expansion of relief work is

$$dw_a/dN_g = kw_a \qquad (7A.13)$$

Consider now the effect of public works employment on total rural income $Y = w_a(N_a + N_g) = w_a(1 - N_u)$ by equation 7A.8. However, since $w_a N_u$ is fixed by the manufacturing wage, the effect of a change in N_g on Y is identical to its effect on w_a as given by equation 7A.13. By inspection, it follows that

$$dY/dN_g \gtreqqless w_a \text{ as } \varepsilon N_a + N_u \lesseqqgtr 1$$

as claimed in Section 7.6. Also note that $\varepsilon N_a + N_u \geq 1$ implies (with equation 7A.9) that $\varepsilon \geq 1 + N_g/N_a > 1$. So $dY/dN_g > w_a$ as long as $\varepsilon \leq 1$.

Notes

1. On the latter, see Alston (1984). Other possible arguments for treating human survival as a policy objective in this setting can be based on John Rawls' (1972) idea of 'primary social goods' and Amartya Sen's (1984) concept of a 'metaright'. On the relationship between survival maximization and expected utility theory see Karni and Schmeidler (1986).
2. An old example is the well-known Biblical account of Joseph's advice to Pharoah to store grain during good harvests in anticipation of bad ones. Aykroyd (1974, 52) reports that the East India Company built a large granary in Bihar in 1784 with the inscription: 'For the perpetual prevention of famines in these provinces'. But the granary was never filled and public storage was not widely pursued as a famine relief policy in India until Independence in 1947. Since then governments in India have, at various times, held quite large stocks (for detailed discussion see Chopra, 1981).
3. Witness the common practice of using the inverse price elasticity of demand as an estimate of the effect on market price of a change in public storage. This is only valid if private storage is unresponsive to price changes and, as this chapter will show, the practice may be highly misleading otherwise.
4. See Manetsch (1981). The emergency feeding programme introduced by CARE during the 1967 famine in Bihar is an example (Singh, 1975). The 'Vulnerable Group Feeding Project' in Bangladesh, operated by the World Food Programme is an example in which food is

allocated between districts according to indicators of distress, including food output, degree of flooding and rural unemployment. Attempts are currently being made to allocate aid according to indicators of need in Ethiopia and Sudan; for example, see Roger Cans' report in 'The Guardian Weekly', 21 July, 1985, 11. Oxfam Health Unit (1984) has advocated the use of need indicators such as weight-to-height ratios.

5. Gender is an interesting example in this setting. The observed sex differentials in childhood survival rates in favour of boys in the Indian sub-continent have been attributed to the response of intrafamily resource allocations to the fact that differential future earnings opportunities favour males (Rosenzweig and Schultz, 1982; Bardhan, 1984, chapter 15). Thus it can be expected that parents will transfer some of their food handouts to their male children. This implies that if food handouts are equal (and other attributes constant) then parents will be in greater need than girls who will, in turn, be in greater need than boys.

6. The assumption that z is predetermined precludes incentive compatibility problems, but I doubt if they are likely to arise in this setting.

7. Strict concavity of s in x implies that M is strictly quasi-convex in x thus guaranteeing an interior solution. Although simplifying the analysis, the concavity assumption is a little stronger than necessary for interior solutions since quasi-convexity is also possible with a limited amount of non-concavity in the individual survival functions.

8. A natural measure of the contribution of inequality in food consumption to famine mortality is the Atkinson (1970) index $I = 1 - \bar{x}/\bar{x}^e$ where $\bar{x}^e$ is the equally distributed equivalent food consumption which, in this setting, is given by the solution of $M(x_1, \ldots, x_N, z) = M(\bar{x}^e, \ldots, \bar{x}^e, z)$ with M defined by equation 7.2. The analogous concept to Atkinson's 'inequality aversion parameter' is the elasticity of famine vulnerability (γ) discussed in Chapter 2. As was pointed out in that chapter, the relatively high values of γ (exceeding two) during the Madras and Bangladesh famines suggest that mortality would have been relatively sensitive to inequality in food consumption.

9. This can be interpreted as a variation on Lerner's (1944) argument that social welfare maximization justifies an equal distribution of income when, although marginal utilities of income vary between people with the same income, one is ignorant about who has which utility function and all possibilities are equally likely. For a proof of Lerner's claim see Sen (1973).

10. This has been argued by Peck (1977–8); Helmberger and Weaver (1977), Chisholm (1982), and Sarris (1982), amongst others.

11. Although there has been some work on other sources of market failure; see Sarris (1982) and Newbery (1984).

12. See, for example, Weckstein (1977), Bigman and Reutlinger (1979), and Reutlinger (1982).

13. The interests of British industrialists (particularly Lancashire textile manufactures keen to expand their markets in the sub-continent) were probably the main motivation for the free trade policy; for detailed discussions see Gopal (1963), Griffiths (1965), and Grampp (1982). On the trade during this period see Latham and Neal (1983). On the domestic economy see Heston (1983), McAlpin (1985).

14. As was noted in Chapters 1 and 5, income effects are likely to reinforce this, at least in the short run.

15. Although clearly hypothetical in this setting, the policy discussed here is not unlike Thailand's taxation of its rice exports over recent decades. Thailand attempted to stabilize domestic rice prices by adjusting its export tax in accordance with fluctuations in world prices. To test their success, I obtained the following result by regressing Thailand's export premium (EPREM) for rice (white 5 per cent broken) on the corresponding export price (EP) using annual data over the period 1955 to 1977.

$$\text{EPREM} = 1.6 + 0.35\text{EP} - 0.36t$$
$$(0.69)\,(5.7) \qquad (2.0)$$

$$R^2 = 0.65;\ D{-}W = 2.24;\ Q(4) = 3.3$$

(The data are from Tolley *et al.*, 1982, chapter 4, which includes a detailed discussion of the policy). It can be seen that the tax had a stabilizing influence on domestic price (since the tax responded positively to changes in export price) although, since the coefficient is significantly less than unity, the export tax did not completely stabilize domestic price. Indeed, on average about 65 per cent of an increase in foreign rice price was passed on to domestic consumers. However, this conclusion may hide significant non-linearity in the relationship; for example, about 90 per cent of the export price increase between 1973 and 1974 was reflected in the export premium (Tolley *et al.*, 1982).

16. This is a three stage least squares estimate obtained jointly with a domestic aggregate demand function. Lagged exports were tried but proved insignificant. For details, including tests of alternative models, see Ravallion (1986*b*).

17. For further discussions and an evaluation of the IMF's food financing programme see Huddleston *et al.* (1984).

18. Grossman (1976) shows that if the errors made by each agent in predicting the price of a risky asset are standard normal white noise and each agent's risk aversion is a constant (although variable across agents) then the price observed in a REE is a sufficient statistic for

inferring relevant aspects of all private information in the economy. Under these conditions, market price is an invertable function of the mean of private information which is all each individual needs to know. Of course, only partial revelation is possible in equilibrium when information is costly (Grossman and Stiglitz 1980).

19. There have been some recent attempts to identify key indicators for early warning on food crises in Bangladesh. See, for example, Eusuf and Currey (1979), Crow (1984) and Cutler (1985). The idea is not new. The Madras Famine Code of 1883 strongly recommended monitoring grain prices as an indicator of famine (see Rangasami 1985) and the Bengal Famine Code of 1913 outlined an elaborate early warning system (Currey, 1984). On the dynamics of peasants' responses to drought and the implications for the choice of indicators see Jodha's (1975) comments on Morris (1974).

20. Crow (1984, 1755) reports that rice prices appear to be the only famine indicator monitored on a continuous basis by the present government.

21. The possibility of a 'transfer paradox' in a stable competitive economy has received considerable recent attention; see Gale (1974), Chichilnisky (1980), Ravallion (1983), Dixit (1983), DeMeza (1983). On the paradox in an economy with 'distortionary' taxes see Brecher and Bhagwati (1982) and (when aid is tied) Kemp and Kojima (1985). Other examples of a transfer paradox have emerged in analyses of imperfect labour markets (Apps, 1981; Ravallion, 1984), models with endogenous voluntary transfers (Warr, 1982; Ravallion, 1983), and in recent literature on optimal income taxation with production (Allen, 1982, Stern, 1982).

22. They need not vanish; the left hand side of the inequality in equation 7.18 places an upper bound on the aggregate substitution effect consistent with the transfer having an adverse effect on the recipient's welfare.

23. The above argument concerning the general equilibrium effects of transfers when there are two goods and three income groups can also be applied to relief work. For this application the two goods are reinterpreted as 'labour' and a composite consumption good. However, since unemployment is such an obvious feature of situations in which relief work is provided (and it is, of course, precluded by competitive equilibrium with flexible prices), I prefer the following model.

24. While I have not seen comparable estimates for Bangladesh, this is the range of elasticities obtained by Evenson and Binswanger (1984) for India.

25. Nor does it follow that an increase in aggregate food availability will fail to stop a famine which was *not* caused by a decline in aggregate availability; see Sen's (1986) clarification of this point.

References

Ahmed, E. (ed.) (1980). *Bangladesh Politics*, Centre for Social Studies, Dhaka University.

Ahmed, R. (1979). *Foodgrain Supply, Distribution and Consumption Policies within a Dual Pricing Mechanism: A Case Study of Bangladesh*, Research Report 8, Washington: International Food Policy Research Institute.

——(1981). *Agricultural Price Policies Under Complex Socioeconomic and Natural Constraints*, Research Report 27, Washington: International Food Policy Research Institute.

Akerlof, G. A. (1980). 'A Theory of Social Custom, of Which Unemployment May Be One Consequence', *The Quarterly Journal of Economics*, 94: 749–75.

—— and Dickens, W. T. (1982). 'The Economic Consequences of Cognitive Dissonance', *The American Economic Review*, 92: 307–39.

Alamgir, M. (1978). *Bangladesh: A Case of Below Poverty Level Equilibrium Trap*, Bangladesh Institute of Development Studies, Dhaka.

—— (1980). *Famine in South Asia: Political Economy of Mass Starvation*, Cambridge, MA: Oelgeshlager, Gunn and Hain.

—— *et al.*, (1977). 'Famine 1974: Political Economy of Mass Starvation in Bangladesh: A Statistical Annex', Dhaka, Bangladesh Institute of Development Studies.

Alexander, J. (1986). 'Information and Price Setting in Rural Javanese Markets', *Bulletin of Indonesian Economic Studies*, 22: 88–112.

Allen, F. (1982). 'Optimal Linear Income Taxation with General Equilibrium Effects on Wages', *Journal of Public Economics*, 17: 135–43.

Allingham, M. (1975). *General Equilibrium*, London: Macmillan.

Alston, P. (1984). 'International Law and the Human Right to Food', in Alston and Tomasevski (1984).

—— and Tomasevski, K. (eds.) (1984). *The Right to Food*, Martinus Nijhoff Publishers.

Ambirajan, S. (1978). *Classical Political Economy and British Policy in India*, Cambridge: Cambridge University Press.

Anderson, R. S. (1976). 'Impressions of Bangladesh: The Role of Arms and the Politics of Exhortation', Montreal: Center for Developing Area Studies, McGill University.

Apps, P. (1981). *A Theory of Inequality and Taxation*, Cambridge: Cambridge University Press.

Arnold, D. (1984). 'Famine in Peasant Consciousness and Peasant Action: Madras, 1876–8', in Guha (1984).

Arrow, K. J. (1982a). 'Review of "Poverty and Famines" by A. K. Sen', *The New York Review of Books*, 29: 24–6.

—— (1982b). 'Risk Perception in Psychology and Economics', *Economic Inquiry*, 20: 1–9.

—— and Debreu, G. (1954). 'Existence of an Equilibrium in a Competitive Economy', *Econometrica*, 22: 265–90.

—— and Hahn, F. H. (1971). *General Competitive Analysis*, San Francisco: Holden-Day.

Atkinson, A. B. (1970). 'On the Measurement of Inequality', *Journal of Economic Theory*, 2: 244–63.

Aykroyd, W. R. (1974). *The Conquest of Famine*, London: Chatto and Windus.

Bailey, R. W., Baillie, R. T., and McMahon, P. C. (1984). 'Interpreting Econometric Evidence on Efficiency in the Foreign Exchange Market', *Oxford Economic Papers*, 36: 67–85.

Baishya, P. (1974). 'Man-Made Famine', *Economic and Political Weekly*, 10 (24 May): 821–22.

Banerjee, T. (1966). *Internal Markets of India 1834–1900*, Calcutta: Academic Publishers.

Bang, F. B. (1981). 'The Role of Disease in the Ecology of Famine', in Robson (1981).

Bangladesh Bureau of Statistics (1984). *Statistical Yearbook of Bangladesh 1983–84*, Dhaka: Government of Bangladesh.

Bangladesh Rural Advancement Committee [BRAC] (1979). 'Peasant Perceptions: Famine', Dhaka, Bangladesh: BRAC.

Bardhan, P. K. (1984). *Land, Labour and Rural Poverty*, Delhi: Oxford University Press.

——, and Rudra, A. (1981). 'Terms and Conditions of Labour Contracts in Agriculture: Results of a Survey in West Bengal in 1979', *Oxford Bulletin of Economics and Statistics*, 43: 89–111.

Bates, J. M., and Granger, C. W. J. (1969). 'The Combination of Forecasts', *Operational Research Quarterly*, 20: 451–68.

Beach, C. M., and MacKinnon, J. G. (1978). 'A Maximum Likelihood Procedure for Regressions with Autocorrelated Errors', *Econometrica*, 46: 51–8.

Begg, D. K. H. (1982). *The Rational Expectations Revolution in Macroeconomics*, Oxford: Philip Allan.

Bellanti, J. A. (ed.) (1983). *Acute Diarrhea: Its Nutritional Consequences in Children*, New York: Raven Press.

Bentham, J. (1982). 'Manual of Political Economy', in Stark (1982).

Bhatia, B. M. (1967). *Famines in India: A Study of some Aspects of the Economic History of India, (1860–1965)*, London: Asia Publishing House.

Bigman, D., and Reutlinger S. (1979). 'National and International Policies Toward Food Security and Price Stabilization', *American Economic Review (Proceedings)*, 69: 159–63.

Binswanger, H. P., and Rosenzweig, M. R. (eds.) (1984). *Contractural Arrangements, Employment, and Wages in Rural Labor Markets in Asia*, New Haven: Yale University Press.

Blanchard, O. J. (1979). 'Speculative Bubbles, Crashes and Rational Expectations', *Economics Letters*, 3: 387–89.

Bliss, C., and Stern, N. (1978). 'Productivity, Wages and Nutrition' (Two Parts), *Journal of Development Economics*, 5: 331–62 and 363–98.

Blyn, G. (1966). *Agricultural Trends in India, 1891–1947: Output Availability and Productivity*, Philadelphia: University of Pennsylvania Press.

—— (1973). 'Price Series Correlation as a Measure of Market Integration', *Indian Journal of Agricultural Economics*, 28: 56–9.

Booth, A., and Sundrum, R. M. (1985). *Labour Absorption in Agriculture*, Oxford: Oxford University Press.

Bose, S. R. (1968). 'Trend of Real Income of the Rural Poor in East Pakistan, 1949–66', *Pakistan Development Review*, 8: 452–88.

Bowden, R. O. (1978). *The Econometrics of Disequilibrium*, Amsterdam: North-Holland Publishing Company.

Boyce, J. K. (1986). *Agricultural Growth in Bangladesh and West Bengal*, Oxford: Oxford University Press, forthcoming.

Bray, M. (1983). 'Convergence to Rational Expectations Equilibrium', in Frydman and Phelps (1983).

—— (1985). 'Rational Expectations, Information and Asset Markets: An Introduction', *Oxford Economic Papers*, 37: 161–95.

Brecher, R. A., and Bhagwati, J. N. (1982). 'Immiserizing Transfers from Abroad', *Journal of International Economics*, 13: 353–64.

Burmeister E. (1980a). 'On Some Conceptual Issues in Rational Expectations Modelling', *Journal of Money Credit and Banking*, 12: 800–16.

—— (1980b). *Capital Theory and Dynamics*, Cambridge: Cambridge University Press.

Cagan, P. (1956). 'The Monetary Dynamics of Hyperinflation', in Friedman (1956).

Centre for Development Studies, Trivandrum, (1975). *Poverty, Unemployment and Development Policy*, New York: United Nations, Department of Economic and Social Affairs.

Chambers, R., Longhurst, R., and Pacey, A. (eds.) (1981). *Seasonal Dimensions to Rural Poverty*, London: Francis Pinter.

Chandra, P. K. (1983). 'Malnutrition and Immunocompetence: An Overview', in J. A. Ballanti (ed.) *Acute Diarrhea: Its Nutritional Consequences*, New York: Raven Press.

Chen, L. C. (ed.) (1973). *Disaster in Bangladesh*, New York: Oxford University Press.

Chen, L. C., Emdadul, H., and D'Souza, S. (1981). 'Sex Bias in the

Family Allocation of Food and Health Care in Rural Bangladesh', *Population and Development Review*, 7: 55–70.

Chichilnisky, G. (1980). 'Basic Goods, the Effects of Commodity Transfers and the International Economic Order', *Journal of Development Economics*, 7: 505–19.

Chisholm, A. H. (1982). 'Commodity-Price Stabilization: Microeconomic Theory and Policy Issues', in Chisholm and Tyers (1982).

—— and Tyers, R. (eds.) (1982). *Food Security: Theory, Policy, and Perspectives from Asia and the Pacific Rim*, Lexington, Mass: Lexington Books.

Chopra, R. N. (1981). *Evolution of Food Policy in India*, Delhi: Macmillan.

Chowdhury, A. K. M., and Chen, L. C. (1977). 'The Interaction of Nutrition, Infection, and Mortality During Recent Food Crises in Bangladesh', *Food Research Institute Studies*, 16: 47–62.

Chowdhury, O. H. (1983). 'Profile of Workers in the Food-for-Work Programme in Bangladesh', *The Bangladesh Development Studies*, 11: 111–34.

Clay, E. J. (1976). 'Institutional Change and Agricultural Wages in Bangladesh', *Bangladesh Development Studies*, 4: 423–40.

—— (1981). 'Seasonal Patterns of Agricultural Employment in Bangladesh', in Chambers *et al.* (1981).

Crow, B. (1984). 'Warnings of Famine in Bangladesh', *Economic and Political Weekly*, 40: 1754–58.

Cummings, R. W. (1967). *Pricing Efficiency in the Indian Wheat Market*, New Delhi: Impex.

Cuny, F. C. (1983). *Disasters and Development*, New York: Oxford University Press.

Currey, B. (1981). 'The Famine Syndrom: Its Definition for Relief and Rehabilitation in Bangladesh', in Robson (1981).

—— (1984). 'Coping with Complexity in Food Crisis Management', in Currey and Hugo (1984).

——, and Hugo, G. (eds.) (1984). *Famine as a Geographical Phenomenon*, Dordrecht, Holland: D. Reidel Publishing Company.

Cutler, P. (1984). 'Famine Forecasting: Prices and Peasant Behaviour in Northern Ethiopia', *Disasters*, 8: 48–56.

—— (1985). 'Detecting Food Emergencies. Lessons from the 1979 Bangladesh Crisis', *Food Policy*, 10: 207–24.

Cyert, R. M., and DeGroot, M. H. (1974). 'Rational Expectations and Bayesian Analysis', *Journal of Political Economy*, 82: 521–36.

Dandekar, V. M., and Pethe, V. P. (1972). *A Survey of Famine Conditions in the Affected Regions of Maharashtra and Mysore*, Poona: Gokhale Institute.

Darling, M. (1947). The Punjab Peasant in Prosperity and Debt, Bombay: Oxford University Press.

Das, T. (1949). *Bengal Famine (1943): As Revealed in a Survey of the Destitutes in Calcutta*, Calcutta: University of Calcutta.

Davidson, J. E. H., Hendry, D. F., Srba, F., and Yeo, S. (1978). 'Econometric Modelling of the Aggregate Time Series Relationship between Consumers' Expenditure and Income in the UK', *The Economic Journal*, 88: 661–92.

Davidson, M. (1974). 'Starvation: Pointing the Finger', *Far Eastern Economic Review*, 86: 26.

De Bondt, W. F. M., and Thaler, R. (1985). 'Does the Stock Market Overreact?', *The Journal of Finance*, 40: 793–805.

Debreu, G. (1959). *The Theory of Value: An Axiomatic Analysis of Economic Equilibrium*, New Haven: Yale University Press.

De Groot, M. H. (1970). *Optimal Statistical Decisions*, New York: McGraw-Hill.

de Leeuw, F., and McKelvey, M. (1984). 'Price Expectations of Business Firms: Bias in the Short and Long Run', *The American Economic Review*, 74: 99–110.

De Meza, D. (1983). 'The Transfer Problem in a Many-Country World: Is it Better to Give than Receive?', *The Manchester School*, September: 266–75.

de Vylder, S. (1982). *Agriculture in Chains. Bangladesh: A Case Study in Contradictions and Constraints*, London: Zed Press.

Dietrich, J. K., and Joines, D. H. (1983). 'Rational Expectations, Informational Efficiency and Tests Using Survey Data: A Comment', *Review of Economics and Statistics*, 65: 525–31.

Digby, W. (1878). *The Famine Campaign in Southern India*, vol. 2, London: Longmans Green and Co.

Dixit, A. (1976). *The Theory of Equilibrium Growth*, Oxford: Oxford University Press.

—— (1983). 'The Multi-Country Transfer Problem', *Economics Letters*, 13: 49–53.

Domberger, S. (1979). 'Price Adjustment and Market Structure', *The Economic Journal*, 89: 96–108.

Drasar, B. S., Tomkins, A. M., and Feachem, R. G. (1981). 'Diarrhoeal Diseases' in Chambers, Longhurst and Pacey (1981).

Dreze, J. (1986). 'Famine Prevention in India', Paper presented at the Food Strategies Conference, World Institute for Development Economics Research, Helsinki.

Dutt, R. (1950). *The Economic History of India in the Victorian Age*, London: Routledge and Kegan Paul.

Easterlin, R. A. (ed.) (1980). *Population and Economic Changes in*

Developing Countries, Chicago: The University of Chicago Press.

Epstein, S. (1967). 'Productive Efficiency and Customary Systems of Reward in Rural South India', in Firth (1967).

Eusuf, A. N. M., and Currey, B. (1979). 'The Feasibility of a Famine Warning System for Bangladesh', Ministry of Relief and Rehabilitation, Government of Bangladesh.

Evans, G., and Gulamani, R. (1984). 'Tests for Rationality of the Carlson–Parkin Inflation Expectations Data', *Oxford Bulletin of Economics and Statistics*, 46: 1–19.

Evenson, R. E., and Binswanger, H. P. (1984). 'Estimating Labor Demand Functions for Indian Agriculture', in Binswanger and Rosenzweig (1984).

Fama, E. F. (1970). 'Efficient Capital Markets: A Review of Theory and Evidence', *Journal of Finance*, 25: 383–417.

Farruk, M. O. (1972). *Structure and Performance of the Rice Marketing System in East Pakistan*, Cornell International Agricultural Development Bulletin 23, Ithaca: Cornell University.

Fase, M. M. G. (1981). 'The Linkage of Stock Exchange Markets between Countries', *Economics Letters*, 7: 363–9.

Fei, J. C. H., and Ranis, G. (1964). *Development of the Labor Surplus Economy*, Homewood, Illinois: Irwin.

Feiwel, G. R. (ed.) (1985). *Issues in Contemporary Microeconomics and Welfare*, London: Macmillan.

Festinger, L. (ed.) (1964). *Conflict, Decision, and Dissonance*, London: Tavistock Publications.

Figlewski, S., and Wachtel, P. (1981). 'The Formation of Inflationary Expectations', *Review of Economics and Statistics*, 63: 1–10.

Firth, R. (ed.) (1967). *Themes in Economic Anthropology*, London: Tavistock for ASA.

Flood, R. P. and Garber, P. M. (1980). 'Market Fundamentals versus Price-Level Bubbles: The First Tests', *Journal of Political Economy*, 88: 745–70.

Friedman, B. M. (1979). 'Optimal Expectations and the Extreme Information Assumptions of "Rational Expectations" Macromodels', *Journal of Monetary Economics*, 5: 23–41.

—— (1980). 'Survey Evidence on the "Rationality" of Interest Rate Expectations', *Journal of Monetary Economics*, 6: 453–65.

Friedman, M. (ed.) (1956). *Studies in the Quantity Theory of Money*, Chicago: Chicago University Press.

Frydman, R., and Phelps, E. S. (eds.) (1983). *Individual Forecasting and Aggregate Outcomes*, Cambridge: Cambridge University Press.

Fuchs, V. R. (1980). 'Comment', in Easterlin (1980).

Gandolfo, G. (1971). *Mathematical Methods and Models in Economic Dynamics*, Amsterdam: North-Holland.

Gale, D. (1974). 'Exchange Equilibrium with Coalitions: An Example', *Journal of Mathematical Economics*, 1: 63–6.

George, P. S. (1984). 'Some Aspects of Public Distribution of Foodgrains in India', *Economic and Political Weekly*, 19 (29 September): A106–A110.

Ghose, A. K. (1982). 'Food Supply and Starvation: A Study of Famines with Reference to the Indian Sub-Continent', *Oxford Economic Papers*, 34: 368–89.

Goldstein, J. S. (1985). 'Basic Human Needs: The Plateau Curve', *World Development*, 13: 595–609.

Goodwin, R. M. (1947). 'Dynamical Coupling with Especial Reference to Markets having Production Lags', *Econometrica*, 15: 181–204.

Gopal, R. (1963). *British Rule in India: An Assessment*, London: Frank Cass.

Gracey, M., and Falkner, F. (eds.) (1985). *Nutritional Needs and Assessment of Normal Growth*, New York: Raven Press.

Grampp, W. D. (1982). 'Economic Opinion when Britain Turned to Free Trade', *History of Political Economy*, 14: 496–520.

Granger, C. W. J. (1969). 'Prediction with a Generalized Cost of Error Function', *Operations Research Quarterly*, 20: 199–207.

—— and Newbold, P. (1974). 'Spurious Regression in Econometrics', *Journal of Econometrics*, 2: 111–20.

—— and —— (1977). *Forecasting Economic Time Series*, New York: Academic Press.

Gray, R. W., and Peck, A. E. (1981). 'The Chicago Wheat Futures Market: Recent Problems in Historical Perspective', *Food Research Institute Studies*, 43: 89–116.

Greenough, P. R. (1982). *Prosperity and Misery in Modern Bengal: The Famine of 1943–49*, Oxford: Oxford University Press.

Griffin, K., and James, J. (1981). *The Transition to Egalitarian Development*, London: Macmillan.

Griffin, K., and Khan, A. R. (eds.) (1977). *Poverty and Landlessness in Rural Asia*, Geneva: International Labour Organization.

Griffiths, P. (1965). *The British Impact on India*, London: Frank Cass.

Griliches, Z. (1967). 'Distributed Lags: A Survey', *Econometrica*, 35: 16–49.

—— and Intriligator, M. D. (eds.) (1984). *Handbook of Econometrics*, vol. 2, Amsterdam: North-Holland.

Grossman, S. J. (1976). 'On the Efficiency of Competitive Stock Markets Where Traders Have Diverse Information', *Journal of Finance*, 31: 573–85.

—— (1981). 'An Introduction to the Theory of Rational Expectations under Asymmetric Information', *The Review of Economic Studies*, 48: 541–59.

—— and Stiglitz, J. E. (1980). 'On the Impossibility of Informationally Efficient Markets', *The American Economic Review*, 70: 393–408.

Guha, R. (ed.) (1984). *Subaltern Studies 3*, Delhi: Oxford University Press.

Hall, B. H., and Hall, R. E. (1980). 'Time Series Processor: Version 3.5, User's Manual', 204 Junipero Serra Blvd., Stanford, Cal.

Harris, J. R., and Todaro, M. P. (1970). 'Migration Unemployment and Development: A Two-Sector Analysis', *American Economic Review*, 60: 126–42.

Harriss, B. (1979). 'There is Method in My Madness: Or is it Vice Versa? Measuring Agricultural Market Performance', *Food Research Institute Studies*, 17: 197–218.

Hart, P. E., Mills, G., and Whitaker, J. K. (eds.) (1964). *Econometric Analysis for National Economic Planning*, London: Butterworths.

Hartmann, B., and Boyce, J. K. (1979). *Needless Hunger: Voices from a Bangladesh Village*, San Francisco: Institute for Food and Development Policy.

—— and —— (1983). *A Quiet Violence: View from a Bangladesh Village*, London: Zed Press.

Harvey, A. C. (1981). *The Econometric Analysis of Time Series*, Oxford: Philip Allan.

Hassan, N., and Ahmad, K. (1984). 'Studies on Food and Nutrient Intake by Rural Population of Bangladesh: Comparison Between Intakes of 1962–64, 1975–76 and 1981–82', *Ecology of Food and Nutrition*, 15: 143–58.

Haugh, L. D. (1976). 'Checking the Independence of Two Covariance-Stationary Time-Series: A Univariate Residual Cross-Correlation Approach', *Journal of the American Statistical Association*, 71: 378–85.

Heiner, R. A. (1983). 'The Origin of Predictable Behavior', *The American Economic Review*, 83: 560–95.

Helmberger, P. G., Campbell, G. R., and Dobson, W. D. (1981). 'Organization and Performance of Agricultural Markets', in Martin (1981).

—— and Weaver, R. (1977). 'Welfare Implications of Commodity Storage under Uncertainty', *American Journal of Agricultural Economics*, 59: 639–51.

Hendry, D. F., and Mizon, G. E. (1978). 'Serial Correlations as a Convenient Simplification, not a Nuisance: A Comment on a Study of the Demand for Money by the Bank of England', *The Economic Journal*, 88: 549–63.

—— Pagan, A. R., and Sargan, J. D. (1984). 'Dynamic Specification', in Griliches and Intriligator (1984).

—— and Richard, J.-F. (1983). 'The Econometric Analysis of Time Series', *International Statistical Review*, 51: 111–63.

Herring, R. J., and Edwards, R. M. (1983). 'Guaranteeing Employment to the Rural Poor: Social Functions and Class Interests in the Employment Guarantee Scheme in Western India', *World Development*, 11: 575–92.

Heston, A. (1983). 'National Income', in Kumar and Desai (1983).

Hey, J. D. (1984). 'The Economics of Optimism and Pessimism: A Definition and some Applications', *Kyklos*, 37: 181–205.

Huddleston, B., Johnson, D. G., Reutlinger S., and Valdés A. (1984). *International Finance for Food Security*, Baltimore: Johns Hopkins University Press.

Hurd, J. (1975). 'Railways and the Expansion of Markets in India, 1861–1921', *Explorations in Economic History*, 12: 263–88.

Hussein, A. M. (ed.) (1976). *Rehab: Drought and Famine in Ethiopia*, London: International African Institute.

International Center for Diarrhoeal Disease Research, Bangladesh (1979). *Annual Report*, Dhaka: ICDDR.

Jacobs, R. L., and Jones, R. A. (1980). 'Price Expectations in the United States: 1947–75', *The American Economic Review*, 70: 269–76.

Jahan, R. (1974). 'Bangladesh in 1973: Management of Factional Politics', *Asian Survey*, 14: 125–35.

Januzzi, F. T., and Peach, J. T. (1980). *The Agrarian Structure of Bangladesh: An Impediment to Development*, Boulder: Westview Press.

Jodha, N. S. (1975). 'Famine and Famine Policies: Some Empirical Evidence', *Economic and Political Weekly*, 10: 1609–23.

Jones, W. O. (1972). *Marketing Staple Food Crops in Tropical Africa*, Ithaca: Cornell University Press.

Jordan, J. S., and Radner, R. (1982). 'Rational Expectations in Microeconomic Models: An Overview', *Journal of Economic Theory*, 26: 201–23.

Kahneman, D., Slovic, P., and Tversky, A. (eds.) (1982). *Judgment Under Uncertainty: Heuristics and Biases*, Cambridge: Cambridge University Press.

Kamaluddin, S. (1973). 'Dacca's Dragnet', *Far Eastern Economic Review*, 32: 41.

Kanbur, S. M. R. (1984). 'How to Analyse Commodity Price Stabilization? A Review Article', *Oxford Economic Papers*, 36: 336–58.

Karni, E., and Schmeidler, D. (1986). 'Self-Preservation as a Foundation of Rational Behavior Under Risk', *Journal of Economic Behavior and Organization*, 7: 71–81.

Katona, G. (1975). *Psychological Economics*, New York: Elsevier.

Kemp, M. C., and Kojima, S. (1985). 'The Welfare Economics of Foreign Aid', in Feiwell (1985).

Khan, A. R. (1977). 'Poverty and Inequality in Rural Bangladesh', in Griffin and Khan (1977).

Khan, Q. (1985). 'Household Wealth, Mother's Education and Child Mortality in South Asia', Discussion Paper, Center for Analysis of Developing Countries, University of Pennsylvania, Philadelphia.

Khusro, A. M. (1973). *Buffer Stocks and Storage of Foodgrains in India*, Bombay: Tata McGraw-Hill.

Kindleberger, C. P. (1978). *Manias, Panics and Crashes: A History of Financial Crises*, London: Macmillan.

Koopmans, T. C. (1957). *Three Essays on the State of Economic Science*, New York: McGraw-Hill.

Kumar, D., and Desai, M. (eds.) (1983). *The Cambridge Economic History of India*, vol. 2, Cambridge University Press.

Kumar, G. (1986). 'Ethiopian Famines 1973–1985: A Case Study', Paper presented at the Food Strategies Conference, World Institute for Development Economics Research, Helsinki.

Kynch, J. and Sen, A. K. (1983). 'Indian Women: Well-being and Survival', *Cambridge Journal of Economics*, 7: 363–80.

Labys, W., and Granger, C. W. J. (1970). *Speculation, Hedging and Commodity Price Forecasting*, Lexington MA: Health-Lexington.

Lardinois, R. (1985). 'Famine, Epidemics and Mortality in South India: A Reappraisal of the Demographic Crisis of 1876–1878', *Economic and Political Weekly*, 20: 454–65.

Latham, A. J. H., and Neal, L. (1983). 'The International Market in Rice and Wheat, 1964–1974', *Economic History Review*, 36: 260–80.

Lechtig, A. (1985). 'Early Malnutrition, Growth and Development', in Gracey and Falkner (1985).

Leibenstein, H. (1957). *Economic Backwardness and Economic Growth*, New York: Wiley.

Lele, U. J. (1971). *Food Grain Marketing in India*, Ithaca: Cornell University Press.

Lent, J. A. (1982). *Newspapers in Asia*, Hong Kong: Heinemann.

Lerner, A. P. (1944). *The Economics of Control*, London: Macmillan.

Lewis, W. A. (1954). 'Economic Development with Unlimited Supplies of Labour', *Manchester School*, 20: 139–91.

Lieberman, S. S. (1985). 'Field-level Perspectives on Maharashtra's Employment Guarantee Scheme', *Public Administration and Development*, 5: 109–27.

Lifschultz, L. (1974a). 'Bothersome Friends', *Far Eastern Economic Review*, 83: 20.

——(1974b). 'Bangladesh: A State of Siege', *Far Eastern Economic Review*, 85: 47–51.

——(1974c). 'Reaping a Harvest of Misery', *Far Eastern Economic Review*, 86: 28–30.

——(1979). *Bangladesh: The Unfinished Revolution*, London: Zed Press.

Lipton, M. (1977). *Why Poor People Stay Poor*, London: Temple Smith.

Loveday, A. (1914). *The History and Economics of Indian Famines*, London: G. Bell and Sons.

Lucas, R. E., and Sargent, T. J. (eds.) (1981). *Rational Expectations and Econometric Practice*, London: George Allen and Unwin.

McAlpin, M. B. (1975). 'The Effects of Expansion of Markets on Rural Income Distribution in Nineteenth Century India', *Explorations in Economic History*, 12: 289–302.

——(1983). 'Price Movements and Fluctuations in Economic Activity (1860–1947)' in Kumar and Desai (1983).

McCallum, B. T. (1976). 'Rational Expectations and the Natural Rate Hypothesis: Some Consistent Estimates', *Econometrica*, 44: 43–52.

McCloskey, D. and Nash, J. (1984). 'Corn at Interest: The Extent and Cost of Grain Storage in Medieval England', *The American Economic Review*, 74: 174–87.

McHenry, D. F., and Bird, K. (1977). 'Food Bungle in Bangladesh', *Foreign Policy*, 27: 72–8.

Maddala, G. S. (1983). *Limited-Dependent and Qualitative Variables in Econometrics*, Cambridge: Cambridge University Press.

Mahmud, W. (1982). 'Income and Price Responses to Changes in Food Availability in a Low-Income Economy', Bureau of Economic Research, University of Dhaka.

Maital, S., and Maital, S. (1981). 'Individual-Rational and Group-Rational Inflation Expectations: Theory and Cross-Section Evidence', *Journal of Economic Behaviour and Organization*, 2: 179–86.

Malinvaud, E. (1972). *Lectures on Microeconomic Theory*, Amsterdam: North Holland.

Manetsch, T. J. (1981). 'On Strategies and Programs for Coping with large-scale Food Shortages' in Robson (1981).

Maniruzzaman, T. (1975). 'Bangladesh in 1974: Economic Crisis and Political Polarization', *Asian Survey*, 15: 117–28.

Mankiw, N. G., Romer, D., and Shapiro, M. D. (1985). 'An Unbiased Re-examination of Stock Market Volatility', *The Journal of Finance*, 40: 677–87.

Marriott, F. H. C., and Pope, J. A. (1954). 'Bias in the Estimation of Autocorrelations', *Biometrika*, 41: 390–402.

Martin, L. R. (ed.) (1981). *A Survey of Agricultural Economics Literature*, Minneapolis: University of Minnesota Press.

Means, G. C. (1972). 'The Administered-Price Thesis Reconfirmed', *The American Economic Review*, 62: 292–306.

Mellor, J. W., and Desai, G. M. (eds.) (1985). *Agricultural Change and Rural Poverty*, Baltimore: Johns Hopkins University Press.

Meng-Try, E. (1984). 'War and Famine: The Example of Kampuchea', in

Currey and Hugo (1984).

Mills, E. (1962). *Price, Output and Inventory Policy*, New York: John Wiley and Sons.

Minford, P., and Peel, D. (1984). 'Testing for Unbiasedness and Efficiency under Incomplete Current Information', *Bulletin of Economic Research*, 36: 1–7.

Mirrlees, J. A. (1975). 'A Pure Theory of Underdeveloped Economies', in L. G. Renolds (ed.) *Agriculture in Development Theory*, New Haven: Yale University Press.

Mitra, A. (1982). 'The Meaning of Meaning', *Economic and Political Weekly*, 27: 488–9.

Moore, J. R., Johns, S. S., and Khusro, A. M. (1973). *Indian Foodgrain Marketing*, New Delhi: Prentice-Hall.

Morris, M. D. (1974). 'What is Famine?', *Economic and Political Weekly*, 9: 1855–64.

Mullineaux, J. (1978). 'On Testing for Rationality: Another Look at the Livingston Price Expectations Data', *Journal of Political Economy*, 86: 329–36.

Muqtada, M. (1981). 'Poverty and Famines in Bangladesh', *Bangladesh Development Studies*, 9: 1–34.

Muth, J. F. (1961). 'Rational Expectations and the Theory of Price Movements', *Econometrica*, 29: 315–35.

—— (1981). 'Estimation of Economic Relationships Containing Latent Expectations Variables', in Lucas and Sargent (1981).

Nankervis, J. C., and Savin, N. E., (1985). 'Testing the Autoregressive Parameter with the t Statistic', *Journal of Econometrics*, 27: 143–62.

Nelder, J. A. (1975). *GLIM Manual Release 2*, Oxford: Numerical Algorithms Group.

—— and Wedderburn, R. M. W. (1972). 'Generalized Linear Models', *A Journal of the Royal Statistical Society A*, 135: 370–84.

Nelson, C. R. (1973). *Applied Time Series Analysis for Managerial Forecasting*, San Francisco: Holden–Day.

Nerlove, M. (1958). *The Dynamics of Supply: Estimation of Farmers' Response to Price*, Baltimore: The Johns Hopkins Press.

—— (1983). 'Expectations, Plans, and Realizations in Theory and Practice', *Econometrica*, 51: 1251–79.

Newbery, D. M. G. (1984). 'Commodity Price Stabilization in Imperfect or Cartelized Markets', *Econometrica*, 52: 563–78.

—— and Stiglitz, J. E. (1981). *The Theory of Commodity Price Stabilization*, Oxford: Oxford University Press.

—— and —— (1982a). 'Optimal Commodity Stock-Piling Rules', *Oxford Economic Papers*, 34: 403–27.

—— and —— (1982b). 'The Choice of Techniques and the Optimality of

Market Equilibrium with Rational Expectations', *Journal of Political Economy*, 90: 223–46.

—— and —— (1984). 'Pareto Inferior Trade', *The Review of Economic Studies*, 51: 1–12.

Nickel, S. (1985). 'Error Correction, Partial Adjustment and All That: An Expository Note', *Oxford Bulletin of Economics and Statistics*, 47: 119–30.

Obstfeld, M., and Rogoff, K. (1983). 'Speculative Hyperinflations in Maximizing Models: Can We Rule Them Out?', *Journal of Political Economy*, 91: 675–87.

Osmani, S. R. (1982). *Economic Inequality and Group Welfare*, Oxford: Oxford University Press.

—— (1986). 'The Food Problems of Bangladesh', Paper presented to the Food Strategies Conference, World Institute for Development Economics Research, Helsinki.

—— and Chowdhury, O. H. (1983). 'Short Run Impacts of Food for Work Programme in Bangladesh', *The Bangladesh Development Studies*, 11: 135–90.

Oughton, E. (1982). 'The Maharashtra Droughts of 1970–73: An Analysis of Scarcity', *Oxford Bulletin of Economics and Statistics*, 44: 169–97.

Oxfam Health Unit (1984). *Oxfam's Practical Guide to Selective Feeding Programmes*, Oxford: Oxfam.

Peck, A. E. (1977–78). 'Implications of Private Storage of Grains for Buffer Stock Schemes to Stabilize Prices', *Food Research Institute Studies*, 16: 125–40.

Pinstrup-Anderson, P. (1985). 'Food Prices and the Poor in Developing Countries', *European Review of Agricultural Economics*, 12: 69–85.

Pitt, M. (1983). 'Food Preferences and Nutrition in Rural Bangladesh', *The Review of Economics and Statistics*, 65: 105–14.

—— and Rosenzweig, M. R. (1985). 'Health and Nutrition Consumption Across and Within Farm Households', *The Review of Economics and Statistics*, 67: 212–24.

Praetz, P. D. (1975). 'Testing the Efficient Markets Hypothesis on the Sydney Wool Futures Exchange', *Australian Economic Papers*, 14: 240–9.

Preston, S. H. (1975). 'The Changing Relation Between Mortality and Level of Economic Development', *Population Studies*, 29: 231–48.

—— (1980). 'Causes and Consequences of Mortality Declines in Less Developed Countries during the Twentieth Century', in Easterlin (1980).

Radhakrishna, R. (1978). 'Demand Functions and Their Development Implications in a Dual Economy: India', *The Developing Economies*, 16: 199–210.

Rahman, M., and Hasan, N. (1980). *Iron Bars of Freedom*, London: News and Media.

Ram, N. (1986). 'An Independent Press and Anti-Hunger Strategies', paper presented at the Food Strategies Conference, World Institute for Development Economics Research, Helsinki.

Rangasami, A. (1985). ' "Failure of Exchange Entitlements" Theory of Famine', *Economic and Political Weekly*, 20: 1747–52 and 1797–1801.

Rashid, S. (1980). 'The Policy of Laissez-Faire during Scarcities', *The Economic Journal*, 90: 493–503.

Ravallion, M. (1982). 'Agricultural Wages in Bangladesh before and after the 1974 Famine', *The Bangladesh Development Studies*, 10: 75–89.

—— (1983). 'Commodity Transfers and the International Economic Order: A Comment', *Journal of Development Economics*, 13: 205–12.

—— (1984). 'How much is a Transfer Payment Worth to a Rural Worker?', *Oxford Economic Papers*, 36: 478–89.

—— (1985a). 'The Performance of Rice Markets in Bangladesh during the 1974 Famine', *The Economic Journal*, 95: 15–29.

—— (1985b). 'The Informational Efficiency of Traders' Price Expectations in a Bangladesh Rice Market', *Oxford Bulletin of Economics and Statistics*, 47: 171–84.

—— (1985c). 'Are Informationally Unbiased Expectations Necessarily Rational?', Australian National University, Working Paper in Economics and Econometrics No. 121 (*Kyklos*, fothcoming).

—— (1985d). 'Towards a Theory of Famine Relief Policy', Australian National University Working Paper in Economics and Econometrics No. 127 (*Journal of Public Economics*, forthcoming).

—— (1986a). 'Testing Market Integration', *American Journal of Agricultural Economics*, 68: 102–9.

—— (1986b). 'Trade and Stabilization: Another Look at British India's Controversial Foodgrain Exports', *Explorations in Economic History*, (forthcoming.)

—— and van de Walle, D. (1984). 'Measuring Ex-Ante Information: What the Newspapers said during the 1974 Famine in Bangladesh', *Review of Public Data Use*, 12: 169–84.

Rawls, J. (1972). *A Theory of Justice*, Oxford: Oxford University Press.

Raychaudhuri, T. (1985). 'Historical Roots of Mass Poverty in South Asia: A Hypothesis', *Economic and Political Weekly*, 20: 801–6.

Reddaway, W. B., and Rahman, M. (1975). 'The Scale of Smuggling out of Bangladesh', Research Report, New Series No. 2, Dhaka: Bangladesh Institute of Development Studies.

Reutlinger, S. (1977). 'Malnutrition: A Poverty or a Food Problem', *World Development*, 5: 715–24.

—— (1982). 'Policies for Food Security in Food-importing Developing Countries', in Chisholm and Tyres (1982).

Rob, R. (1985). 'Equilibrium Price Distributions', *Review of Economic Studies*, 52: 487–504.

Robson, J. R. K. (ed.) (1981). *Famine: Its Causes Effects and Management*, New York: Gordon and Breach.

Rodgers, G. B. (1979). 'Income and Inequality as Determinants of Mortality: An International Cross-section Analysis', *Population Studies*, 39: 343–51.

Rosenberg, I. H. (1973). 'Nutrition: Food Production, Dietary Patterns, and Nutritional Deficiencies', in Chen (1973).

Rosenzweig, M. R., and Schultz, T. P. (1982). 'Market Opportunities, Genetic Endowments and Intrafamily Resource Distribution: Child Survival in Rural India', *The American Economic Review*, 72: 803–15.

Rothschild, M. (1973). 'Models of Market Organization with Imperfect Information', *Journal of Political Economy*, 81: 1283–1308.

Rudra, A. (1982). *Indian Agricultural Economics: Myths and Realities*, New Delhi: Allied Publishers.

Saith, A. (1981). 'Production, Prices and Poverty in Rural India', *Journal of Development Studies*, 17: 196–213.

Salmon, M. (1982). 'Error Correction Mechanisms', *The Economic Journal*, 92: 615–29.

Samuelson, P. A. (1947). *Foundations of Economic Analysis*, Cambridge, Mass.: Harvard University Press.

—— (1957). 'Intertemporal Price Equilibrium: A Prologue to the Theory of Speculation', *Weltwirtschaftliches Archiv*, 79: 181–219.

Sargan, J. D. (1964). 'Wages and Prices in the United Kingdom: A Study in Econometric Methodology', in Hart, Mills, and Whitaker (1964).

—— (1980). 'Some Tests of Dynamic Specification for a Single Equation', *Econometrica*, 48: 879–97.

Sarris, A. H. (1982). 'Commodity-Price Theory and Public Stabilization Stocks', in Chisholm and Tyers (1982).

Schultz, T. P. (1979). 'Interpretation of Relations Among Mortality, Economics of the Household and the Health Environment', Working Paper No. 78, Population and Labour Policies Programme, International Labour Office, Geneva.

Seaman, J., and Holt, J. (1980). 'Markets and Famines in the Third World', *Disasters*, 4: 283–97.

Sen, A. K. (1973). 'On Ignorance and Equal Distribution', *The American Economic Review*, 63: 1022–4.

—— (1977). 'Starvation and Exchange Entitlements: A General Approach and its Application to the Great Bengal Famine', *Cambridge Journal of Economics*, 1: 33–60.

—— (1981a). *Poverty and Famines: An Essay on Entitlement and Deprivation*, Oxford: Oxford University Press.

—— (1981b). 'Ingredients of Famine Analysis: Availability and Entitlements', *Quarterly Journal of Economics*, 95: 433–64.

—— (1984). 'The Right Not to be Hungry', in Alston and Tomasevski (1984).

—— (1985). 'Dharm Narain on Poverty: Concepts and Broader Issues', in Mellor and Desai (1985).

—— (1986). 'The Causes of Famine: A Reply', *Food Policy*, 11: 125–32.

Shiller, R. J. (1981). 'Do Stock Prices Move Too Much to be Justified by Subsequent Changes in Dividends?', *The American Economic Review*, 71: 421–36.

Silverman, B. W. (1985). 'Some Aspects of the Spline Smoothing Approach to Non-parametric Regression Curve Fitting', *Journal of the Royal Statistical Society B*, 47: 1–52.

Singh, K. S. (1975). *The Indian Famine 1967: A Study in Crisis and Change*, New Delhi: People's Publishing House.

Smith, A. (1961). *An Inquiry Into the Causes of the Wealth of Nations*, London: Methuen.

Sobhan, R. (1980). 'Politics of Food and Famine in Bangladesh', in Ahmed (1980).

Srinivasan, T. N. (1983). 'Review of Sen, A. K., "Poverty and Famines: An Essay of Entitlement and Deprivation"', *American Journal of Agricultural Economics*, 65: 200–1.

—— (1985). 'Agricultural Production, Relative Prices, Entitlements, and Poverty', in Mellor and Desai (1985).

Srivastava, H. S. (1968). *The History of Indian Famines 1858–1918: And Development of Famine Policy*, Agra: S. R. Mehra.

Stark, W. (ed.) (1982). *Jeremey Bentham's Economic Writings*, London: George Allen and Unwin.

Steele, J. (1985). 'Millionaire "Grain Barons" Hoarding Supplies in Sudan', *The Guardian Weekly*, 133: (20 October): 8.

Stein, Z., Susser, M., Saenger, G., and Marolla, F. (1975). *Famine and Human Development. The Dutch Hunger Winter of 1944–45*. New York: Oxford University Press.

Stepanek, J. F. (1979). *Bangladesh: Equitable Growth?* New York: Pergamon Press.

Stern, N. (1982). 'Optimal Taxation with Errors in Administration', *Journal of Public Economics*, 17: 181–211.

Stiglitz, J. E. (1976). 'The Efficiency Wage Hypothesis, Surplus Labour and the Distribution of Income in LDCs', *Oxford Economic Papers*, 28: 185–207.

Stokes, E. (1978). *The Peasant and the Raj*, Cambridge: Cambridge University Press.

Struth, F. K. (1984). 'Modelling Expectations Formation with Parameter-Adaptive Filters: An Empirical Application to the Livingston Forecasts', *Oxford Bulletin of Economics and Statistics*, 46: 211–39.

Svedberg, P. (1986). 'Famine in Sub-Saharan Africa', Paper presented at the Food Strategies Conference, World Institute for Development Economics Research, Helsinki.

Swamy, G., and Binswanger, H. P. (1983). 'Flexible Consumer Demand Systems and Linear Estimation: Food in India', *American Journal of Agricultural Economics*, 65: 675–84.

Takayama, T., and Judge, G. G. (1971). *Spatial and Temporal Price and Allocation Models*, Amsterdam: North Holland.

Tarakchandra, D. (1949). *Bengal Famine (1943); As Revealed in a Survey of the Destitutes in Calcutta*, Calcutta: Calcutta University Press.

Theil, H. (1966). *Applied Economic Forecasting*, Amsterdam: North Holland.

Thomas, V. (1980). 'Regional Differences in Foodgrain Production and Distribution in Bangladesh', *The Bangladesh Development Studies*, 8: 93–106.

Tolley, G. S., Thomas, V., and Wong C. M. (1982). *Agricultural Price Policies and the Developing Countries*, Baltimore: Johns Hopkins University Press.

Townsend, R. M. (1978). 'Market Anticipations, Rational Expectations, and Bayesian Learning', *International Economic Review*, 19: 481–94.

Turnovsky, S. J. (1970). 'Empirical Evidence on the Formation of Price Expectations', *Journal of the American Statistical Association*, 65: 1441–54.

—— Shalit, H., and Schmitz, A. (1980). 'Consumer Surplus, Price Instability and Consumer Welfare', *Econometrica*, 48: 135–52.

Tversky, A., and Kahneman, D. (1982). 'Judgement Under Uncertainty: Heuristics and Biases', in Kahneman, Slovic and Tversky (1982).

Uri, N. D., and Rifkin, E. J. (1985). 'Georgraphic Markets, Causality and Railroad Deregulation', *The Review of Economics and Statistics*, 67: 422–28.

Vallin, J. (1968). 'La Mortalité dans des pays du Tiers Monde: évolution et perspectives', *Population*, 23: 845–68.

van de Walle, D. (1985). 'Population Growth and Poverty: Another Look at the Indian Time Series Data', *Journal of Development Studies*, 21: 429–39.

van Schendel, W. (1981). *Peasant Mobility: The Odds of Life in Rural Bangladesh*, Assen, The Netherlands: Van Gorcun and Co.

Varian, H. R. (1978). *Microeconomic Analysis*, New York: Norton.

—— (1979). 'Catastrophe Theory and the Business Cycle', *Economic Inquiry*, 17: 14–28.

Visco, I. (1984). *Price Expectations in Rising Inflation*, Amsterdam: North Holland.

Warr, P. G. (1982). 'Pareto Optimal Redistribution and Private Charity',

Journal of Public Economics, 19: 131–8.

Waugh, F. V. (1944). 'Does the Consumer Benefit from Price Instability?', *Quarterly Journal of Economics*, 58: 602–14.

Weckstein, R. S. (1977). 'Food Security: Storage vs. Exchange', *World Development*, 5: 613–21.

Wickens, M. R. (1982). 'The Efficient Estimation of Econometric Models with Rational Expectations', *The Review of Economic Studies*, 49: 55–68.

Wicklund, R. A., and Brehm, J. W. (1976). *Perspectives on Cognitive Dissonance*, New York: John Wiley and Sons.

Williamson, J. G. (1984). 'British Mortality and the Value of Life, 1781–1931', *Population Studies*, 38: 157–72.

Woodham-Smith, C. (1962). *The Great Hunger: Ireland 1845–49*, London: Hamish Hamilton.

Working, H. (1949a). 'The Theory of the Price of Storage', *The American Economic Review*, 39: 1254–62.

—— (1949b). 'The Investigation of Economic Expectations', *The American Economic Review*, 39: 150–66.

Wright, B. D., and Williams, J. C. (1982). 'The Economic Role of Commodity Storage', *The Economic Journal*, 92: 596–614.

—— (1984). 'Anti-Hoarding Laws: A Stock Condemnation Reconsidered', *American Journal of Agricultural Economics*, 66: 447–55.

Zeeman, E. C. (1974). 'On the Unstable Behaviour of Stock Exchanges', *Journal of Mathematical Economics*, 1: 39–49.

Index